Enhancing Psychodynamic Therapy with Cognitive-Behavioral Techniques

Enhancing Psychodynamic Therapy with Cognitive-Behavioral Techniques

Edited by

Terry Brumley Northcut, Ph.D.,
and
Nina Rovinelli Heller, Ph.D.

JASON ARONSON INC.
Northvale, New Jersey
London

This book was set in 11 pt. New Century Schoolbook.

Copyright © 1999 by Jason Aronson Inc.

10 9 8 7 6 5 4 3 2 1

Library of Congress Cataloging-in-Publication Data

Enhancing psychodynamic therapy with cognitive-behavioral techniques / edited by
  Terry Brumley Northcut and Nina Rovinelli Heller.
     p. cm.
  Includes bibliographical references and index.
  ISBN 0-7657-0181-2
  1. Psychodynamic psychotherapy. 2. Cognitive therapy.
3. Behavior therapy. I. Northcut, Terry Brumley. II. Heller, Nina
Rovinelli.
  [DNLM: 1. Mental Disorders—therapy. 2. Cognitive Therapy. WM
425.5.C6 C6768 1999]
RC489.P72C64 1999
616.89'142—dc21
DNLM/DLC
for Library of Congress   98–21443

Printed in the United States of America on acid-free paper. For information and cata-
log write to Jason Aronson Inc., 230 Livingston Street, Northvale, New Jersey 07647-
1726. Or visit our website: http://www.aronson.com

Contents

II: APPLICATIONS TO PRACTICE POPULATIONS IN DIVERSE SETTINGS

Preface

Enhancing Psychodynamic Therapy with Cognitive-Behavioral Techniques is an important and timely book for several reasons. First, the reality of today's clinical practice requires all of us in the mental health professions to treat our clients in a more focused, definable, and accountable way. Taking a rigid position about defending our theoretical turfs is one way to cope with the external impingements on our practice. Ultimately, however, we all lose, clients included, if we don't consider advances made in other approaches that may enhance and inform our own work. Clinicians, both individually and as professional groups, are experiencing a developmental crisis of sorts in terms of finding how to best meet clients' needs.

Our professional experiences in the field and in the classroom have demonstrated the strength of psychodynamic theory in appreciating the complexities of human behavior. A reexamination is warranted given the recent advances in understanding the effects of trauma, biological contributors of psychological problems, and the role of culture. By taking a closer look at these areas, we can understand both the strengths and weaknesses of our theoretical framework and forge new accommodations. Social work is well poised to forge these accommodations given the historical emphases on the biopsychosocial approach to practice that builds on the strengths and resiliency of clients and client groups. What has often been overlooked as a strength in the psychodynamic field are cognitive capabilities in general and cognitive-behavioral techniques in particular.

It is true that many clinicians practice in a manner that is integrative and more eclectic. The time has come to discuss which kinds of integrations make the best use of available knowledge and the strengths of clients and theories. Cognitive theory seems to us to offer the most in terms of clinically and empirically validated technique.

Readers will gain an understanding of the strengths and limitations of both psychodynamic and cognitive approaches as well as the potential of combining the two. They will also gain an understanding of how to determine when the two should be combined. The challenges and opportunities of certain populations for integration will also be discussed. What has been omitted from this practice dialogue is the comprehensive historical overview of both approaches. This kind of overview has been thoroughly covered in prior literature (e.g., Beck et al. 1990, Berzoff et al. 1996, Goldstein 1995, Woods and Hollis 1990, Zastrow 1992).

We assume the reader's familiarity with the basic tenets of psychodynamic theory and practice. Our contributors represent academics and clinicians with records of scholarly inquiry. They also demonstrate an interest and commitment to the integration of theory and practice. This commitment extends to a continuing reevaluation of what works, with whom, and why. In Part I, the contributors take a look at why integration is essential and in what ways. Part II extends the look by illustrating this integration with contemporary clinical examples from diverse populations and settings.

The primary audience we hope to reach will be experienced clinicians and advanced graduate students since we assume some prior knowledge of psychodynamic theory and practice experience. Skovholt and Ronnestad (1992) discuss the stages prominent in therapists' development. The new graduate struggles with the realization of the limitations of his or her training program in terms of preparation for the characteristics of "real" practice. Also, the experience of graduate training relies heavily on "assimilation" of new information. Once graduated, the professional is confronted with the need to "accommodate" or integrate prior knowledge. As the post-graduate professional is "assimilating," he or she is also challenged to explore new techniques and theories in order to cope with the limitations of what has been learned. It is at this point that clinicians often look for new ways of doing therapy in order to fill in the gaps. The more seasoned professional is also looking to supplement or reevaluate current ways of practicing, albeit for different reasons. The experienced clinician is strongly influenced by clients' feedback regarding the effectiveness of clinician's interventions. Consequently, one of the tasks for the experienced clinician is to evaluate his or her conceptual framework. Enough experience has been achieved to determine in what areas the theoretical approach is most lacking. At this more experienced level the therapist is also confronted with the dilemma of stagnation versus professional development. Wachtel (1985), a psychodynamic therapist, has stated, "If your theoretical perspective has remained constant throughout your career, it's a good sign that you've been looking at too narrow a range of data" (p. 16). One of the determinants of professional development, according to Skovholt and Ronnestad, is the awareness of the complexity of intrapsychic, interpersonal, and systemic phenomena. For this reason, a seasoned clinician often looks to expand his or her own theoretical framework with treatment theories that allow for this complex understanding.

We therefore believe our book has two target audiences: the recent or soon-to-graduate professional who is coping with limitations of clinical preparation, and the seasoned clinician who is evaluating practice for issues related to professional development and increased clinical effectiveness. Advanced practice students have enough field experience and theoretical foundational knowledge to have interest and ability to utilize an integrative model. And experienced professionals have seen their share of successes and failures and are ready to reexamine their current ways of practicing.

REFERENCES

Beck, A. T., Freeman, A., and Associates. (1990). *Cognitive Therapy of Personality Disorders.* New York: Guilford.

Berzoff, J., Flanagan, L. M., and Hertz, P. (1996). *Inside Out and Outside In: Psychodynamic Clinical Theory and Practice in Contemporary Multicultural Contexts.* Northvale, NJ: Jason Aronson.

Goldstein, E. (1995). *Ego Psychology and Social Work Practice,* 2nd ed. New York: Free Press.

Skovholt, T. M., and Ronnestad, M. H. (1992). *The Evolving Professional Self.* Chichester, England: Wiley.

Wachtel, P. L. (1985). Need for theory. *International Newsletter of Paradigmatic Psychology* I:15–17.

Woods, M. E., and Hollis, F. (1990). *Casework: A Psychosocial Therapy.* New York: McGraw-Hill.

Zastrow, C. (1992). *The Practice of Social Work.* Belmont, CA: Wadsworth.

Acknowledgments

It is a daunting challenge to thank all of those who have assisted us along the way. Our families are due an enormous amount of gratitude for their support, love, and consistent good humor through all of the phone calls, visits, and take-out and missed dinners. Our friends and colleagues have provided us with the intellectual stimulation and collaborative support at Loyola University of Chicago, the University of Connecticut, Smith College, and the Brattleboro, Vermont, clinical community. The writers in this volume have been a pleasure to work with in terms of their wonderful ideas and their cheerful accommodation to the task at hand. Our students' and our clients' contributions are immeasurable. Without their willingness to work with us in the learning and growing process, we would not have written this book. In particular, we thank those clients who have felt understood by our psychodynamic perspective as well as challenged us to see its limitations. We especially remember and thank Karen.

Specifically, we want to thank Marcia and David Spira for their thoughtful ideas and responses to our many questions. Carolyn Saari's willingness to answer often ill-formed questions has been a source of ongoing encouragement. Dana Northcut and Dan Heller deserve an acknowledgment in bold letters for their patient technical support in trying to assist us in joining this technological era. We appreciate Gerry Schamess's and Bob and Cynthia Shilkret's continued support of our academic and writing careers. We also thank Randy Lucente, Martin Bloom, Dean Joseph Walsh, and Dean Kay Davidson for their support of our writing. Our graduate assistants, Kari Dana, Pat Farrell, and Kris Pomeroy, performed numerous essential tasks, often on short notice.

It is awkward to thank each other. However, the opportunity to collaborate on our work and on our lives has provided us with an experience that has enriched us. Our professional selves and our personal selves have benefited beyond measure.

Contributors

Kathryn Basham, Ph.D., LICSW: Assistant Professor, Smith College School for Social Work, Northampton, MA

Adin DeLaCour, LICSW: Private Practice, Northampton, MA

James W. Drisko, DSW, LICSW: Associate Professor, Smith College School for Social Work, Northampton, MA

Donald K. Granvold, Ph.D.: Professor, School of Social Work, University of Texas at Arlington

Emily Lyon Gray, Ph.D.: Clinical Psychologist, Director, Spring Center, Brattleboro, VT

Nina Rovinelli Heller, Ph.D.: Assistant Professor, University of Connecticut, School of Social Work, West Hartford

Thomas W. Johnson, Ed.D., MSW.: University of Medicine and Dentistry of New Jersey, New Brunswick

Dennis Miehls, Ph.D.: King's College, Department of Social Work, London, Ontario, Canada

Terry Brumley Northcut, Ph.D.: Assistant Professor, Loyola University of Chicago, School of Social Work, Chicago

Clayton T. Shorkey, Ph.D., LMSW-ACP: Cullen Trust Centennial Professor in Alcohol Studies and Education, School of Social Work, University of Texas at Austin

Cheryl Springer, Ph.D.: Associate Professor, School of Social Work, Salem State College, MA

1

Introduction: Bringing Together Theory and Experience

Terry Brumley Northcut and Nina Rovinelli Heller

Theory without experience is mere intellectual play. Experience without theory is blind.

—IMMANUEL KANT

Undoubtedly, professional clinical social workers can recall their first practice course in which they learned not only to start where the client is, but also to examine the context of the client system. With that training as our foundation, it seems appropriate to present the context, and thereby the motivation, for this book. Both editors entered the social work profession as clinicians committed to effecting change on the micro and macro level. After years of practice we entered into doctoral graduate programs to advance our theoretical understanding of human behavior. Having practiced enough in the field, we felt compelled to reevaluate why certain interventions were not effective and why certain techniques were more effective. One of the achievements of this education was a better understanding of the contributions of psychodynamic theory for assessing and treating complex human behavior. While we each maintained our practice both in agency settings and in private practice, we began to teach social work practice. Our experience both as clinicians and as academics has led us to collaborate regarding the need for an integration of cognitive-behavioral approaches with psychodynamic practice. Our belief that the time has come for this integration is based on several factors.

First, we discovered in our own practice with clients often labeled as borderline that cognitive-behavioral interventions were helpful in enhancing our psychodynamic practice (Heller and Northcut 1996). The clients we worked with often defied theoretical purity and likewise reacted negatively to an eclectic approach that provided no continuity or structure.

Second, graduate students in field placements reported client scenarios that challenge even the most experienced clinicians. Practice in the '90s has been strongly influenced by managed care and limited resources for clients most in need. Consequently, by the time some clients enter a therapeutic system, the crisis has reached dramatic proportions, having been confounded by numerous societal infringements (poverty, violence, etc.). In addition, clients' presenting problems usually include multiple diagnoses, such as substance abuse, thought disorders, personality disorders, and physical illnesses. In addition to these complex problems, our practices reflect the influence of restricted mental health resources requiring short-term treatment.

Third, we reached a professional developmental level necessitating a reexamination of our current way of practicing while still believing that psychodynamic theory is a viable and necessary foundation for good practice. The postmodern influence has provided a wake-up call to clinicians to look at their own biases and influence on clients. While we do not practice from a constructivist position, we do believe our knowledge of "truth" is continually being redefined by our own experience, our clients' lives, and the culture we live in.

Fourth, as we have worked in several academic arenas, we have observed what appears to be a common polarization within the therapeutic community in general and the social work profession in particular. There is often a competition for who has the corner on "true psychotherapy" or the "real social work identity" that is positioned in terms of allegiances to certain theories, treatment modalities, or social work specializations. It is quite clear: we all lose when we attempt to convince our colleagues that we have found *the* way. Perhaps most alarming and discouraging is the reality that the people whom we entered the profession to help bear the greatest disadvantage from these types of debates. It is in our clients' best interest and the best interests of our profession to find common ground in which we can capitalize on the strengths each position brings to the practice arena.

In choosing to integrate two theoretical frameworks, we are maintaining and advocating the need for practice that continues to be informed by theory. Unfortunately, there is often a tendency to react to all the contextual complexities of today's practice with an attitude that questions the relevance of theory. We often tell students that now, more than ever, theory is important. When we are called upon to assess client strengths and needs more quickly and with greater finesse, we must know all that we can about human behavior and influences, whether it be an understanding of cultural values, cognitive schemas, familial patterns, or psychodynamic underpinnings. Our position is that we can maintain what has been useful about psychodynamic theory, its appreciation of the complexity of behavior, and incorporate selectively the tools that do the most to enhance client competence and sense of mastery. It is this position that is reflected in our book.

HISTORICAL REVIEW

The utilization of several points of view and various points of intervention is not new to the social work profession. In fact, it is this incorporation of the biological, social, and psychological that has held lasting appeal for generations of social workers. Despite differences in emphasis, virtually all beginning and advanced social work texts have purported to ascribe to the biopsychosocial model (e.g., Germain and Gitterman 1996, Hollis 1964, Richmond 1917, Woods and Hollis 1990). Because of this appreciation of the complexity of the transactions between an individual and his or her environment, multipronged approaches to the alleviation of suffering have always been valued.

The uniqueness of the biopsychosocial model does presuppose, however, an approach that posits the need of the client before the theoretical "belief" of the worker. Typically, clinical social workers have specialized in either the sociological or the psychological arenas, borrowing theories from other disciplines when necessary. In our view, this "borrowing" represents a strength of our profession in the sense that we have been able to accommodate appropriate advances in other fields in the service of our work with clients. For example, social work intervention with the mentally ill has benefited enormously from advances in the biological fields and from systems theory. This accommodation does not result in a relinquishment of social work knowledge or values, but rather enhances our burgeoning knowledge base and is essential to evolving theory and practice models, particularly as we are challenged to "do more" in less time. With the ability to selectively choose in which arena to intervene, the social worker is most advantaged by understanding and being able to integrate a variety of perspectives. Unfortunately, what can result is a type of practice "eclecticism" that loses sight of the strengths of particular theories. Consequently, we propose an integration that builds on the psychodynamic tradition in social work and capitalizes on cognitive contributions.

The influence of psychoanalytic thinking on clinical social work practice is well documented (e.g., Berzoff et al. 1996, Goldstein 1995, Woods and Hollis 1990, Zastrow 1992) and will not be reviewed here. However, with the growing attention to integrative approaches comes the need to assess the limitations of psychodynamic theory and the areas in which integration is most productive. Within the field of social work, two recent noteworthy texts from two very different theoretical points of view propose the need for integration. Goldstein (1990), in *Borderline Disorders*, notes that "no one theoretical formulation does justice to the complexity of personality development" (p. 192). She proposes that the integrative perspective allows the clinician to tailor the treatment to the client's developmental needs using a variety of techniques. Granvold (1994), in *Cognitive and Behavioral Treatment: Methods and Applications*, makes a persuasive case for the integration of cognitive therapy and constructivism. This latter work is particularly interesting in that some social workers view constructivism as another area conducive to integration. Both texts present a clear theoretical foundation with excellent clinical applications, making the texts suited for advanced specializations in social work.

Two other social work academicians/clinicians have also contributed to this integrative movement. Weisz (1997) compared self psychology and cognitive therapy, particularly in the area of "self-nurturing." Dungee-Anderson (1992) focused on self-nurturing as well, with a cognitive-behavioral treatment approach for the borderline client that capitalized on the developmental object relations literature.

The profession of psychology, and the specific area of cognitive-behavioral theory, has placed a great deal of emphasis on advanced integrative approaches. As evidence of the widespread interest in integration, the Society for the Exploration of Psychotherapy Integration (SEPI) was developed in 1983. Around that same time, the National Institute of Mental Health (NIMH) instituted a collaborative research program for the treatment of depression (Elkin et al. 1985). The investment of NIMH continues to be in the area of interdisciplinary research, thus influencing not only clinical practice and research but also mental health policies. Professional psychology journals also continue to demonstrate this widespread interest in integration. *The Journal of Cognitive Psychotherapy* featured a special issue (fall 1995) on "Psychotherapy Integration and Cognitive Psychotherapy," with a look at how cognitive theory has changed and what direction it should take in the future.

Several authors are particularly noteworthy in the field of psychology in their attempts to advance integrative theory and practice. Donald Meichenbaum (1993) has proposed that the field of cognitive behavior modification (CBM) is part of an "evolutionary process" that has attempted to "integrate the clinical concerns of psychodynamic and systems-oriented psychotherapists with the technology of behavior therapists" (p. 202). Mardi Horowitz (1994) suggested that modern cognitive science offers a shared language that could help revitalize the field of psychotherapy. He further stated that

> Psychodynamic, interpersonal, cognitive, and behavioral therapies need not be investigated from defensively isolated camps. The effectiveness of each brand name of psychotherapy has been proven. Psychotherapy research has failed on any consistent basis to distinguish the effects of different schools and many theorists now call for an integrative approach. . . . We can move from encouraging the competition of one therapy against another to systematically studying how change occurs. With knowledge about change we can plan sets of techniques that, together, facilitate adaptive change. [p. 8]

Michael J. Mahoney (1995) also has offered a timely integration of cognitive and constructivist theories. Marvin R. Goldfried (1995) placed his focus on the changes in thinking and practice of cognitive-behavior therapy, a critical step necessary before an integrative model can be built. Meichenbaum, Horowitz, Mahoney, and Goldfried have provided the theoretician and practitioner with relevant, cutting-edge ideas. These authors and others will be discussed more fully throughout the text.

OVERVIEW OF THE TEXT

The organization of this book reflects our belief that practice must be based on the clear articulation of theory as well as comprehensive assessment. Part I begins with the two theoretical frameworks and describes the limits of both approaches, particularly in the areas of cognition and affect from a psychodynamic perspective. Granvold continues the focus on theory by examining cognitive theory and its evolution as it impacts potential for integration. Building on that theoretical discussion, Heller and Northcut propose a model for assessment that includes both psychodynamic and cognitive-behavioral dimensions.

In Part II, contributors apply cognitive-behavioral interventions in their psychodynamic practice with a variety of populations, modalities, and settings. Each chapter includes an overview of literature specific to that population and setting, with guidelines for interventions. Case material and vignettes demonstrate the application of theory and technique to client groups. By offering the reader a look at theory *and* practice, we hope to provide a complete picture of how integration can be accomplished. The writers in this section are experienced clinicians who demonstrate the challenges in "teasing out" what is often practiced automatically. Experienced practitioners practicing from an integrative framework will find it helpful to struggle to articulate the points of their integration.

It is time for clinical social workers to continue to utilize the best of our specialized knowledge, from within and outside the profession, and orchestrate greater integrative practice models. While we move to examine both the psychodynamic and cognitive-behavioral theories and practice models, we will confront the questions regarding the compatibility or complementariness of the two approaches. What can one offer the other? Does one approach work better with one population or problem than another? More specifically, can cognitive social workers learn something from the psychodynamic understanding of the roles of affect, transference, and developmental history? Can psychodynamic social workers learn something about the role of thought processes in influencing behavior and creating change, or in the focus on evaluation of treatment outcome from their cognitive-oriented counterparts? Importantly, how can this proposed integration further our understanding and intervention of clients not just in the individual psychic realm, but in the interpersonal, cultural, and societal realms?

REFERENCES

Berzoff, J., Flanagan, L. M., and Hertz, P. (1996). *Inside Out and Outside In: Psychodynamic Clinical Theory and Practice in Contemporary Multicultural Contexts*. Northvale, NJ: Jason Aronson.

Dungee-Anderson, D. (1992). Self nurturing: a cognitive behavioral treatment approach for the borderline client. *Clinical Social Work Journal* 20(3):295–312.

Elkin, I., Parloff, M. B., Hadley, S. W., and Autrey, J. H. (1985). NIMH treatment of depression collaborative research program: background and research plan. *Archives of General Psychiatry* 42:305–316.

Germain, C., and Gitterman, A. (1996). *The Life Model of Social Work Practice: Advances in Theory and Practice*, 2nd ed. New York: Columbia University Press.

Goldfried, M. R. (1995). *From Cognitive-Behavior Therapy to Psychotherapy Integration*. New York: Springer.

Goldstein, E. (1990). *Borderline Disorders: Clinical Models and Techniques*. New York: Guilford.

——— (1995). *Ego Psychology and Social Work Practice*, 2nd ed. New York: Free Press.

Granvold, D. K. (1994). *Cognitive and Behavioral Treatment: Methods and Applications*. Belmont, CA: Wadsworth.

Heller, N. R., and Northcut, T. B. (1996). Utilizing cognitive-behavioral techniques in psychodynamic practice with clients diagnosed as borderline. *Clinical Social Work Journal* 24(2):203–215.

Hollis, F. (1964). *Casework: A Psychosocial Therapy*. New York: Random House.

Horowitz, M. (1994). Psychotherapy integration: implications for research standards. *Psychotherapy and Rehabilitation Research Bulletin* 3:8–9.

Mahoney, M. J. (1995). *Cognitive and Constructive Psychotherapies: Theory, Research, and Practice*. New York: Springer.

Meichenbaum, D. (1993). Changing conceptions of cognitive behavior modification: retrospect and prospect. *Journal of Consulting and Clinical Psychology* 61(2):202–204.

Richmond, M. (1917). *Social Diagnosis*. New York: Russell Sage Foundation.

Weisz, A. N. (1997). Models for treatment: a comparison of cognitive therapy and self psychology. *Journal of Analytic Social Work* 4(2):51–67.

Woods, M. E., and Hollis, F. (1990). *Casework: A Psychosocial Therapy.* New York: McGraw-Hill.

Zastrow, C. (1992). *The Practice of Social Work.* Belmont, CA: Wadsworth.

I

TOOLS FOR INTEGRATION

2

Integrating Psychodynamic and Cognitive-Behavioral Theory: A Psychodynamic Perspective

Terry Brumley Northcut

INTRODUCTION

The union of psychodynamic and cognitive-behavioral theories appears to be a star-crossed romance with allegiances to each staunchly defended. Interestingly enough, the relationship has qualities of both the first blush of attraction and the subsequent disillusionment phase in a committed relationship. For example, in the excitement of finding ways to integrate the two theories, we tend to believe we are doing what has never been done, not unlike an adolescent who has "reinvented" love. The reality appears to be that clinicians integrate all the time. In studies of clinicians from a variety of disciplines in the last twenty years, the trend is clearly one that demonstrates that psychotherapists "utilize procedures and views from more than one theoretical orientation" (Garfield and Bergin 1994, p. 6). What the contributors to this text are trying to achieve is a greater understanding of how and when to integrate these two approaches effectively and the ramifications of such an integration.

As our integrative relationship surpasses the honeymoon phase, clinicians may also experience the eventual disillusionment of an "opposites attract" relationship: what we admire initially may annoy us later on. Additionally, we may devalue the other to camouflage what is lacking in ourselves. At this point in the relationship it is easiest to buy into the stereotypes long proffered for each theory: behavior therapists are "cold, calculating, and manipulative" and psychodynamic therapists are "aloof, woolly-headed, and overly speculative" (Goldfried 1995, p. 4). By focusing on the mechanics and consequences of incorporating another approach into our psychodynamic practice, we hope to avoid any irreconcilable differences.

To facilitate as clearly as possible the points at which integration is possible we need to do several things. First, the parameters and/or caveats of attempting integration will be considered. Second, I will focus on the strengths and weaknesses of both approaches. Ideally, an integrative model will retain the strengths of each theory, and perhaps use the strengths of the second theory to repair or minimize the weaknesses of the first. It is important to be clear about what the strengths are that must be preserved/respected. In clinical work an essential piece of the diagnostic assessment is identifying strengths so as to use them for addressing problems. I will draw on this list of strengths when possible to address the weaknesses of each theory, and will conclude with the key focus areas that must be balanced in a thoughtful assessment, paving the way for future chapters that offer guidelines for assessing when and how to integrate. An essential caveat must be offered. These theoretical schools are continually evolving and wide in scope. Therefore, this summary is like a snapshot of a waterfall—the overall picture captures the essence, but individual details may be obscured. I will try to comment on general themes or trends, but in so doing I do these theories a disservice. It is impossible to thoroughly credit all of the theorists who have worked diligently through the years to engage in a dynamic exploration of human behavior. These ideas are complex and do not lend themselves easily to sweeping generalizations. Their very complexity also demands continual revisions of the theories, which hopefully retains that which provides the most value. All theoretical frames allow us do some things (in terms of explanation) and hinder us from doing others (Flax 1997). Our challenge is to be clear on what the theories allow us to do and what they prevent us from doing.

PARAMETERS AND CAVEATS OF INTEGRATION

There have been three major ways to approach reconciling different theoretical approaches in psychotherapy: emphasizing common factors, theoretical integration, and technical eclecticism (Messer and Warren 1995). The first way, emphasizing common factors, requires examining what different approaches accomplish that is similar. According to Frank (1982) and Frank and Frank (1991), all therapeutic models attempt to combat the demoralization that clients bring into treatment through providing four essential features (Messer and Warren 1995). These four features are:

1. An emotionally charged, confiding relationship with a helping person, that inspires confidence and increases expectancies of success, thereby improving morale;
2. A healing setting, which provides safety, and other special attributes which distinguish it from the rest of the person's surroundings (e.g., a hospital, clinic, or consulting room, which carry the aura of science);
3. A rationale or conceptual scheme that provides a plausible explanation for the patient's symptoms;
4. A ritual or procedure that requires the active participation of both client and therapist and that is believed by both to be the means of restoring the patient's health. [Frank and Frank 1991, pp. 42–44]

It is clear that both psychodynamic therapy and cognitive-behavioral approaches provide all four factors. However, there are very clear differences in terms of how they are executed. Schacht's (1984) analogy clearly demonstrates the problem: "Salt in one's soup is quite different from salt in one's gas tank" (p. 121). While there may be a common element of a relationship, setting, rationale, and ritual, the contexts are so different that one cannot make a direct comparison. A relationship that is neutral to foster transference has qualities very different from one that is didactic in order to best teach (Messer and Warren 1995). However, when combining two seemingly disparate approaches, the inconsistencies clarify the limits of each and should not stop the attempt. It is in their incongruence that greater clarity and utility will be found (Flax 1997). One way the contributors to this text will attempt to deal with this problem is by not using the second for its explanatory power—rather as technique that can facilitate improved ego functioning (see Chapter 4). If client functioning can be improved by incorporating cognitive-behavioral techniques into psychodynamic treatment as we propose, then we must revisit psychodynamic theory for areas of expansion.

A second way to reconcile different theoretical approaches is through theoretical integration. Theoretical integration appears to be a most promising means for reconciliation, but also the most difficult. Integration can be defined as "a systematic attempt at combining elements of two or more forms of psychotherapy" (Garfield and Bergin 1994, p. 8). Several prominent clinicians have been in the forefront of attempting integration: Goldfried (1980, 1982, 1991, 1995) from a behavioral perspective and Arkowitz and Messer (1984), Birk and Brinkley-Birk (1974), Marmor (1971), and Wachtel (1977, 1997) from a psychoanalytic perspective. Wachtel has reminded us that while certainly childhood experiences, fantasies, and so forth establish patterns or cycles, these patterns are maintained in the present by "a reality which the person has helped to create: both internal reality and external events are crucial" (Messer and Warren 1995, p. 236). Behavioral techniques provide a means to alter these present-day interpersonal patterns and to manage debilitating anxiety or affect. The drawbacks to theoretical integration of this kind are many. First, what is included from another approach or theory may require the minimization of aspects of the first theory. For example, Wachtel has to minimize the role of drives to effectively incorporate behavioral interventions. Also, there is no common language between therapeutic schools that would allow terms to be used interchangeably. In addition, the philosophy undergirding the different approaches can work to hinder integration. The psychodynamic approach is subjective, and currently seems to rely on the construction of meanings between client and therapist, or at least an understanding that "problems" are multidetermined (Moore and Fine 1990). Historically, behaviorism has relied on a scientific approach that defines and selects an observable problem to empirically study for identifiable solutions. However, constructivism has influenced the behavioral schools as well, making this an ideal time to attempt a rapprochement. This influence will be discussed further by Granvold in Chapter 3.

Technical eclecticism, a third and final effort at integration, generally means choosing a treatment method or approach based on the needs of the individual client or client groups depending on theory, experience, or research (Garfield and Bergin 1994, Messer and Warren 1995). While this approach appears pragmatic and may appeal to managed care companies in their continuing quest to keep costs down, there are some fundamental problems with this approach. "Eclecticism does not represent any truly systematic view, and thus research on this approach has been minimal and in fact is not really possible. It seems likely that eclecticism actually may be a stage in the development of a more refined and efficacious type of psychotherapy" (Garfield and Bergin 1994, p. 7). An eclectic approach means a clinician practices from one approach and then imports many others without necessarily examining the conceptual fit between the different approaches; consequently, any explanatory or predictive power is lost (Hall 1987, personal communication). Also, what has been empirically proven to work within one treatment approach is not necessarily going to be as effective when the context, meaning, and protocols are changed (as mentioned earlier). Any empirical validity of the efficacy of any approach must be established anew (Messer and Warren 1995). With further refinements and knowledge about how and when clinicians import other approaches, it is likely that we will be able to practice from an integrative perspective as opposed to an eclectic one.

A more practical problem with technical eclecticism has to do with the number of approaches one clinician can be expected to master. For example, the profession of social work expects graduates of its training programs to be competent in individual, couples, family, and group approaches in addition to being an effective policy advocate. In a sense, our professional identity relies on an understanding of the impact of multiple systems and our ability to intervene in each of these areas. Realistically it is not feasible to be all things to all clients, and the challenge is to know what we do well and whom to refer to for the rest. But referring is not always the solution either. How likely is it that one therapeutic setting has "therapists of different orientations and personality styles . . . that will match the many possible dimensions of relevant client characteristics" (Messer and Warren 1995, p. 234)?

As can be seen, the term *integration* poses a number of conundrums for the clinician attempting to practice from several theoretical frameworks. At the very least, we may be guilty of "folding in" cognitive-behavioral therapy (CBT) techniques into psychodynamic practice, as a "true" theoretical integration seems premature at this stage of theory development. Nevertheless, to avoid obsessive navel gazing, we will use the terms *integration* and *incorporation* interchangeably as they are terms commonly used within the practice community. At the conclusion of the application chapters we will revisit this dilemma and invite readers to make their own assessments. Ongoing dialogue is essential in advancing the progress of theoretical and practice integration.

Since we are proposing that incorporation of cognitive understandings and technique should occur within the context of psychodynamic treatment, we will begin with examining psychodynamic practice more in detail. According to Gabbard (1994), "psychodynamic psychiatry is an approach to diagnosis and treatment characterized by a way of thinking about both patient and clinician that includes unconscious conflict, deficits and distortions of intrapsychic structures, and internal object relations" (p. 5). We are using the term to include all theories and approaches that focus on or are based on an understanding of the intrapsychic processes. There are a variety of theories that can be considered psychodynamic, including but not limited to classical psychoanalysis, ego psychology, object relations, self psychology, and intersubjective approaches. The diversity of psychodynamic theories vividly demonstrates why it is impossible to adequately summarize the contributions of each. However, when psychotherapy builds on a foundation of psychodynamic theory, certain assumptions are made about the internal world of client(s). The logical first assumption is that there is indeed an internal world that shapes how we think, behave, and feel. The different psychodynamic approaches vary in terms of what is emphasized, ideas about psychic structure, description of a "self," and attempts at integration (Lifson 1996). Beliefs about what is "curative" also range in scope. Insight has historically meant "understanding the dynamic factors contributing to conflict resolution . . . essential for therapeutic change" (Moore and Fine 1990, p. 98). "True" insight includes affect and cognition because "cognitive awareness alone does not lead to therapeutic change" (Moore and Fine 1990, p. 98). The need for affective and cognitive components will be important as we move to discuss assessment in the next chapter. Further thoughts about therapeutic change include the effects of transmuting internalization of the empathic therapeutic relationship (e.g., Elson 1986, Kohut 1984) and facilitating clients' developing their own narrative that allows for "identity complexity" (Saari 1993). Both self psychology and narrative approaches underscore the primacy of the therapeutic relationship which will be critical in assessing when and how to incorporate cognitive techniques.

STRENGTHS AND WEAKNESSES OF PSYCHODYNAMIC THEORY

All psychodynamic approaches rely on or react to some of the major strengths of classical psychoanalytic theory. The strengths that will be discussed briefly are the importance of the unconscious, emphasis on human sexuality, function of defenses, adaptability of the ego, role of developmental lines and object relations, primacy of the therapeutic relationship and the transference, and the idiosyncratic, important stories clients possess and need to construct. The weaknesses include "adultomorphization" of the theories, limited sample populations, errors in focus on separation-individuation, "mother-blaming" aspects, limitations of terms such as object relations, emphasis on insight and transference neurosis, and ambivalent alliance with science. I am assuming that the reader has a basic understanding of psychodynamic theories. The goal is to highlight the high points to establish the context from which we are operating. It is not possible, or more importantly, practical, to list everyone who has written about each of these areas. Only key players will be given so that the reader will be "on the same page." Integrative theorists will be discussed according to their primary orientation.

Perhaps the single most defining strength of psychodynamic theory is the appreciation of the unconscious as mentioned above. Freud attempted to provide a scientific means of understanding the unconscious world, including dreams, while building on prior philosophical and historical writers such as Aristotle, Virgil, and Kant (Freud 1900). He also went on to elaborate the various structural and topographical aspects of the consciousness that have influenced clinicians and theoreticians for decades. The extent to which this common belief has pervaded not only our clinical arena, but also western society, can be seen in language and marketing: for example, the "Freudian slip" and the "selling" of sexual satisfaction that is the backdrop for products as varied as toothpaste, cars, and cigarettes.

In the sociocultural era in which he was operating, Freud's emphasis on human sexuality represents a second area of strength. Up to this time sexuality was not appreciated as a critical factor in human functioning. Such a recognition did much to "normalize" sexual wishes, fantasies, and behavior.

Some errors and assumptions, of course, derailed progress in understanding human behavior, particularly female sexuality, desire, and homosexuality, but his interest and emphasis did much to open a window on a subject that had been previously closed. This contribution, like others, clearly demonstrates the inescapable cultural influences that shape and determine which piece of the puzzle of human behavior we focus on. "It was Freud who brought the sexual outcasts back into the family of humanity and showed us the common themes in all the complicated dances of our erotic life" (Stone 1997, p. 37).

Freud and his daughter, Anna Freud, contributed understanding of the action of the ego to defend against unacceptable impulses from the unconscious and protect the individual from the experience of anxiety (A. Freud 1966, Goldstein 1995). Whether clinicians today are practicing short-term or long-term treatment, the need for a clear understanding of defenses is critical for assessing adaptive and maladaptive coping strategies. Without this understanding, clinicians waste time and energy trying to suggest techniques that are beyond the person's ability to perform. Clear understanding and assessment of client functioning allows the clinician to accurately determine when to focus on the therapeutic relationship and/or when there may be a need for a concrete, didactic intervention.

Hartmann (1958) emphasized the human ability to adapt to one's surroundings given an "average expectable environment." This focus shifted the emphasis on human pathology to one of adaptability, paving the way for future work on ego strengths and resiliency. Using this concept of adaptation, Erikson extended ego psychology to include the broader psychosocial arena, studying, for example, the Sioux and Yurok people to explore lives of nonclinical populations and children from different cultural contexts (Crain 1992). In so doing, he was able to focus not only on Freud's psychosexual stages, but also on the way in which the ego "meets the social world." Freud, A. Freud, and Erikson emphasized the idea that certain tasks are central at particular times in our lives. Erikson, of course, extended developmental tasks through adulthood, an important extension given Freud's emphasis on early childhood. By providing a framework to understand what "usually" happens during certain time frames, clinicians could explain and predict some courses of behavior whether it was in the area of psychosexual tasks or psychosocial tasks.

The contribution of the unconscious, sexuality, and developmental lines facilitated a greater understanding of clinical problems, paving the way for an elaboration of Freud's concept of the transference as a critical factor in the clinical relationship. Early experiences form an imprint that influences future relationships. Freud and numerous others have written extensively about transference and its role in psychotherapy. The concept of transference has important ramifications in terms of understanding that we don't just interact with the here and now but we also are reacting to a pattern established in childhood. In a sense, we continue a dance by unconsciously fulfilling roles we learned to fill as children. These early relationships and transferences are not only dyadic, as the construct of the oedipal conflict underscores. Regardless of whether we believe the oedipal conflict is essential to "normal" development, a by-product of early pathological development, or a culturally biased anomaly, it does appear that children use relationships with multiple adults to understand and negotiate triadic relations.

Mahler (Mahler et al. 1975) also contributed much work on understanding the relationship with the immediate social environment by elaborating on the role of early object relations in shaping human development. Her ideas emphasized development in preoedipal years, elucidating the "psychological birth of the human infant." Later theoreticians and clinicians expanded her concepts to focus on the role of early object relations in the development of pathology and consequently on adult functioning (e.g., Blanck and Blanck 1974, Kernberg 1975, Masterson 1976).

If you were to ask a large group of clinicians, regardless of theoretical orientation, what is curative about psychotherapy, many would undoubtedly cite the treatment relationship, another primary strength of psychodynamic theory. The emphasis on the relationship goes back to Freud as well as to numerous early social workers (e.g., Garrett 1949, Richmond 1917, Towle 1940). The focus on the relationship varies in emphasis from being considered essential for the transference neurosis to develop, or in the context of therapeutic empathy to ameliorate prior empathic failures (Kohut 1984). "Although Freud (1912/ 1958) developed a one-person, drive-based theory of personality development and of therapy, his theoretical position was inconsistent from the outset. He acknowledged the therapist's emotional involvement, albeit reactive and inconstant, calling it countertransference" (Natterson and Friedman 1995, p. x). "One-person psychologies" evident in Freud's writings and in the classic Strachey paper (1934) emphasized insight and the importance of an interpretation in facilitating insight to the point that insight has been deified as curative mutative factors in treatment. Following Freud and extending these ideas, Ferenczi (1988) focused on the "mutual analysis" of client and therapist. Alexander and French (1946) shifted the pendulum away from the fantasy that a therapist could be neutral and objective and provide technically correct techniques. They "believed that the therapist should discern the attitude required by the patient and that the adoption of this attitude by the therapist would establish the corrective emotional experience needed by the patient" (Natterson and Friedman 1995, p. 133). Sullivan (1953) also focused on fitting the technique to the client, emphasizing the therapist as both a real figure and different from the transference figure in the client's earlier life (DeLaCour 1996). The ideas of Ferenczi, Alexander and French, and Sullivan's interpersonal school paved the way for an intersubjective orientation: a two-person psychology. "Mitchell (1993) has pointed out that the emphasis of this relational perspective shifts from uncovering the truth through insight (as was the case in drive theory and ego psychology), toward restoring the client's core subjective truths" (DeLaCour 1996, p. 216).

Historically, the profession has extended theory to incorporate new knowledge, albeit sometimes altering the meaning of original terms without changing the actual word, leaving much room for confusion (Greenberg and Mitchell 1983). Social workers, while incorporating many contributions from psychodynamic theory, have traditionally emphasized the complexity of individual problems with the focus on the "person-in-the-environment." The assessment of individual development was juxtaposed on an appreciation for the wider social system (usually emphasizing that the role of the clinician was to help the individual to adapt in more effective ways). Certainly an understanding of the impact of social impingements facilitated an appreciation for the complexity of human experience. Without the influence of psychodynamic theory there would not have been the understanding that, given the same deplorable social situations, there are individual ways of understanding and making meaning of those experiences. While it is certainly useful and imperative to be aware of the broad effects of negative social factors, it is also true that in the meantime we need to address crises that occur situation by situation. For this reason, psychodynamic theory has paved the way for the importance of listening to clients' stories and experience, leading the way for constructivist, narrative perspectives (Saari 1991, 1993, Schafer 1981, Spence 1984). When you allow that each client has a particular understanding and experience of certain life events, you are also mindful that the provision of services has meaning as well (Altman 1995).

It is important to remember that psychodynamic theory began with Freud trying to understand a clinical population—a population presenting with complex problems. Therein lies one of its major weaknesses. He tried to develop a theory that described normal development from looking at himself and his patients, usually adults. Eagle (1984) has cautioned that "under no circumstances are we ever justified in using our creative fictional 'constructions' about origins of pathology in the first year of life to serve as data for theorizing about early psychological development" (p. 38). Freud (1899) even had warned about the questionable ability to ever accurately "remember" events in our childhood. Peterfreund (1978) spoke also to the fallacy of characterizing "early states of normal development in terms of . . . later states of psychopathology" (p. 427). This adultomorphization assumes that adult pathology is really a persistence of normal childhood issues. Eagle goes on to say that a "normal infant is not an arrested or defective version of the completed adult, but an organism whose responses are highly adaptive, given its capacity and level of organization" (p. 139).

In addition to this adultomorphization, the populations on which these theories are based are very limited. Consequently, the theories have limited applications when comparing development between cultures. The focus on autonomy and separation has been found to vary from culture to culture, raising the question of whether there is a meaningful concept of "normality" and what the limitations of such standards are. Any time you prescribe "normality," you are introducing a "knowledge power nexus" that can result in confusion between what "normal" behavior is needed to fit in with certain societal demands and what is basic human nature (Flax 1997, Lyotard 1984). For example, the idea that psychological separation is critical for "normal" development is linked to western cultures that rely on autonomous behavior for the societal good (Flax 1997). Such a view is ethnocentric in that it labels cultural, gender, and sexual orientation differences as inferior development. This ethnocentrism also spills over into issues of technique.

I once worked with a young Vietnamese client with whom I tried to use free association as the "appropriate" technique for transference to develop. After a painfully (for us both) quiet session I was finally able to talk about the meaning of the silence for him, and the cultural mandate not to initiate conversations related to feelings. It was culturally syntonic to respond to inquiries by the "doctor," but not to talk spontaneously about such matters. Once we were able to discuss this we worked out a reasonable balance of giving him enough room for elaboration and spontaneity and enough structure from me to allow him to feel he wasn't "out of line." As mental health professionals we often make judgments about confidence and self-esteem based on nonverbal communications (e.g., looking the clinician in the eye, assertions about needs). All of these behaviors have prescriptive guidelines based on culture, and there are enormous implications whether trying to construct an idea of normal human development or establishing guidelines for technique. It is now understood that the emphasis on neutrality in psychodynamic approaches is not achievable given that any comment, interpretation, and/or other form of intervention or the lack of a comment, interpretation, and/or other form of intervention represents a choice based on the clinician's theoretical framework, cultural perspective, and past experiences.

Anna Freud's classic paper (1965) on developmental lines also emphasizes a fundamental premise in psychodynamic theories: the importance of development for understanding normal and abnormal behavior. Object relations theories in particular focus on developmental stages that stand on a number of assumptions as summarized by Westen (1990). The assumptions are:

1. A continuum of development is isomorphic with a continuum of pathology (Peterfreund 1978, Westen 1989).
2. The origin of severe character pathology lies in the first three years of life.
3. There is a discontinuity between the pre-oedipal and oedipal years, such that certain fundamental phenomena (such as splitting, poorly integrated self-structure and narcissism) are transcended by the oedipal period.
4. "Object relations" refers to a unitary phenomenon or developmental line.
5. Developmental sequences in object relations are culturally invariant, and
6. Clinical data from pathological adults are necessary and largely sufficient for constructing and evaluating theories of object-relational pathology and development. [p. 662]

Empirical studies in the areas of infant research, social cognition, and cross-cultural development have challenged these assumptions. Stern's (1985) work challenged the assumption of infant autism and symbiosis. There also has been intense debate, as a result of Mahler's ideas about "normal" psychological development, about whether it is necessary for males and females to "separate and individuate" in order to have psychological health (e.g., Chodorow 1978, Gilligan 1982, Jordan and Surrey 1986).

Mothers have taken the lion's share of the blame when it comes to our interpretation of what goes wrong in development. There has been an overemphasis on maternal failure as the origin of psychopathology, granting mothers the power to "cause" schizophrenia, manic depression, and so on. It would seem the time has come to free ourselves from this deterministic approach to understanding human frailties. In so doing we also can give mothers a break from the omnipotence we have historically afforded them. "Idealization and blaming the mother are two sides of the same belief in the all-powerful mother. . . . Blame and idealization of mothers have become our cultural ideology" (Chodorow and Contratto 1982, p. 65). The assumption that the mother–child dyad is central to all psychological, relational, affective, behavioral aspects of a child's life, both as a child and later as an adult, has led to "psychological determinism and reductionism that argues that what happens in the earliest mother–infant relationship determines the whole of history, society, and culture" (p. 64). Because some psychoanalysts took Freud's ideas as scientific truth, generations of men and women have been labeled deviant in terms of gender and/or sexual orientation patterns. It is hoped that we have learned from the errors of our deterministic philosophies and can recognize that the complexity of growth and development defies a unitary theory linking cause and effect.

Just as the idea of a developmental line for psychological functioning is challenged by the very complexity of growth and change, terms like object relations don't capture the full range of personality factors that contribute to human behavior. Empirical studies of responses of clients diagnosed as borderline yield results that demonstrate the often confusing aspects of the term *object relations* (Lerner and St. Peter 1984, Westen 1990). For example, when borderlines are compared with schizophrenics and neurotics, findings suggest that the borderlines produce more malevolent Rorschach responses than schizophrenics. Interestingly enough, these respondents also demonstrate more inaccurately perceived percepts that are nonetheless of high cognitive-developmental level (Blatt et al.'s 1976 system). In other words, clients diagnosed as borderline demonstrate more advanced cognitive skills than the neurotic subjects in some areas. This is in contradiction to the prevailing ideology about borderline development originating in the preoedipal developmental level either via fixation or regression. Additional studies by Stuart and colleagues (1990) also indicate that while borderlines score high on attributional level (assumptions of others), they do so on human figures viewed as most malevolent. The complexity of attributions indicates more advancement than a toddler or latency-age skill level. Taking this complexity into consideration, and using clinical observation, social cognition, and object relations theory and research, Westen and colleagues (Westen and Segal 1988, Westen et al. 1985, 1988) developed a set of measures of dimensions of object relations. The scales include

> complexity of representations of people (tendency to represent people in rich and elaborate ways and to distinguish clearly their subjective experience and points of view), affect-tone of relationship paradigms (affective quality of the object world, from malevolent to benevolent); capacity for emotional investment in relationships and moral standards (need-gratifying orientation to the object world vs. investment in values, ideals and committed relationships), and understanding of social causality (tendency to attribute causes of behaviors, thoughts and emotions in complex, logical, accurate and psychologically minded ways). [Westen 1990, p. 677]

Findings indicate tremendous variability among these dimensions in the subjects diagnosed as borderline. The traditionally used term *object relations* does not allow for the complexity and variability in affect and cognition demonstrated in empirical studies such as these.

The historical emphasis on insight and analysis unfortunately resulted in a minimization of diverse opportunities for change outside the therapeutic office/relationship. Emphasis on fostering the transference neurosis meant "forcing" the symptoms/pathology to surface in therapy so that it could be altered. But this focus minimized and obscured the reality that people can change via many ways. This required time for the transference neurosis to both surface and be worked through—which realistically required an enormous commitment from client and therapist—emotionally, and economically. While not necessarily bad, such exclusiveness can make the theory hard to translate into other practice arenas and classes. Freud did acknowledge that with phobias extra means are necessary. "One can hardly ever master a phobia if one waits till the patient lets the analysis influence him to give it up. He will never in that case bring into the analysis the material indispensable for a convincing resolution of the phobia. One must proceed differently. . . . One succeeds only when one can induce them by the influence of the analysis . . . to go into the street and to struggle with their anxiety while they make the attempt" (Freud 1919, p. 166).

Historically, psychoanalysis has struggled with an identity crisis regarding which professional community was home, natural sciences or arts and humanities. While professing to be a science, there has been reluctance to incorporate advances in biological research in regard to the origins of mental disorders (e.g., schizophrenia, bipolar disorders). Giving biology its rightful place in terms of influence on development does call into question the role of development in understanding psychopathology. Stone (1997) concludes that despite Freud's belief that psychoanalysis could cure neurosis and patients could then deal with "ordinary human suffering" on their own, the reverse may be true. When we help clients deal with their symptoms, then psychoanalysis may help deal with "ordinary human suffering" (p. 39). The potential seems greatest in allowing psychoanalysis to take its rightful place, as numerous theorists have tried to do, as a hermeneutic discipline. Capitalizing on the constructivist movement, we can step away from the need to discern what actually happened in childhood to helping clients construct some meaningful narrative that helps them organize and understand their behavior and feelings. Numerous authors have taken that step (e.g., Saari 1991, 1993, Schafer 1981, Spence 1984).

In summary then, psychodynamic theory has contributed theories that dictate that human behavior is multidetermined and has multiple meanings. Influences on behavior include the unconscious, biology (including sexuality), family environment, human relationships, development in early childhood, and individual resiliencies and strengths. Historically lacking has been the empirical support for these suppositions and for the therapeutic techniques stemming from such beliefs. While clearly demonstrating an appreciation of the treatment relationship, also missing has been the capitalization on all of a client's strengths, including cognitive capabilities that are demonstrated in studies illuminating the many facets included in internal representations of relationships.

Numerous authors, theoreticians, and clinicians have endeavored to strengthen psychodynamic theories. Writers such as Wachtel (1977, 1997), Horowitz (1991), Strupp and Binder (1984), Luborsky and Crits-Christoph (1990), and Weiss and Sampson (1986) have worked to preserve the contributions of psychodynamic theory and incorporate new ways of thinking about the internal world that are consistent with the complexity we experience clinically and in empirical research. Pérez Foster and colleagues (1996), Comas-Diaz and Jacobsen (1991), and Roland (1988) also have challenged psychodynamic clinicians to rethink how the lens of culture reshapes our theories.

Readers interested in ongoing efforts at "preservation and in-corporation" will find much to savor in the writings of these authors. Interestingly, by drawing on the contributions of the theory, we see areas in which integration might occur. For ex-ample, the emphasis on the complexity of behavior paves the way toward eliminating the ethnocentrism of the theory if the complexity of meaning of other cultures is appreciated. Like-wise, understanding the multitude of meanings possible for be-havior prevents us from letting a biological understanding of a disease lose the human idiosyncratic factor. Extending the meaning of terms such as *object relations* also conveys some of the complexity in terms such as *cognition*. Perhaps early ideas about what can be included in conflict-free spheres can be elabo-rated on in ways that address these cognitive complexities. What is clear, however, is that much work remains in advancing and capitalizing on the strengths of psychodynamic theory.

STRENGTHS AND WEAKNESSES OF COGNITIVE-BEHAVIORAL THEORIES

Cognitive-behavioral theories and techniques offer many strengths. First, it is important to clarify what is meant by cog-nitive-behavioral. We are combining the two terms in this text, but in fact they represent two different developmental histories.

The cognitive interventions were typically developed by dynami-cally trained theorists and tend to emphasize the role of mean-ing. In these approaches, what a person thinks (or says) is not so important as what he or she believes. The cognitive-behav-ioral interventions were typically developed by theorists trained as behaviorists. In these approaches, thinking tends to be con-ceptualized in a more concrete fashion and is often regarded as a set of covert self-statements (private behaviors) that can be influenced by the same laws of conditioning that influence other overt behaviors. The cognitive theorists have led in developing strategies for examining the rationality or validity of existing beliefs, whereas the cognitive-behavioral theorists have focused on the development of strategies for teaching specific cognitive skills.

In fact, both approaches combine cognitive and behavioral elements, albeit in different ways and to different extents, and both legitimately belong to the larger family of cognitive-behavioral interventions. Moreover, each approach has borrowed from the other over the years, blurring the distinctions between them. Finally, there has been a growing interest among the cognitive-behavioral theorists in a constructivist approach that suggests that reality is a product of the personal meanings that people create (Mahoney 1993, Meichenbaum and Fitzpatrick 1993). This has led them to eschew the emphasis on rationality or empiricism that is the hallmark of the original cognitive theorists. As a consequence, some of the cognitive-behavioral theorists have become even more cognitive in their perspectives than the original cognitive theorists, further blurring the distinctions between the approaches. [Hollon and Beck 1994, p. 429]

By combining the two terms we are trying to capture the broad array of interventions that have come to be associated with cognitive and cognitive-behavioral theories. This also allows us to capture some of the shifts in theory and practice through the years. Suffice it to say, the lines are blurry at this point, and use of the term *cognitive-behavioral therapy* appears to be the most inclusive and accurate. Granvold elaborates further on the philosophical underpinnings and advancements in the following chapter.

As with psychodynamic theories, any attempt to summarize strengths and weaknesses of cognitive-behavioral theories runs the risk of distorting and misrepresenting the enormous efforts of leaders in this ever-expanding field. The reader should remember that this summary is written from the perspective of a psychodynamic practitioner, which clearly reflects a bias. From my perspective the strengths worth noting include empirical support for efficacy of treatment, emphasis on self-revision of theory and technique, targeting technique with specific client populations, educational aspects of the approach, collaboration between clinician and client, emphasis on relapse prevention, use of out-of-session time, structure and problem-solving aspects, focus on alliance with theoretical cognitive revolution, and new interest in the role of affect in behavior and cognition. Weaknesses in the field are the lack of focus on the role of trauma in the formation of schemas, differentiation in origin of core and peripheral schemas, lack of conceptual scaffolding for different experiences of mental dysfunctional states (including internal factors and external or cultural factors), and the historical minimization of the treatment relationship (including transference and countertransference effects).

One of the greatest strengths of cognitive-behavioral approaches is the emphasis on verifying the efficacy of its approaches with clinical populations. Recent years have produced a prolific body of literature that has demonstrated "carefully controlled, high-quality studies, most supporting the efficacy of these approaches" (Hollon and Beck 1994, p. 456). Theorists such as A. T. Beck, while trained psychodynamically, were frustrated by the lack of proof that what they were trying to accomplish in therapy was effective over time (J. Beck 1997). Over time we have seen dramatic support for the effectiveness of CBT in the treatment of panic and anxiety disorders. There is also indication that CBT is at least as effective as other methods with depression, bipolar disorder, bulimia, and conduct-disordered children. Perhaps the most significant factor in all of the literature is the commitment not to rest on assumptions about effectiveness and continue to refine and reshape treatment methods for improved empirical support for interventions. While there is no strong empirical support yet for treatment with personality disorders, much effort has gone into developing a model that lends itself well to evaluation (Beck et al. 1990).

Theorists and practitioners of CBT have continued to revise both theory and technique to take into account progress and setbacks in research. Such self-examination is another strength of this approach. In so doing, emphasis has remained on targeting specific problem areas of clients and contracting around those problem areas. "The articulation of a more explicit contract between patient and therapist need not exclude a concern with conflict or with examining the compromises and self-deceptions in the patient's life. But it does permit the patient to be a partner more fully in the therapeutic effort" (Wachtel 1984, p. 41). Particularly compatible with the social work profession's emphasis on strengths (e.g., Saleebey 1992), CBT is an approach that enlists the client as a partner in the process. Clients also gain through the emphasis on teaching within CBT via active participation (homework, thought records, prioritizing problems). Historically, one of the essential features of CBT has been the emphasis on active intervention (Wachtel 1984). While both psychodynamic therapy and CBT strive for understanding of the client's problems, CBT applies the understanding via a variety of techniques geared to change the identified problems. Terminology and rationale for treatment are presented as accessible tools for clients to use that can be experienced as empowering. By presenting an educational component in the treatment, client cognitive strengths are capitalized upon and strengthened (i.e., ego functioning).

When treatment goals are specific and mutually agreed upon by client and therapist, therapeutic outcome can be more easily measured. Measurable behavioral outcomes that are incorporated into the assessment process lend themselves to an evaluation of the efficacy of treatment. Certainly these features are appreciated, and now required, by third-party payers and others. Clients also benefit by the attention to demonstrating effectiveness. They learn usable tools for posttreatment that will enhance relapse prevention. CBT typically builds into the treatment process an emphasis on ongoing efforts by clients to monitor their own problems once treatment has ceased.

A major philosophical difference with classical psychoanalytic theory is the use of "out-of-session" time. Instead of trying to intensify the therapeutic relationship to re-create interpersonal conflicts, the therapist considers out-of-session time an appropriate arena to test solutions and identify problems, which is particularly important in the shorter treatments mandated today (see Chapter 13). This approach can also be interpreted by the client as a connection to the therapist, a way to continue thinking about and preserving the relationship beyond the in-session experience. The psychodynamic perspective offers a framework for understanding the meaning clients may make of "assignments" in terms of expectations of compliance or rebelling. However, the same behaviors can be understood from a CBT perspective and shared with the client, via understandings about attributions, self schemas, and so forth. Again, the client is brought into the process as a collaborator in observation and determining solutions (which minimizes blaming the client for resistance).

CBT also lends itself well to the tremendous variety of client populations and problems we serve. For example, for clients diagnosed as schizoid who are experiencing anxiety, the therapeutic relationship is often frightening and experienced as "too close." CBT can provide necessary structure and distance for clients who need it. For clients experiencing debilitating depression that is impairing daily functioning, CBT, in combination with psychotropic medications when appropriate, can mobilize behavior. For clinical practice with clients who have been marginalized in our society, CBT can provide a user-friendly framework that demystifies the therapeutic process. Boyd-Franklin (1989) speaks to the important therapeutic gains made when problem solving is an essential feature of the early phases in treatment with African-American families. She suggests that there are at least three benefits of specific, focused interventions: they (1) educate families new to the therapeutic process, (2) empower families with multiple problems by identifying and prioritizing problems, and (3) build credibility and trust for the clinician as problems are "addressed and solved" (p. 141).

Cognitive-behavioral models have kept pace with the "cognitive revolution" within psychology (Dobson and Craig 1996, p. vii). A prime example of changes within this area include revisions in ideas about information processing, motivation, and emotion. Of particular interest for integrative efforts between CBT and psychodynamic theories and practices are the last two areas—motivation and emotion. A precursor to understanding motivation were the efforts to supplement understanding of environmental behavior with models of self-regulation (Kanfer 1996). Current work recognizes that motivation in therapy and other areas is not limited to a personal characteristic, but includes "the capacity of the human organism for self-direction and continuing adjustment to the fluctuating environmental and biological conditions at any moment and also over the course of therapy" (Kanfer 1996, p. 2). The foundation of motivational models is in general systems theory with the understanding that for goal-directed behavior to take place, a current sequence of functioning must be interrupted either by succeeding at a previous goal or establishing a new goal of higher priority. "In clients who come to therapy, the interruptions are often created by environmental demands (extrinsic motivation) such as the loss of a job or referral by a physician. It is the first task of the therapist to develop self-generated goals (intrinsic motivation) for which therapy represents the instrumental pathways. Frequently, these personal goals are more distant, more abstract, and of lower value than the desire for immediate removal of a current distress" (p. 4). Consequently, the first task involves self-monitoring, which for many clients is a significant part of treatment: to get them to introduce the step of thinking about their behavior. Once clients are able to observe their behavior, they are well on their way to finding a more effective means of managing affect and behavior, which includes self-evaluation and self-consequation stages in CBT treatment.

While previously thought not to value the role of affect in understanding behavior, CBT has moved to viewing emotion as having a central role in explaining behavior (Kanfer 1996). Many schools of therapy, including psychodynamic therapy, have focused on how emotions can be disorganizing and disruptive. A critical issue in therapy is what interferes with clients' abilities to regulate their own impulses/behavior. "[I]ntense emotions tend to bypass self-regulatory processes, much as cognitively demanding tasks do [Kanfer and Stevenson 1985], and can reduce the effectiveness of self-control techniques. Thus therapists work for recognition of early cues of emotional arousal to which new behaviors can be attached before the client progresses to a highly aroused state" (Kanfer 1996, p. 23). These therapeutic tasks of CBT are quite similar to the efforts of therapy informed by ego psychology: supporting the ego's highest level of development, building an observing ego, and supporting the ego functions of impulse and affective regulation. Anticipating emotional arousal disrupts the automatic response sequences and allows clients to self-monitor prior to debilitating emotion-driven behavior. Awareness of the cues that lead to emotional arousal facilitate interactional improvement and intrapsychic change (Greenberg and Safran 1987). In an effort to compensate for the lack of historical attention to the role of affect, CBT has moved from the management of affect to the purposive and selective eliciting of affect (see Chapter 3). By shifting the narrow focus away from a view that emotional arousal is disruptive, clients can learn to distinguish between "good" (or ego-enhancing) emotional arousal and "bad" (or ego-impairing) emotional arousal.

Historically, Freud emphasized catharsis as essential to "chimney sweeping" of emotional trauma. Empirical research has indicated that "when the expression of affect merely recapitulates ancient patterns, it may be ineffective or even harmful in strengthening a patient's destructive interpersonal patterns" (Kanfer 1996, p. 24). Work with trauma survivors has emphasized that it is not just the reexperiencing of the trauma that is beneficial. Actions that allow for management of the unacceptable and intrusive memories as well as the extremely evocative affects are critical to the amelioration of the trauma (Heller and Northcut 1996). It is in this area of trauma that one of the weaknesses of CBT appears. There has been little attention to the role of trauma in the formation of schemas, core beliefs, and the like. Nor has much attention been paid to a clearer articulation of when certain events/experiences coalesce into core schema and when these same events may result only in peripheral schemas. What this deficit in the literature points to is the gap in understanding for layers of consciousness beyond what is immediately retrievable. Consequently, CBT is left without a conceptual understanding of the many ways in which clients may resist or block schema revisions. For example, without the concept of defenses and the unconscious, CBT has been missing a "tenable theory of personality" (Beck 1995, p. 29). As Westen points out (1991), CBT lacks the conceptual scaffolding for understanding the difference between "neurotic" depression, for example, and the depression experienced by clients diagnosed as borderline. There is a great deal of variability between clients in terms of how affect is experienced. Another example is noted in the use of a core belief of "I feel worthless." The "neurotic" affective experience of that core belief is distinct from the same expression "I feel worthless" from a client diagnosed as schizoid. It is critical to respect the internal world of the client as distinct, powerful, and idiosyncratic from client to client. Focus on the external world alone can be experienced by clients as reductionistic and nonempathic. Likewise it would be important to investigate the possibility of "cultural schemas" that capture commonalities of experience within different cultural groups. What appears to be needed is a consideration and balance of emphasis on internal and external factors that contribute to the formation of schemas and affects.

Making a distinction between different qualitative experiences of events and affects, CBT is freer to move in the realm of the treatment relationship. Attention to the therapeutic relationship and its effect has been minimized in the cognitive-behavioral literature. Recently, Beck and colleagues (1990) instructed that the treatment relationship must be considered in order to be therapeutically helpful. Particularly in work with clients diagnosed as personality disordered, the treatment relationship has to move to a primary position or else any therapeutic progress is blocked. Along these same lines is the need to take into account the therapist's feelings, attitudes, and cognitions toward their clients (countertransference). It seems likely that therapists have relevant schemas and attributions about themselves and others that impact the treatment process.

To summarize the contributions of cognitive-behavioral theory and technique, we can focus on the emphasis on empirical validation of effectiveness of treatment methods, which contributes to numerous revisions in theory; the fit between specific populations and specific techniques found to be applicable; the empowering aspects of didactic qualities of theory; the multiple avenues for growth, including out-of-session time and efforts to prevent relapse; and, finally, a commitment to keeping abreast of the research in the area of cognition and social cognition, especially in the areas of motivation and emotion. These strengths have contributed to the self-scrutiny of this theoretical school, enabling advancement particularly in the area of constructivism. As part of the cognitive revolution, writers have begun to alter the historical information processing view of the mind as a passive receptacle to one that considers the action involved with "knowing" (Bruner 1990). "Among other things, constructive perspectives emphasize the operation of tacit (unconscious) ordering processes, the complexity of human experience, and the merits of a developmental, process-focused approach to knowing" (Mahoney 1995, p. 7). It is fascinating to see the recent acknowledgment of the importance and the role of the unconscious in directing behavior. Despite the fact that the current view of the unconscious in cognitive-behavioral arenas is different from Freud's classical view (more along the lines of the constructivist view of tacit processes), this still represents a fundamental shift in theory.

There are numerous constructive approaches to psychotherapy (e.g., Guidano 1987, 1991, Mahoney 1988a,b, 1991, 1995, Neimeyer 1993, Neimeyer and Mahoney 1995). An emphasis on clients' construction of meaning makes room for considering different perspectives on core and peripheral beliefs.

Specifically, with a shift in philosophical stance, the cognitive-behaviorist can allow himself or herself to "hear" the multiple layers of meaning behind statements that previously may have sounded alike. This constructivist stance will allow further work in providing "conceptual scaffolding" for the many different stories our clients have to share.

KEY FOCUS AREAS NEEDED FOR BALANCED ASSESSMENT AND TREATMENT

What is evident from a closer look at the contributions of both psychodynamic and cognitive-behavioral approaches is that both approaches have moved to a point that considers the complexity present in the understanding of client affects, behaviors, and thoughts. While coming at theory development from different vantage points, it is striking that both psychodynamic and cognitive-behavioral fields have been influenced by postmodernism and thereby are making way for constructivist perspectives. While appreciating the interconnectedness of cognition, affect, and behavior, both perspectives place central value on the meaning clients place on each of these areas and on their own narrative history.

If we allow ourselves to consider the strengths and weaknesses of both theoretical schools, we find that perhaps a fuller assessment and practice would take into account several critical areas. First, the role of the internal world in negotiating and understanding external actions and events. For example, attention to the strengths of psychodynamic theory reminds the clinician to appreciate that the action of trying to incorporate another perspective into ongoing psychodynamic treatment has meaning for clients. Consequently, space must be allowed for clinician and client to examine the shifts as they occur. What is the meaning for a client when a clinician shifts from an analytic stance to a didactic position?

Second, it is important to keep on searching for ways to evaluate the effectiveness of our treatment, regardless of theoretical orientation. There are qualitative and quantitative means for doing so that can prevent empirical study from reducing variables to single dimensions; for example, did behavior change? Both schools demonstrate that a fuller understanding of our clients involves cognition, affect, and behavior.

Third, another variable critical to assess in addition to cognition, affect, and behavior is the role of the environment in instigating, contributing to, and perpetuating client problems. For example, ignoring the societal context of our theories prevents us from seeing the ways in which our therapeutic approaches prevent us from hearing the larger context of client narratives. In addition, when we open our theoretical "ears" we can listen for larger cultural schemas that may influence cognition, affect, and behavior.

It is clear that the psychodynamic theory and cognitive-behavioral theories have much to offer each other. Continued courtship and partnerships will give us room to evaluate how to purposefully and effectively integrate these historically important perspectives.

REFERENCES

Alexander, F., and French, T. (1946). *Psychoanalytic Therapy*. New York: Ronald.

Altman, N. (1995). *The Analyst in the Inner City*. Hillsdale, NJ: Analytic Press.

Arkowitz, H., and Messer, S. B., eds. (1984). *Psychoanalytic Therapy and Behavior Therapy: Is Integration Possible?* New York: Plenum.

Beck, A. T. (1995). Cognitive therapy: past, present, and future. In *Cognitive and Constructive Psychotherapies: Theory, Research, and Practice*, ed. M. J. Mahoney, pp. 29–40. New York: Springer.

Beck, A. T., Freeman, A., and Associates (1990). *Cognitive Therapy of Personality Disorders*. New York: Guilford.

Beck, J. (1997). *Cognitive-behavior treatment with anxiety disorders*. Presentation at Northwestern University Psychiatric Grand Rounds, Chicago, February.

Birk, L., and Brinkley-Birk, A. (1974). Psychoanalysis and behavior therapy. *American Journal of Psychiatry* 131:499–510.

Blanck, G., and Blanck, R. (1974). *Ego Psychology in Theory and Practice.* New York: Columbia University Press.

Blatt, S. J., Brenneis, L. B., Schimek, J., and Glick, M. (1976). Normal development and the psychopathological impairment of the concept of the object on the Rorschach. *Journal of Abnormal Psychology* 85:364–373.

Boyd-Franklin, N. (1989). *Black Families in Therapy: A Multisystems Approach.* New York: Guilford.

Bruner, J. (1990). *Acts of Meaning.* Cambridge, MA: Harvard University Press.

Chodorow, N. (1978). *The Reproduction of Mothering: Psychoanalysis and the Sociology of Gender.* Berkeley, CA: University of California Press.

Chodorow, N., and Contratto, S. (1982). The fantasy of the perfect mother. In *Rethinking the Family: Some Feminist Questions*, ed. B. Thorne and M. Yalom, pp. 54–75. New York: Longman.

Comas-Diaz, L., and Jacobsen, F. M. (1991). Ethnocultural transference and countertransference in the therapeutic dyad. *American Journal of Orthopsychiatry* 61:392–402.

Crain, W. (1992). *Theories of Development: Concepts and Applications*, 3rd ed. Englewood Cliffs, NJ: Prentice-Hall.

DeLaCour, E. (1996). The interpersonal school and its influence on current relational theories. In *Inside Out and Outside In: Psychodynamic Clinical Theory and Practice in Contemporary Multicultural Contexts*, ed. J. Berzoff, L. M. Flanagan, and P. Hertz, pp. 199–219. Northvale, NJ: Jason Aronson.

Dobson, K. S., and Craig, K. D. (1996). *Advances in Cognitive-Behavioral Therapy.* Thousand Oaks, CA: Sage.

Eagle, M. N. (1984). *Recent Developments in Psychoanalysis.* Cambridge, MA: Harvard University Press.

Elson, M. (1986). *Self Psychology in Clinical Social Work.* New York: Norton.

Ferenczi, S. (1988). *The Clinical Diary of Sandor Ferenczi*, trans. J. Dupont. Cambridge, MA: Harvard University Press.

Flax, J. (1997). *Taking multiplicity seriously.* Paper presented at the meeting of the Chicago Institute for Clinical Social Work, Chicago, June.

Frank, J. D. (1982). Therapeutic components shared by all psychotherapies. In *The Master Lecture Series: Vol. 1: Psychotherapy Research and Behavior Change*, ed. J. H. Harvey and M. M. Parks, pp. 73–122. Washington, DC: American Psychological Association.

Frank, J. D., and Frank, J. B. (1991). *Persuasion and Healing*, 3rd. ed. Baltimore, MD: Johns Hopkins University Press.

Freud, A. (1965). *Normality and Pathology in Childhood: Assessments of Development*. New York: International Universities Press.

—— (1966). *The Ego and the Mechanisms of Defense*. New York: International Universities Press.

Freud, S. (1899). Screen memories. *Standard Edition* 3:301–322.

—— (1900). The interpretation of dreams. *Standard Edition* 4/5.

—— (1912). Observations on transference love. *Standard Edition* 12:159–171.

—— (1919). Lines of advance in psychoanalytic therapy. *Standard Edition* 17:159–168.

Gabbard, G. (1994). *Psychodynamic Psychiatry in Clinical Practice: The DSM-IV Edition*. Washington, DC: American Psychiatric Press.

Garfield, S. L., and Bergin, A. E. (1994). Introduction and historical overview. In *Handbook of Psychotherapy and Behavior Change*. New York: Wiley.

Garrett, A. (1949). The worker–client relationship. *American Journal of Orthopsychiatry* 19(2):224–238.

Gilligan, C. (1982). *A Different Voice: Psychological Theory and Women's Development*. Cambridge, MA: Harvard University Press.

Goldfried, M. R. (1980). Psychotherapy as coping skills training. In *Psychotherapy Process: Current Issues and Future Directions*, ed. M. J. Mahoney, pp. 89–119. New York: Plenum.

—— (1991). Research issues in psychotherapy integration. *Journal of Psychotherapy Integration* 1:5–25.

—— (1995). *From Cognitive-Behavior Therapy to Psychotherapy Integration*. New York: Springer.

——, ed. (1982). *Converging Themes in Psychotherapy: Trends in Psychodynamic, Humanistic, and Behavioral Practice*. New York: Springer.

Goldstein, E. (1995). *Ego Psychology and Social Work Practice*. New York: Guilford.

Greenberg, J., and Mitchell, S. (1983). *Object Relations in Psychoanalytic Theory*. Cambridge, MA: Harvard University Press.

Greenberg, L. S., and Safran, J. D. (1987). *Emotion in Psychotherapy: Affect and Cognition in the Process of Change*. New York: Guilford.

Guidano, V. F. (1987). *Complexity of the Self*. New York: Guilford.

—————— (1991). *The Self in Process: Toward a Post-Rationalist Cognitive Therapy*. New York: Guilford.

Hartmann, H. (1958). *Ego Psychology and the Problem of Adaptation*. New York: International Universities Press.

Heller, N. R., and Northcut, T. B. (1996). Utilizing cognitive-behavioral techniques in psychodynamic practice with clients diagnosed as borderline. *Clinical Social Work Journal* 24(2):203–215.

Hollon, S. D., and Beck, A. T. (1994). Cognitive and cognitive-behavioral therapies. In *Handbook of Psychotherapy and Behavior Change*, ed. A. E. Bergin and S. L. Garfield, pp. 428–466. New York: Wiley.

Horowitz, M. (1991). *Person Schemas and Maladaptive Interpersonal Patterns*. Chicago: University of Chicago Press.

Jordan, J., and Surrey, J. (1986). The self-in-relation: empathy and the mother–daughter relationship. In *The Psychology of Today's Woman: New Psychoanalytic Visions*, ed. T. Bernay and D. Cantor, pp. 81–105. Hillsdale, NJ: Analytic Press.

Kanfer, F. H. (1996). Motivation and emotion in behavior therapy. In *Advances in Cognitive-Behavioral Therapy*, ed. K. S. Dobson and K. D. Craig, pp. 1–30. Thousand Oaks, CA: Sage.

Kanfer, F. H., and Stevenson, M. K. (1985). The effects of self-regulation on concurrent cognitive processing. *Cognitive Therapy and Research* 9:667–684.

Kernberg, O. F. (1975). *Borderline Conditions and Pathological Narcissism*. New York: Jason Aronson.

Kohut, H. (1984). *How Does Analysis Cure?* Chicago: University of Chicago Press.

Lerner, H. D., and St. Peter, S. (1984). Patterns of object relations in neurotic, borderline, and schizophrenic patients. *Psychiatry* 47:77–92.

Lifson, L. E., ed. (1996). *Understanding Therapeutic Action: Psychodynamic Concepts of Cure*. Hillsdale, NJ: Analytic Press.

Luborsky, L., and Crits-Christoph, P. (1990). *Understanding Transference: The CCRT Method*. New York: Basic Books.

Lyotard, J-F. (1984). *The Postmodern Condition: A Report on Knowledge*, trans. G. Bennington and B. Massumi. Minneapolis: University of Minnesota Press.

Mahler, M. S., Pine, F., and Bergman, A. (1975). *The Psychological Birth of the Human Infant*. New York: Basic Books.

Mahoney, M. J. (1988a). Constructive metatheory: I. Basic features and historical foundations. *International Journal of Personal Construct Psychology* 1:1–35.

—— (1988b). Constructive metatheory: II. Implications for psychotherapy. *International Journal of Personal Construct Psychology* 1:299–315.

—— (1991). *Human Change Processes: The Scientific Foundations of Psychotherapy*. New York: Basic Books.

—— (1993). Theoretical developments in the cognitive psychotherapies. *Journal of Consulting and Clinical Psychology* 61:187–193.

——, ed. (1995). *Cognitive and Constructive Psychotherapies: Theory, Research, and Practice*. New York: Springer.

Marmor, J. (1971). Dynamic psychotherapy and behavior therapy. *Archives of General Psychiatry* 24:22–28.

Masterson, J. (1976). *Psychology of the Borderline Adult*. New York: Brunner/Mazel.

Meichenbaum, D. H. (1990). Paying homage: providing challenges. *Psychological Inquiry* 1(1):96–100.

Meichenbaum, D. H., and Fitzpatrick, D. (1993). A constructive narrative perspective of stress and coping: stress inoculation applications. In *Handbook of Stress*, ed. L. Goldberger and S. Breznitz, pp. 706–723. New York: Free Press.

Messer, S. B., and Warren, C. S. (1995). *Models of Brief Psychodynamic Therapy: A Comparative Approach*. New York: Guilford.

Mitchell, S. A. (1993). *Hope and Dread in Psychoanalysis*. New York: Basic Books.

Moore, B. E., and Fine, B. D. (1990). *Psychoanalytic Terms and Concepts*. New Haven, CT: Yale University Press.

Natterson, J. M., and Friedman, R. J. (1995). *A Primer of Clinical Intersubjectivity*. Northvale, NJ: Jason Aronson.

Neimeyer, R. A. (1993). An appraisal of constructivist psychotherapies. *Journal of Consulting and Clinical Psychology* 61:221–234.

Neimeyer, R. A., and Mahoney, M. J. eds. (1995). *Constructivism in Psychotherapy*. Washington, DC: American Psychological Association.

Perez Foster, R., Moskowitz, M., and Javier, R. A. (1996). *Reaching Across Boundaries of Culture and Class*. Northvale, NJ: Jason Aronson.

Peterfreund, E. (1978). Some critical comments on psychoanalytic conceptions of infancy. *International Journal of Psycho-Analysis* 59:427–441.

Richmond, M. (1917). *Social Diagnosis*. New York: Russell Sage Foundation.

Roland, A. (1988). *In Search of Self in India and Japan: Toward a Cross-Cultural Psychology*. Princeton, NJ: Princeton University Press.

Saari, C. (1991). *The Creation of Meaning in Clinical Social Work*. New York: Guilford.

——— (1993). Identity complexity as an indicator of health. *Clinical Social Work Journal* 21(1):11–23.

Saleebey, D. (1992). Introduction: power in the people. In *The Strengths Perspective in Social Work Practice*, pp. 3–17. New York: Longman.

Schacht, T. E. (1984). The varieties of integrative experience. In *Psychoanalytic Therapy and Behavior Therapy: Is Integration Possible?*, ed. H. Arkowitz and S. B. Messer, pp. 107–131. New York: Plenum.

Schafer, R. (1981). Narration in the psychoanalytic dialogue. In *On Narrative*, ed. W. J. Mitchell, pp. 212–253. Chicago: University of Chicago Press.

Smith-Benjamin, L. (1990). Interpersonal analysis of the cathartic model. In *Emotion: Theory, Research and Experience: Vol. 5: Emotion, Psychopathology and Psychotherapy*, ed. R. Plutchick and H. Kellerman, pp. 209–229. New York: Academic Press.

Spence, D. (1984). *Narrative Truth and Historical Truth: Meaning and Interpretation in Psychoanalysis*. New York: Norton.

Stern, D. (1985). *The Interpersonal World of the Infant*. New York: Basic Books.

Stone, A. A. (1997). Where will psychoanalysis survive? *Harvard Magazine*. Jan/Feb, pp. 35–39.

Strachey, J. (1934). The nature of the therapeutic action of psychoanalysis. *International Journal of Psycho-Analysis* 15:127–159.

Strupp, H., and Binder, J. (1984). *Psychotherapy in a New Key*. New York: Basic Books.

Stuart, J., Westen, D., Lohr, N., et al. (1990). Object relations in borderlines, major depressives, and normals: analysis of Rorschach human figure responses. *Journal of Personality Assessment* 55:296–311.

Sullivan, H. S. (1953). *The Interpersonal Theory of Psychiatry*. New York: Norton.

Towle, C. (1940). Some uses of relationship. In *Helping: Charlotte Towle on Social Work and Social Casework*, ed. H. H. Perlman, pp. 66–73. Chicago: University of Chicago Press, 1969.

Wachtel, P. (1977). *Psychoanalysis and Behavior Therapy: Toward an Integration*. New York: Basic Books.

—— (1984). On theory, practice, and the nature of integration. In *Psychoanalytic Therapy and Behavior Therapy: Is Integration Possible?* ed. H. Arkowitz and S. B. Messer, pp. 31–52. New York: Plenum.

—— (1997). *Psychoanalysis, Behavior Therapy, and the Relational World*. Washington, DC: American Psychological Association.

Weiss, J., and Sampson, H. (1986). *The Psychoanalytic Process*. New York: Guilford.

Westen, D. (1989). Are "primitive" object relations really preoedipal? *American Journal of Orthopsychiatry* 59:331–345.

—— (1990). Toward a revised theory of borderline object relations: contributions of empirical research. *International Journal of Psycho-Analysis* 71:661–693.

—— (1991). Cognitive-behavioral interventions in the psychoanalytic psychotherapy of borderline personality disorders. *Clinical Psychology Review* 11:211–230.

Westen, D., Barends, A., Leigh, J., et al. (1988). Assessing object relations and social cognition from interview data. Unpublished manuscript.

Westen, D., Lohr, N., Silk, K., and Kerber, K. (1985). Measuring object relations and social cognition using the TAT: Scoring manual. Unpublished manuscript.

Westen, D., and Segal, H. (1988). Assessing object relations and social cognition from Picture Arrangement stories: Scoring manual. Unpublished manuscript.

3

Integrating Cognitive and Constructive Psychotherapies: A Cognitive Perspective

Donald K. Granvold

Cognitive psychotherapy methods were introduced and initially developed during the 1950s and 1960s when behaviorists and psychodynamicists were at the height of their debates. Three individuals stand out as the most noteworthy pioneers: George Kelly (1955) introduced personal construct psychology, Albert Ellis (1955a, 1958, 1962) created rational-emotive therapy, and Aaron T. Beck (1963, 1964, 1967) developed cognitive therapy out of his work with depression. The collective efforts of these clinicians and contributions from countless others produced a cognitive revolution in psychology. While there was resistance within the ranks of both the behaviorists and psychodynamicists, many found cognitive methods to be intriguing. Established therapists and a mass of newly trained clinician researchers, drawing upon the work of the early cognitivists, began to expand and further develop cognitive treatment procedures and to apply them to an array of clinical problems and populations. Many of these clinicians proceeded from an empirical orientation in which they sought research support for the efficacy of their interventions. The research findings generated by a multitude of outcome studies provided support for the effectiveness of cognitive therapy, and with the accumulation of research support came a proliferation of cognitive therapies. To date, more than twenty distinct varieties of cognitive therapy have been identified (Mahoney and Lyddon 1988). While cognitive therapies share the common distinction that cognitive factors are the primary focus in psychotherapy, behavioral procedures have been incorporated in most cognitive interventions.

Cognitive and cognitive-behavioral approaches are among the most frequently used intervention procedures by psychotherapists of various disciplines. This popularity is due in part to the trend toward the selection of interventions that have been found to produce rapidly effective and resilient (long-lasting and relapse-resistant) change. The strength of cognitive and cognitive-behavioral methods lies in their treatment efficacy and broad applicability.[1]

Cognitivists, while strongly committed to the efficacy of their methods, have been active participants in the psychotherapy integration movement. The idea that even greater effectiveness may result from the cross-fertilization of psychotherapeutic systems is enticing. This chapter introduces the reader to cognitivism and the formidable constructivism movement within cognitivism. The theoretical bases of cognitive and constructive treatment methods are delineated to facilitate the reader's consideration of integrating these methods with psychodynamic psychotherapy. In the latter section of this chapter, several important features of psychotherapy integration are presented and selected points of convergence and contrast between cognitive/constructive and psychodynamic therapies are discussed.

COGNITIVE METATHEORY

There appears to be no singular, succinct theory of cognitive therapy. Rather, cognitive therapists draw upon several established theories and integrate them with cognitive concepts. To this extent, a more accurate term for the theoretical foundation of cognitive therapies is metatheory—a related group of theories sharing assumptions and assertions. The following is a brief

---

1. See end of chapter for examples.

discussion of the most common theories evident in the clinical formulations of cognitivists.

Systems Theory

Most cognitivists ascribe to systems theory in which humans are viewed as living systems characterized as purposive, ever-evolving, steady-state seeking, and self-perpetuating. Consistent with this theory, a change in any component of the system is considered to effect change in other system components. Cognitivists have abandoned "one-sided determinism" in which human behavior is explained as the product of either environmental forces or internal dispositions (Bandura 1985). Instead, behavior, cognition, and personal factors (emotion, motivation, physiology, and physical factors) are considered to interact in a social/environmental context. According to this "reciprocal determinism" conceptualization, each factor is interactive, overlapping, and mutually influential (Bandura 1978). The constant flux of the system and its recursive nature result in the potential of any variable to be antecedent, mediating process, or outcome. Accordingly, human behavior cannot be attributed to any singular *cause*.

Systems theory posits that the human system seeks to sustain its integrity while continuing to evolve. To preserve its integrity and simultaneously to facilitate its evolution, the system operates with mechanisms to govern change. As extreme change is considered to be threatening to the system, core elements of the system remain change resistant. Cognitivists have identified these elements as core ordering processes (Mahoney 1991) or deep structures of self-knowledge (Guidano 1988). While operating at a tacit (unconscious) level, these structures have abstract ordering capabilities and function both to govern the individual's conscious processes and to constrain the individual's sense of self and the world.

The process of change is inherent in the human living system. Life is an ongoing recursion of perturbation and adaptation, disorganization and distress, and emerging complexity and differentiation (Granvold 1996b). The process is one of evolutionary self-organization—a dynamic organization–reorganization activity. Knowledge development, specifically self-knowledge, is assumed to follow this pattern. More complex and integrated levels of self-identity are achieved through the assimilation of perturbations produced by interactions with the world (Mahoney and Lyddon 1988). The human system seeks a dynamic balance between the comfort of maintenance and the drive to evolve described by Mahoney (1991) as "a 'moving balance' between familiarity (confirmation) and novelty" (p. 152).

Life-Span Development

Another contemporary trend that has had a remarkable impact on the theory and practice of counseling is the focused interest on human psychosocial development across the life span (Guidano 1987, 1991; Guidano and Liotti 1983; Kegan 1982; Mahoney 1991; Mahoney and Lyddon 1988). As noted above, the living system continues to evolve and develop. In systems terms, this development is the product of a reciprocal interdependence among the human's systems/subsystems in which a dynamic developmental and codevelopmental process occurs (Mahoney and Lyddon 1988). This dynamic evolutionary process takes place in and is a part of a social/ecological context. Historically, attempts to provide clarity to this process have been made by a number of noteworthy theorists who have conceptualized stages of human development (e.g., Erikson 1968, A. Freud 1953–1966, Maslow 1962, Piaget 1926, 1928, 1929). More recently there has been a "conceptual shift from stages and structures to systems and processes" (Mahoney 1991, p. 147). Interest has focused on the emerging, ever-evolving self and the proactive role the individual takes in his own development. Guidano (1991) notes that life-span human development is regulated by an orthogenetic progression. Periods of systemic relative stability are punctuated by growth periods in which the self system experiences upheaval, the result of which is a more complex and highly differentiated self. Ever-expanding knowledge of self, the world, and one's place in it relies on this process. Furthermore, this process is lifelong.

Attachment Theory

Attachment theory is considered by cognitivists as a viable way of conceptualizing the impact of early developmental experiences on identity, personality development, and psychopathology. While others have contributed, Bowlby (1969, 1973, 1980) continues to be the predominant figure in the articulation of attachment theory. According to the theory, an attachment figure provides a base from which early development takes place. While the individual develops degrees of self-reliance, the quality of trust and security provided in the primary bonding experience is highly influential in the establishment of a life pattern of functioning and development. In cognitive terms, these early bonding experiences result in the formation of self-schemas—relatively inflexible, general rules or silent assumptions (beliefs, attitudes, concepts) about self and one's relationship with others and the world. Early maladaptive self-schemas are considered by cognitivists to be significantly accountable for psychological disturbance and, furthermore, effective psychotherapy is highly contingent upon accessing and modifying them (Beck 1976, Beck et al. 1979, McGinn and Young 1996, Rush and Beck 1978, Young 1990).

Social Learning Theory

Many behaviorally trained professionals began to incorporate cognitive methods in their treatment procedures during the cognitive revolution when cognitive and cognitive-behavioral approaches gained popularity. A number of early cognitive methods showed evidence of strong behavioral influences. In this group were the covert conditioning therapies including systematic desensitization (Wolpe 1958), thought stopping (Lazarus 1971, Wolpe 1958, 1969), covert control (Homme 1965), covert sensitization (Cautela 1966), and covert modeling (Cautela

1971). Most of these methods soon lost their appeal, however, primarily as a result of a lack of empirical support.

Social learning theory (Bandura 1969, 1977) emphasized the role of cognitive mediation in human behavior. This represented a distinct departure from causal explanations of behavior that focused exclusively on external variables. While operant and respondent conditioning and vicarious learning processes were considered operative, Bandura made a clear statement that mediational variables could not be denied as behavioral determinants. Social learning theory has been highly influential in the shift in thinking of behaviorists whose methods had been focused exclusively on external variables as agents of behavioral control. The acknowledgment of cognitive mediation did not, however, result in the abandonment of behavioral procedures to produce behavior change. Rather, cognitive methods were combined with behavioral change strategies to produce effective interventions.

Cognitivists from this behavioral tradition continue to be sensitive to the role of external variables in their assessment and treatment procedures. Stimulus control, reinforcement control, and vicarious conditioning procedures remain viable considerations in helping people change.

Cognitive Theory

The essence of cognitive theory is that human existence is about meaning making. Inasmuch as cognition is conceptualized as structure, process, and outcome, cognitive functioning plays various roles in shaping human experience (Granvold 1995, Ingram and Kendall 1986). Not only is cognition implicated in psychopathology and in effective psychotherapy (Alford and Beck 1997), likewise, "adaptive, normal" human development is inherently cognitive. By logical extension, the cognitive components of human functioning are considered the critical assessment and intervention points in the theory of cognitive therapy.

A central tenet of cognitive theory is that humans actively

construct their own realities. Environmental stimuli, internally generated stimuli, and physical sensations all vie for the individual's attention. The individual actively selects, filters, and interprets the stimuli that impinge on him (Clark and Steer 1996). The result of this process is the generation of an idiosyncratic meaning. Not only is this meaning a consequence of the reciprocal interaction of variables (reciprocal determinism), but it serves as a key factor in the stimulation of cognitive, emotive, and behavioral consequences. Maladaptive cognitive, emotive, and behavioral responses, therefore, are considered to be largely the consequences of cognitive functioning. Current cognitive theory does not posit that cognition precedes and *causes* emotion in a sequential, unidirectional manner (Beck 1991, Clark and Steer 1996). It is assumed, however, that modifications in cognitive structure, process, or outcomes (e.g., beliefs, attributions, thoughts, images) are the most powerful, efficient, and resilient means to treat psychological disorders, behavioral problems, emotional distress, and unsatisfactory goal achievement.

Cognitive Structure

The structural component of cognitive functioning plays a primary role in the construction of meaning. Meaning making inherently involves abstract cognitive processes "that constrain (but do not specify) the contents of conscious experience" (Mahoney 1991, p. 104). This abstract ordering (cognitive structure) comprises cognitive networks, associative linkages, and other self-organizing processes. Operating at the tacit level, these processes govern the classifications that allow specific meanings to be reached. Hayek (1978) noted that the contents of experience are created by abstract processing far removed from the "experience of the experience." He goes on to state that "all the conscious experience that we regard as relatively concrete and primary, in particular all sensations, perceptions, and images, are the product of a superimposition of many 'classifications' of the events perceived. . . . What I contend, in short, is that the mind must be capable of performing abstract operations in order to be able to perceive particulars, and that this capacity appears long before we can speak of a conscious awareness of particulars" (pp. 36–37). This abstract operations level of knowing is conceptualized as an ensemble of schemas—core rules, meanings, and structures—that operate tacitly and with profound impact on the individual's constructions of self, others, the world, and his or her interactions interpersonally and with the environment. Schemas are viewed as active in biasing perception and memory as they inherently function in the encoding, storage, and retrieval processes (Brewer and Nakamura 1984, Dowd and Pace 1989, Hastie 1981, Taylor and Crocker 1981). These deep cognitive structures (Guidano 1987, 1988) or core ordering processes (Mahoney 1991), many of which have developed during childhood, exist as highly stable, resilient, and strongly defended processes. Cognitivists consider schemas to be difficult to access and, once accessed, they are extremely difficult to change.

From the above, it may appear that cognitivists, like Freudians, maintain the view that what is not conscious is subconscious. Mahoney (1991) notes, however, that Hayek's conceptualization of the abstract "is no seething caldron of repressed impulses and unresolved conflicts, and is not described as necessarily lower than the processes considered conscious" (p. 108). Rather, Hayek (1978) contended that the abstract rules that "govern the conscious processes without appearing in them" proceed not at too low a level but at too high a level, and therefore it is more appropriate that they be called "super-conscious" (p. 45).

Cognitive Processing and Cognitive Outcomes

The cognitive processing and cognitive outcomes components of cognition operate at the surface level of functioning. These explicit levels of self-knowledge are characterized as existing within conscious awareness or at peripheral, easily accessible levels. The cognitive model postulates that people are predisposed to process information in faulty ways, and in so doing arrive at cognitive constructions that lack logical or evidential support, or lack viability. Most humans are socialized to distort meanings and to make evaluative judgments of self, others, and the world in a negative, critical, and/or pejorative manner. Arbitrary inferences, negative causal attributions, and interpretations made from faulty premises represent common errors in information processing. These errors, typically evident in combinations, greatly contribute to negative conceptualizations of self, others, the world, and the future. It is assumed that exposure and modification of faulty information processing will lead to a reduction in the individual's vulnerability to negative bias and distorted elaborations of meanings in the future.

Beliefs, expectations, thoughts, opinions, evaluative standards, attributions, and images represent cognitive outcomes that may operate to promote an individual's well-being or, alternatively, function as determinants of disturbance and dysfunction. As is the case with cognitive processing, many individuals appear to be predisposed toward the construction of maladaptive meanings. These constructions in conjunction with schematic and processing functions are theorized to control psychological functioning.

Cognitive Change as Central to the Human Change Process

It is axiomatic that the pathway to effective change in human functioning is through cognitive change. Cognitive structure, process, and outcomes mediate behavioral, emotional, and, to a remarkable extent, physical and physiological functioning. Treatment of psychological distress, maladaptive behavioral functioning, and interpersonal problems requires changes in cognitive functioning. Likewise, the empowerment objective, described not only as an individual and collective development of understanding, voice, and influence over the social, political, and environmental forces that adversely affect people's lives, requires the promotion of the "power within" (Saleebey 1992). Individually, this "discovery" is a function of cognitive change. (The reader is directed to the following resources for further information on the principles and practice of traditional cognitive and cognitive-behavioral treatment: Beck et al. 1990, J. Beck 1995, Brower and Nurius 1993, Dattilio and Freeman 1994, Dattilio and Kendall 1994, Ellis 1994, Freeman et al. 1989, Granvold 1994, 1997, Salkovskis 1996, Scott et al. 1989, Vallis et al. 1991.)

COGNITIVE METATHEORY AND PRACTICE IMPLICATIONS

The cognitive metatheory articulated above is largely, but not exclusively, representative of orthodox or traditional cognitive therapy. Some of the features are representative of constructive metatheory as well. Early cognitive therapies, consistent with modern psychology, were based on an empiricist philosophy that contends that an invariant, external reality exists independently of the perceiver and that knowledge is sensory-based (Dowd and Pace 1989). This philosophy has come under recent challenge with the advent of constructivism. Mahoney (1993) notes that constructivism is the source of "the first conceptual debate in the [cognitive therapy] field" (p. 189). While this debate has been ongoing for well over a decade, it appears that the boundaries between cognitive and constructive therapies remain "fuzzy" and ill-defined. For example, some of the features described above as part of cognitive metatheory reflect the influence of constructivism on cognitive psychology. In particular, systems theory, life-span development, attachment theory, and much of the cognitive theory content, particularly cognitive structure and processing, are highly consistent with the constructivist perspective. There are, however, remarkable philosophical differences between those cognitivists who remain strongly wedded to empiricism and constructivists. These differences have profound clinical practice implications. Following is a discussion of the distinguishing features of constructive metatheory including a comparison of traditional cognitive and constructive clinical practice.

Constructivist Ontology

At the core of constructivist theory is the ontological position that "humans actively create and construe their personal and social realities" (Mahoney 1988, p. 364). Challenged is the view that an external reality objectively exists and is finitely transferred through the senses to effect personal "reality." According to this objectivist view, it is possible to achieve a "reality check" and "truth" objectively exists. R. A. Neimeyer (1993a) notes that, according to this correspondence theory of truth, "the validity of one's belief systems is determined by their degree of 'match' with the real world, or at least with the 'facts' as provided by one's senses" (p. 222). From a constructivist perspective, this search for validation is ill-conceived for there is no immutable "truth" to be reached or bedrock "reality" to be accessed. In constructivism, validity is rejected in favor of *viability*. The viability of any construction (conceptualized personal reality) "is a function of its consequences for the individual or group that provisionally adopts it (cf. von Glasersfeld 1984), as well as its overall coherence with the larger system of personally or socially held beliefs into which it is incorporated (Neimeyer and Harter 1988)" (R. A. Neimeyer 1993a, p. 222). To further clarify, data are not considered to "justify" or *validate* knowledge, "but selectively eliminate less *viable* explorations and conjectures" (Mahoney et al. 1995, p. 105). This distinction has extremely significant clinical implications. Rather than attempting to seek evidence to validate client constructions, treatment is focused on the generation of alternative conceptualizations and the determination of the viability (consequences and coherence) of· each construction.

Critical Constructivism and Radical Constructivism

Before proceeding with a presentation of other features of constructive metatheory, it should be noted that within the constructivist movement disagreement exists regarding ontology. It has been suggested that referring to "constructivism" as a singular noun is more rhetorical than realistic, for "even within the more narrow scope of psychotherapy, constructivists have been energetically pluralistic in their postulates and procedures" (Neimeyer 1995, p. 30). A significant divergence exists between the "critical constructivists" and "radical constructivists" as follows: "Critical constructivists tend to be realists who assume that there is a definite reality that people increasingly approximate in their constructs, even though they may never be able to 'access' it completely. In contrast, radical constructivists are idealists who do not concern themselves with the ultimate nature of a reality beyond the human experience" (Efran and Fauber 1995, p. 276). For the radical constructivist, "reality" does not exist externally, but is "exclusively a function of the structure of the human cognitive system" (Lyddon 1995, p. 73). Critical constructivism enjoys the greater popularity among clinical practitioners.

Human Knowing as Proactive and Autopoietic

Ontology and epistemology have been described as two sides of the same coin inasmuch as "knowledge is inseparable from existence, and existence is inseparable from knowledge" (Goncalves 1995, p. 204). The consistency in constructive ontology and epistemology is evident in the placement of the locus of knowledge development *within* the individual. A cardinal feature of constructivism is the "assertion that *human knowing* is active, anticipatory, and literally 'constructive' (form-giving)" (Mahoney et al. 1995). Not only is the mind considered to be proactive and generative, but human systems are considered to be *autopoietic*—self-organizing and active in determining their own evolution (Maturana and Varela 1980). To further elucidate, constructivism is based on a motor theory of the mind in which "the mind appears as an active, constructive system, capable of producing not only its output but also to a large extent the input it receives, including sensations that lie at the base of its own constructions" (Guidano 1988, p. 309). Knowledge is an evolutionary result and an interactive process. Further, knowledge development is biased by the self-organizing abilities of human cognitive processing (Guidano and Liotti 1983). This view stands in contrast to sensory theories that assert that information from the external world flows inward through the senses to the mind, where it is maintained. Popper (1972) refers to this view as "the bucket theory of the mind." Behaviorism and information-processing models are examples of psychological approaches based on sensory theory.

Core Ordering Processes

In the earlier section on cognitive structure, the role of abstract functioning in meaning construction was identified. The constructivist view asserts that a two-level model of knowledge processing exists, consisting of a tacit/explicit duality wherein unconscious processes are accorded a central role in the formulation of cognitive structures necessary for the ordering of everyday experience. These structures are critical to the integrity (stability) of the human system and therefore it is theorized that they are heavily protected against challenge. Even though they may promote disadvantageous outcomes for the individual, they remain relatively immutable. As such, they prevent the human system from becoming highly unstable. These deep cognitive structures (schemas) have abstract ordering capabilities and function at the tacit or unconscious level. These tacit ordering rules are considered to govern the individual's conscious processes and operate to constrain the individual's sense of self and the world. Change in these core ordering structures, although difficult to achieve, is assumed to be highly significant in the promotion of pervasive and resilient change.

Practice Implications

The metatheoretical assumptions outlined in this section, along with those constructivist features presented in the section on cognitive metatheory (systems theory, life-span development, and attachment theory), can be combined to shape interventions that range in their differences from slight to great in contrast to traditional cognitive procedures. As noted earlier, the boundaries between these approaches are not sharply delineated. In this section the practice implications derived from constructive metatheory will be briefly presented. (For more detailed descriptions of constructivist metatheory and the practical differences between cognitive and constructive psychotherapy approaches, see Granvold 1996b, Kuehlwein and Rosen 1993, Mahoney 1991, 1995, G. Neimeyer 1993, R. A. Neimeyer 1993a,b, Neimeyer and Mahoney 1995, Rosen and Kuehlwein 1996, Safran et al. 1986).

Life-Span Development

In contrast to the present focus of the traditional cognitivist, individual life-span development is explored in constructivist treatment. Treatment is dedicated to the ongoing emergence of the individual through increased self-awareness and self-actualization. The therapist promotes the proactive participation of the client in his or her own evolution and collaborates with the client in developing strategies to promote goal attainment. Particular attention is given to attachment processes as they relate to the client's contemporary relationships and his or her desire to expand his or her network of intimate social relationships.

Goal of Therapy: Problem or Process

From a systems theory perspective, personal evolution inherently involves a perturbation-assimilation dynamic. Discomfort is considered to be necessary for meaningful change. Thus, rather than framing client concerns as problems, a process orientation is assumed. The goal of therapy based on a problem view is corrective—to modify, minimize, or eliminate the problem. From a process view, a problem is conceptualized as a discrepancy between a client's current capacity and the developmental challenges being experienced. The "problem" may effectively function as the catalyst for systemic change. Eliminating the problem may actually impede the individual's development. Personal meanings are explored as they relate to personal development objectives. Such explorations may provide access to self-schemas and ultimately lead to core structural change. Alternatively, the focus may be on the appraisal of the *viability* of personal constructs and the development of more viable constructions.

Treatment of Emotion

Emotionality and emotional awareness processes are considered by constructivists to be integral to the personal meaning and personal development processes of the individual. Rather than exercising efforts to control, diminish, or terminate emotional expressiveness (considered to be intrusive or counterproductive), clients are encouraged to explore, experience, and express their emotions. An emotion traditionally considered to be "negative" or "maladaptive" (e.g., depression) is construed as potentially adaptive. It may be considered, as noted above, to be a *perturbation* to the self system, a motivating force for change. Emotions are construed as the human system's way of alerting the *self* that change is necessary for the resumption of greater comfort. To expect the perturbation-adaptation recursive to be free of discomfort is faulty unless the change demand is minimal. In sum, emotions serve a vital role in both promoting and effecting personal development.

Therapist Role

While both constructive and traditional cognitive therapists collaborate with their clients in developing an understanding of the idiosyncratic meanings the client brings to therapy, constructive therapists tend to be far less active-directive in the disputation of distorted, "unrealistic," or "irrational" beliefs and opt rather to Socratically guide the client in the development of more viable constructions. The interpretive guidelines (e.g., irrational beliefs, information processing errors) used by more "rational" cognitive therapists to accomplish cognitive restructuring are abandoned in favor of more creative, client-generated meaning-making procedures. Hence, rather than instructing the client in the cognitive model and its application, the therapist and client go exploring together. These expeditions, while reliant on the process expertise of the therapist and his or her knowledge base of the client population (Granvold 1996a), take both therapist and client into less well-charted territory and provide opportunities to creatively use a myriad of alternatives to do the "mapping."

The constructivist movement is strong within the cognitivist ranks. Most cognitivists are philosophical constructivists and have entered the postmodern era having reached the enlightened conclusion, as did Walter Truett Anderson (1990), that *Reality Isn't What It Used to Be.* For me, and many others I trust, the transition has posed a revolutionary challenge to many time-tested and relatively inexorable theoretical and clinical constructs that have served me well in my clinical practice. These traditional constructions have been a "part" of me—central to my professional-personal domain and of axiomatic status. They are, however, merely symbolic representations of an assumptive world and not immutable truths. In the words of George Kelly (1955), I and perhaps others have been suffering from *"hardening of the categories"*!

COGNITIVE AND CONSTRUCTIVE THERAPY INTEGRATION WITH PSYCHODYNAMIC THERAPIES

Intrigue with the possibilities of psychotherapy integration is not just a 1990s phenomenon. Its beginnings can be traced back to the early 1930s (Goldfried 1995). There has been a relatively recent surge of interest in the integration movement, however, evidenced by the founding of the Society for the Exploration of Psychotherapy Integration in 1983 and the initial publication of the *Journal of Psychotherapy Integration* in 1991. The integration movement is in response to the desire of many in the field to move from the competitive relationship among different approaches to therapy to a more open dialogue for the advancement of our collective knowledge of the clinical change process.

Rapprochement and Integration through Mutual Respect and Open Dialogue

I am of the view that efforts at psychotherapy integration should be undertaken with a spirit of openness to the synergistic potential of such endeavors rather than with turf-protecting mechanisms operating "on alert." Integrationists have called for a reduction in "acrimonious debates" (Castonguay and Goldfried 1994), and have encouraged a stance of "open inquiry, mutual respect, and transtheoretical dialogue" (Norcross 1990, p. 298). Whatever the theoretical persuasion, we are all seeking to facilitate the amelioration of client unrest, dysfunction, and dissatisfaction; the empowerment of the disadvantaged and disenfranchised; and the mobilization of an evolving self toward higher-order self-actualization. As noted at the end of the previous section, opening oneself to new perspectives and possibilities is challenging. While confining, there is comfort in the familiar. However, the rewards of expanding one's perspective, while possibly disconcerting, would appear to far outweigh the discomfort costs.

Take Heed of the Dodo Bird

Earlier I made reference to the clinical efficacy of cognitive and cognitive-behavioral therapies applied to many populations, but it is important to note that comparative outcome studies of different psychotherapy systems have failed to find significantly different outcomes. The outcomes appear to be approximately the same; therapists of different persuasions merely use different procedures to produce treatment effects. Drawing on this conclusion from their review of outcome studies, Luborsky and colleagues (1975) declared, as did the Dodo bird after the race in *Alice's Adventures in Wonderland,* "Everyone has won and all must have prizes." This finding of approximate equity in treatment effectiveness has since been referred to as the Dodo bird hypothesis.

Despite the bona fide evidence in support of the Dodo bird hypothesis, cognitivists and psychodynamicists have tended to hold on to the view that their way is *the* effective way to proceed. In George Orwell's *Animal Farm* (1946), one of the seven commandments governing the society was that "All the animals are equal." Over time this dictum became amended to "All the animals are equal but some are more equal than others." The amended form of this dictum appears to be operative among the psychotherapy schools as well: "All psychotherapies are equal; it's just that some are more equal than others."

Approaches to Psychotherapy Integration

Alford and Beck (1997) have identified three formal contemporary approaches to psychotherapy integration: (1) technical eclecticism, (2) theoretical integration, and (3) the common-factors approach. Technical eclecticism involves the use of methods from diverse psychotherapy systems. "Theoretical integrationists" attempt to bring diverse theories together in a synthesized manner. "Common-factors" proponents attempt to delineate and focus on the core features that characterize all approaches. Each approach to integration has meaningful potential but each has its own unique problems as well. Critics caution that technical eclecticism may result in the haphazard selection of techniques applied without benefit of an organizing theory; efforts at theoretical integration of extremely diverse theories may promote theoretical incoherence; and the focus on common factors may displace attention from the rich potential of the unique perspective, as well as reduce complex psychotherapy systems to elementary commonalities (Neimeyer 1995). The charge to the integrationist movement would appear to be to promote the ongoing development of a more highly theoretically integrated and technically multifaceted psychotherapy system.

The Myth of Uniformity

In the sections that follow I will briefly identify some similarities and differences between cognitive/constructive and psychodynamic therapies. First, however, it should be noted that numerous variations exist *within* psychotherapy schools. The "uniformity myth" (Kiesler 1966) is an important factor for one to consider in attempting to compare and contrast psychotherapies. As you read this volume, recognize that the data sources drawn for analysis may represent your construction of the psychotherapies more or less closely.

CONVERGENCE, CONTRAST, AND AREAS OF POTENTIAL MUTUAL INFLUENCE

Many aspects of the psychotherapeutic process deserve consideration in addressing the integration of psychotherapy systems. I have selected several for discussion knowing that, due to space limitations, other highly relevant considerations have been left out.

Schematic Change

Cognitive/constructive and psychodynamic therapies share a common focus on schemas. There is agreement that these meaning structures are at the core of psychological functioning and that psychopathology results from a disturbance of cognitive structures and content (Alford and Beck 1997, Beidel and Turner 1986, Beutler and Guest 1989, Bucci 1997, Dorpat and Miller 1992, Goldfried 1995, Rosen 1993, Soldz 1996). Schemas are represented as the "architecture" of cognition without which meaning construction could not take place. It is further recognized that schematic functioning, as noted earlier in this chapter, exists at an abstract level. Life experiences are filtered through these existing structures producing idiosyncratic meanings (reality). Thus, the past is inherently influential in present meaning making. The role of past (particularly early) life development on the present has always characterized psychodynamic psychotherapy. Proponents of both systems agree that the aim of treatment is cognitive change, and preferentially change in schematic functioning, which is considered to have pervasive effects.

Extratherapy versus Within-Therapy Emphasis

In seeking change at the structural, processing, and content levels of cognitive functioning, cognitive constructivists have tended to utilize behavioral, emotive-evocative (experiential), social-environmental, and an array of alternative cognitive change techniques in their treatment strategies. Socratic questioning methods and inductive reasoning procedures are frequently used to identify and modify cognitive processing, meanings with limited viability, and self-schemas underlying dysfunction. As with psychodynamic approaches, insight into intrapsychic functioning and a greater level of self-awareness are necessary for change. While maintaining the centrality of cognitive factors in human functioning and human change processes, however, many leading cognitivists contend that the inclusion of such behavioral components as behavioral activation and skills development are critical ingredients in the production of effective change (Bandura 1977, Beck 1985, Ellis

1994). Cognitivists utilize extra-session homework assignments and engage the client in discussions of social and environmental stressors. The consequences of behavioral responses are addressed to determine the existence and strength of external reinforcers (e.g., secondary gains). Comparatively, cognitive constructivists seek cognitive change in their clients through the orchestration of extratherapy experiences much more so than do psychodynamicists. Rather than promoting experience outside the session, psychodynamicists emphasize experiences within the therapeutic relationship to provide opportunities for change. Approaches that emphasize transference conceptualize technique and the therapeutic relationship as inseparable (Arkowitz and Hannah 1989). While this tradition of promoting new experiences within therapy continues to prevail, it is noteworthy that there is a movement to integrate psychodynamic and behavioral methods (Arkowitz and Messer 1984, Wachtel 1977).

Focus on Development

As addressed in the section on cognitive metatheory, traditional cognitivists and constructivists alike are attending more to childhood and adult developmental factors in their interventions. It is recognized that many maladaptive schemas have their etiology in early life experiences. Furthermore, these early maladaptive schemas have powerful influence over the change process. Soldz (1996) notes that all psychoanalytic schools emphasize that the "child is the father to the adult," a view that places all adult behavior contingent on childhood development. While maintaining respect for the tremendous impact that early life experiences have on the individual, constructivists, in particular, consider development to cover the life span. They do not view the past as indelibly maintained in the present or destined to be embedded in the future. Hence, change during adulthood may proceed beyond early developmental influences (Guidano 1991, Kegan 1982, 1994, Mahoney 1991). This latter view casts greater optimism on the possibilities of greatly overcoming the untoward effects of childhood mistreatment.

Emotional Arousal in Treatment

Cognitive and psychodynamic approaches to treatment have evidenced significant differences with regard to the role of emotion in the change process. Traditional cognitivists have tended to treat emotional expressiveness as problematic and have often labeled emotions as "negative." Emotional expressions have tended to be conceptualized as intrusive, maladaptive, debilitating, generally unpleasant to experience, and negative in effect (Granvold 1996b). Interventions have been developed and implemented with the purpose to control, alter, or terminate "negative" emotions (e.g., anger, depression, anxiety, guilt, sadness). While it is not uncommon for clients to be emotionally expressive in treatment, cognitivists have tended not to use emotive-evocative procedures in session. Psychodynamic therapy, in contrast, utilizes the therapist–client relationship for the purpose of re-creating emotional experiences in a "safe" context in which the therapist becomes an active participant in therapeutic reenactments. Change is facilitated through the affective reexperiencing of life experiences in which maladaptive behaviors and defensive interpersonal styles were evidenced (Arkowitz and Hannah 1989). The locus of learning is within the therapeutic relationship rather than through extratherapy experiences. Constructivists are aligned far more closely with psychodynamicists than with traditional cognitivists in their views of the role of emotion in human change. Affective experiences are considered to be powerful forms of knowing, and effective therapeutic change is produced through facilitating the experience, expression, and exploration of emotion, not through its control (Greenberg and Safran 1987, 1989, Guidano 1987, 1991, Mahoney and Lyddon 1988). The role of affect in constructivist approaches to therapy reflects far greater consistency with psychodynamic therapy than with orthodox cognitive procedures.

Embodiment Issues and Sexuality

The body and bodily experience have largely been ignored in the cognitive psychotherapy systems. While physical and physiological processes have received mention as reciprocally interactive determinants of human behavior (along with cognition, behavior, and other factors), the role of the body in the human experience (much less human change processes) has not been coherently delineated. Human mentation and human embodiment have remained as apparent dualistic entities. In reference to this neglect of embodiment, Mahoney (1991) suggests that psychotherapy is represented as if it took place between "talking heads."

Freud's theory of psychosexual stages, biological urges, and sexual fantasies, at a minimum, drew attention to the mind–body debate. Recent trends in psychoanalysis, however, have resulted in a deemphasis of the role of sexuality and bodily experiences in psychological and interpersonal functioning (Soldz 1996).

Human sexuality and other bodily experiences are highly significant components of the human experience. A perusal of the "human sexuality" section of your local bookstore will reveal a plethora of books on an amazing array of sexual topics. Or tune in randomly to any midday soap opera and find how little time passes before sexual or body function content is expressed. In my clinical experience it is a rare client whose concerns exist outside the realms of their sexuality or bodily experience. To the contrary, treatment of most individual and relationship problems involve some aspect of sexuality. Bodily experience outside the realm of sexuality is also frequently an important part of treatment (e.g., stress-related physical symptoms, psychosomatic disorders, health or physical aging concerns). In our integrative efforts, there is great need to elevate the importance of embodiment and sexuality aspects of the human condition and to seek their explicit incorporation with other primary components of human change and development.

CONCLUDING REMARKS

The cognitive therapies have developed through the integration of diverse approaches to clinical practice and the evaluation of their clinical efficacy. The influence of postmodernism has produced an evolution within cognitivism resulting in the advent of cognitive constructivism. While there are metatheoretical similarities between them, there are also profound differences between these practice ideologies. Yet many of us who practice cognitive intervention manage, we hope, to integrate the two in a coherent manner. Such integration requires first the inclination, followed by questioning, openness, imagination, and knowledge of the available options.

It is apparent that cognitivists have traditionally been integrationists, although not always gracious in our considerations. The methodologies we have collaboratively developed with our colleagues from diverse psychotherapy systems are testaments to the potential benefits of cross-fertilization. The integration movement is critical to the evolution of psychotherapy and the many other forms of human change processes. Franks (1984) has noted that "good theory, like good therapy, is merely a working approximation until a better theory comes along" (p. 254). It is a commitment to change rather than to the preservation of fixed psychotherapy systems that will allow a better theory, and hence better therapy, to "come along."

Endnote

1. Treatment efficacy has been demonstrated in the treatment of *affective disorders* (Beutler et al. 1987, Blackburn 1988, Bowers 1990, Clark and Steer 1996, Dobson 1989, Hollon and Najavits 1989, Michelson and Ascher 1987, Perris 1989), *anxiety and panic disorders* (Barlow 1988, Barlow et al. 1989, Beck and Emery 1985, Beck et al. 1992, Butler et al. 1991, Clark et al. 1994, Dattilio and Kendall 1994, Michelson and Ascher 1987), *social phobia* (Becker 1992, Emmelkamp et al. 1985, Gelernter et al. 1991, Heimberg 1990, Mattick et al. 1989), *personality disorders* (Beck et al. 1990, Freeman and Leaf 1989,

Layden et al. 1993, Linehan 1991, Linehan et al. 1993, Rothstein and Vallis 1991, Turner et al. 1994), *posttraumatic stress disorder* (Dancu and Foa 1992, Foa et al. 1991, Meichenbaum 1994, Parrott and Howes 1991), *schizophrenia* (Chadwick and Lowe 1990, Kingdon and Turkington 1991, 1994, Perris 1989, Perris et al. 1993, Perris and Skagerlind 1994), *child sexual abuse* (Deblinger 1992, Duehn 1994, Laws 1989, Sgroi 1989), *impulse control disorders* (Hazeleus and Deffenbacher 1986, Lochman et al. 1984, Novaco 1975, 1977a,b), *chronic pain* (Corey 1988, Eimer 1989, Keefe et al. 1990, Kerns et al. 1986, Linton et al. 1989, Miller 1991, Salkovskis 1989, Sanders et al. 1989, Turk et al. 1983), *eating disorders* (Agras et al. 1992, Cooper and Fairburn 1984, Craighead and Agras 1991, Edgette and Prout 1989, Fairburn 1981, Fairburn et al. 1991, Garner 1992, Garner et al. 1993, Mitchell et al. 1990, Smith et al. 1992, Telch et al. 1990, Wilson and Fairburn 1993), *medical disorders* (Dahlquist et al. 1985, Getka and Glass 1992, Jay et al. 1987, Kaplan et al. 1982, Kendall et al. 1979, Meichenbaum 1993, Perry et al. 1991, Telch and Telch 1986), *substance abuse* (Beck et al. 1992, 1993, Chaney et al. 1978, Sanchez-Craig et al. 1984, Schinke and Singer 1994, Shorkey 1994, Woody et al. 1983), *couple problems* (Baucom et al. 1990, 1995, Granvold and Jordon 1994), and *family problems* (Bedrosian and Bozicas 1994, Epstein et al. 1988, Huber and Baruth 1989, Munson 1994).

REFERENCES

Agras, W. S., Rossiter, E. M., Arnow, B., et al. (1992). Pharmacological and cognitive-behavioral treatment for bulimia nervosa: a controlled comparison. *American Journal of Psychiatry* 149:82–87.

Alford, B. A., and Beck, A. T. (1997). *The Integrative Power of Cognitive Therapy*. New York: Guilford.

Anderson, W. T. (1990). *Reality Isn't What It Used to Be*. San Francisco: Harper & Row.

Arkowitz, H., and Hannah, M. T. (1989). Cognitive, behavioral, and psychodynamic therapies. In *Comprehensive Handbook of Cognitive Therapy*, ed. A. Freeman, K. M. Simon, L. E. Beutler, and H. Arkowitz, pp. 143–167. New York: Plenum.

Arkowitz, H., and Messer, S. M., ed. (1984). *Psychoanalytic Therapy and Behavior Therapy: Is Integration Possible?* New York: Plenum.

Bandura, A. (1969). *Principles of Behavior Modification*. New York: Holt, Rinehart & Winston.

———— (1977). *Social Learning Theory*. Englewood Cliffs, NJ: Prentice-Hall.

———— (1978). The self system in reciprocal determinism. *American Psychologist* 33:344–358.

———— (1985). Model of causality in social learning theory. In *Cognition and Psychotherapy*, ed. M. J. Mahoney and A. Freeman, pp. 81–99. New York: Plenum.

Barlow, D. H. (1988). *Anxiety and Its Disorders: The Nature and Treatment of Anxiety and Panic*. New York: Guilford.

Barlow, D. H., Craske, M., Cerny, J. A., and Klosko, J. S. (1989). Behavioral treatment of panic disorder. *Behavior Therapy* 20:261–268.

Baucom, D. H., Epstein, N., and Rankin, L. A. (1995). Cognitive aspects of cognitive-behavioral marital therapy. In *Clinical Handbook of Couple Therapy*, ed. N. S. Jacobson and A. S. Gurman, pp. 65–90. New York: Guilford.

Baucom, D. H., Sayers, S., and Scher, T. G. (1990). Supplementary behavioral marital therapy with cognitive restructuring and emotional expressiveness training: an outcome investigation. *Journal of Consulting and Clinical Psychology* 58:636–645.

Beck, A. T. (1963). Thinking and depression: 1. Idiosyncratic content and cognitive distortions. *Archives of General Psychiatry* 9:324–333.

———— (1964). Thinking and depression: 2. Theory and therapy. *Archives of General Psychiatry* 10:561–571.

———— (1967). *Depression: Clinical, Experimental, and Theoretical Aspects*. New York: Hoeber. (Republished as *Depression: Causes and Treatment*. Philadelphia: University of Pennsylvania Press, 1972.)

———— (1976). *Cognitive Therapy and the Emotional Disorders*. New York: International Universities Press.

———— (1985). Cognitive therapy, behavior therapy, psychoanalysis, and pharmacotherapy: a cognitive continuum. In *Cognition and Psychotherapy*, ed. M. J. Mahoney and A. Freeman, pp. 325–346. New York: Plenum.

———— (1991). Cognitive therapy: a 30-year retrospective. *American Psychologist* 46:368–375.

Beck, A. T., and Emery, G. (1985). *Anxiety Disorders and Phobias: A Cognitive Perspective*. New York: Basic Books.

Beck, A. T., Freeman, A., and Associates (1990). *Cognitive Therapy of Personality Disorders*. New York: Guilford.

Beck, A. T., Rush, A. J., Shaw, B. F., and Emery, G. (1979). *Cognitive Therapy of Depression*. New York: Guilford.

Beck, A. T., Sokol, L., Clark, D. A., et al. (1992). A crossover study of focused cognitive therapy for panic disorder. *American Journal of Psychiatry* 149:778–783.

Beck, A. T., Wright, F. D., and Newman, C. F. (1992). Cocaine abuse. In *Comprehensive Casebook of Cognitive Therapy*, ed. A. Freeman and F. M. Dattilio, pp. 185–192. New York: Plenum.

Beck, A. T., Wright, F. D., Newman, C. F., and Liese, B. S. (1993). *Cognitive Therapy of Substance Abuse*. New York: Guilford.

Beck, J. S. (1995). *Cognitive Therapy: Basics and Beyond*. New York: Guilford.

Becker, J. S. (1992). Social phobia. In *Comprehensive Casebook of Cognitive Therapy*, ed. A. Freeman and F. M. Dattilio, pp. 71–77. New York: Plenum.

Bedrosian, R. S., and Bozicas, G. D. (1994). *Treating Family of Origin Problems: A Cognitive Approach*. New York: Guilford.

Beidel, D. C., and Turner, S. M. (1986). A critique of the theoretical bases of cognitive-behavioral theories and therapy. *Clinical Psychology Review* 6:177–197.

Beutler, L. E., and Guest, P. D. (1989). The role of cognitive change in psychotherapy. In *Comprehensive Handbook of Cognitive Therapy*, ed. A. Freeman, K. M. Simon, L. E, Beutler, and H. Arkowitz, pp. 123–142. New York: Plenum.

Beutler, L. E., Scogin, F., Kirkish, P., et al. (1987). Group cognitive therapy and Alprazolan in the treatment of depression in older adults. *Journal of Consulting and Clinical Psychology* 55:550–556.

Blackburn, I. M. (1988). An appraisal of cognitive trials of cognitive therapy for depression. In *Cognitive Psychotherapy*, ed. C. Perris, I. M. Blackburn, and H. Perris, pp. 329–364. New York: Springer.

Bowers, W. A. (1990). Treatment of depressed in-patients: cognitive therapy plus medication, relaxation plus medication, and medication alone. *British Journal of Psychiatry* 156:73–78.

Bowlby, J. (1969). *Attachment and Loss. Vol. 1, Attachment*. New York: Basic Books.

——— (1973). *Attachment and Loss. Vol. 2, Separation: Anxiety and Anger.* New York: Basic Books.

——— (1980). *Attachment and Loss. Vol. 3, Loss: Sadness and Depression.* London: Hogarth.

Brewer, W. F., and Nakumura, G. V. (1984). The nature and function of schemas. In *Handbook of Social Cognition,* vol. 1, ed. R. S. Wyer, Jr., and T. K. Srull, pp. 119–160. Hillsdale, NJ: Erlbaum.

Brower, A. M., and Nurius, P. S. (1993). *Social Cognition and Individual Change.* Newbury Park, CA: Sage.

Bucci, W. (1997). *Psychoanalysis and Cognitive Science.* New York: Guilford.

Butler, G., Fennell, M., Robson, P., and Gelder, M. (1991). Comparison of behavior therapy and cognitive behavior therapy in the treatment of generalized anxiety disorder. *Journal of Consulting and Clinical Psychology* 59:167–175.

Castonguay, L. G., and Goldfried, M. R. (1994). Psychotherapy integration: an idea whose time has come. *Applied and Preventive Psychology* 3:159–172.

Cautela, J. R. (1966). Treatment of compulsive behavior by covert sensitization. *Psychological Record* 16:33–41.

——— (1971). *Covert modeling.* Paper presented at the Association for the Advancement of Behavior Therapy, Washington, DC, Winter.

Chadwick, P. D. J., and Lowe, C. F. (1990). Measurement and modification of delusional beliefs. *Journal of Consulting and Clinical Psychology* 58:225–232.

Chaney, E. F., O'Leary, M. R., and Marlatt, G. A. (1978). Skill training with alcoholics. *Journal of Consulting and Clinical Psychology* 46:1092–1104.

Clark, D. A., and Steer, R. A. (1996). Empirical status of the cognitive model of anxiety and depression. In *Frontiers of Cognitive Therapy,* ed. P. M. Salkovskis, pp. 75–96. New York: Guilford.

Clark, D. M., Salkovskis, M., Hackmann, A., et al. (1994). A comparison of cognitive therapy, applied relaxation and imipramine in the treatment of panic disorder. *British Journal of Psychiatry* 164:759–769.

Cooper, P. J., and Fairburn, C. G. (1984). Cognitive behavior therapy for anorexia nervosa: some preliminary findings. *Journal of Psychosomatic Research* 28:493–499.

Corey, D. (1988). *Pain: Learning to Live Without It.* New York: Macmillan.

Craighead, L. W., and Agras, W. S. (1991). Mechanisms of action in cognitive-behavioral and pharmacological interventions for obesity and bulimia nervosa. *Journal of Consulting and Clinical Psychology* 59:115–125.

Dahlquist, L. M., Gil, K. M., Armstrong, F. D., et al. (1985). Behavioral management of children's distress during chemotherapy. *Journal of Behavior Therapy and Experimental Psychiatry* 16:325–329.

Dancu, C. F., and Foa, E. G. (1992). Posttraumatic stress disorder. In *Comprehensive Casebook of Cognitive Therapy*, ed. A. Freeman and F. M. Dattilio, pp. 79–88. New York: Plenum.

Dattilio, F. M., and Freeman, A., eds. (1994). *Cognitive-Behavioral Strategies in Crisis Intervention.* New York: Guilford.

Dattilio, F. M., and Kendall, P. C. (1994). Panic disorder. In *Comprehensive Casebook of Cognitive Therapy*, ed. A. Freeman and F. M. Dattilio, pp. 159–167. New York: Plenum.

Deblinger, E. (1992). Child sexual abuse. In *Comprehensive Casebook of Cognitive Therapy*, ed. A. Freeman and F. M. Dattilio, pp. 159–167. New York: Plenum.

Dobson, K. S. (1989). A meta-analysis of the efficacy of cognitive therapy for depression. *Journal of Consulting and Clinical Psychology* 57:414–419.

Dorpat, T. L., and Miller, M. L. (1992). *Clinical Interaction and the Analysis of Meaning: A New Psychoanalytic Theory.* Hillsdale, NJ: Analytic Press.

Dowd, E. T., and Pace, T. M. (1989). The relativity of reality. In *Comprehensive Handbook of Cognitive Therapy*, ed. A. Freeman, K. M. Simon, L. E. Beutler, and H. Arkowitz, pp. 213–226. New York: Plenum.

Duehn, W. D. (1994). Cognitive-behavioral approaches in the treatment of the child sex offender. In *Cognitive and Behavioral Treatment: Methods and Applications*, ed. D. K. Granvold, pp. 125–134. Pacific Grove, CA: Brooks/Cole.

Edgette, J. S., and Prout, M. F. (1989). Cognitive and behavioral approaches to the treatment of anorexia nervosa. In *Comprehensive Handbook of Cognitive Therapy*, ed. A. Freeman, K. M. Simon, L. E. Beutler, and H. Arkowitz, pp. 367–383. New York: Plenum.

Efran, J. S., and Fauber, R. L. (1995). Radical constructivism: questions and answers. In *Constructivism in Psychotherapy*, ed. R. A. Neimeyer and M. J. Mahoney, pp. 275–304. Washington, DC: American Psychological Association.

Eimer, B. N. (1989). Psychotherapy for chronic pain: A cognitive approach. In *Comprehensive Handbook of Cognitive Therapy*, ed. A. Freeman, K. M. Simon, L. E. Beutler, and H. Arkowitz, pp. 449–465. New York: Plenum.

Ellis, A. (1955a). New aproaches to psychotherapy techniques. *Journal of Clinical Psychology Monograph Supplement*, Vol. 11.

——— (1955b). Psychotherapy techniques for use with psychotics. *American Journal of Psychotherapy* 57:452–476.

——— (1958). Rational psychotherapy. *Journal of General Psychology* 59:35–49.

——— (1962). *Reason and Emotion in Psychotherapy*. Secaucus, NJ: Lyle Stuart.

——— (1994). *Reason and Emotion in Psychotherapy: A Comprehensive Method of Treating Human Disturbances*, rev. Secaucus, NJ: Birch Lane.

Emmelkamp, P. M. G., Mersch, P. P., Vissia, E., and van der Helm, M. (1985). Social phobias: a comparative evaluation of cognitive and behavioral interventions. *Behavior Modification* 7:331–344.

Epstein, N., Schlesinger, S. E., and Dryden, W., eds. (1988). *Cognitive-Behavioral Therapy with Families*. New York: Brunner/Mazel.

Erikson, E. H. (1968). *Identity: Youth and Crisis*. New York: Norton.

Fairburn, C. G. (1981). A cognitive behavioral approach to the treatment of bulimia. *Psychological Medicine* 11:707–711.

Fairburn, C. G., Jones, R., Peveler, R. C., et al. (1991). Three psychological treatments for bulimia nervosa: A comparative trial. *Archives of General Psychiatry* 48:463–469.

Foa, E. D., Rothbaum, B. O., Riggs, D., and Murdock, T. (1991). Treatment of PTSD in rape victims: a comparison between cognitive-behavioral procedures and counseling, *Journal of Consulting and Clinical Psychology* 59:715–723.

Franks, C. M. (1984). A rejoinder to Leon Salzman. In *Psychoanalytic Therapy and Behavior Therapy: Is Integration Possible?*, ed. H. Arkowitz and S. B. Messer, pp. 253–254. New York: Plenum.

Freeman, A., and Leaf, R. C. (1989). Cognitive therapy applied to personality disorders. In *Comprehensive Handbook of Cognitive*

Therapy, ed. A. Freeman, K. M. Simon, L. E. Beutler, and H. Arkowitz, pp. 403–433. New York: Plenum.

Freeman, A., Simon, K. M., Beutler, L. E., and Arkowitz, H., eds. (1989). *Comprehensive Handbook of Cognitive Therapy*. New York: Plenum.

Freud, A. (1953–1966). *The Standard Edition of the Complete Psychological Works*, ed. J. Strachey. London: Hogarth.

Garner, D. M. (1992). Bulimia nervosa. In *Comprehensive Casebook of Cognitive Therapy*, ed. A. Freeman and F. M. Dattilio, pp. 169–176. New York: Plenum.

Garner, D. M., Rockert, W., Davis, R., et al. (1993). Comparison of cognitive-behavioral and supportive-expressive therapy for bulimia nervosa. *American Journal of Psychiatry* 150:37–46.

Gelernter, C. S., Uhde, T. W., Cimbolic, P., et al. (1991). Cognitive-behavioral and pharmacological treatments of social phobia: a controlled study. *Archives of General Psychiatry* 48:938–945.

Getka, E. J., and Glass, C. R. (1992). Behavioral and cognitive-behavioral approaches to the reduction of dental anxiety. *Behavior Therapy* 23:433–448.

Goldfried, M. R. (1995). *From Cognitive-Behavior Therapy to Psychotherapy Integration*. New York: Springer.

Goncalves, O. F. (1995). Hermeneutics, constructivism, and cognitive-behavioral therapies: From the object to the project. In *Constructivism in Psychotherapy*, ed. R. A. Neimeyer and M. J. Mahoney, pp. 195–230. Washington, DC: American Psychological Association.

Granvold, D. K. (1995). Cognitive treatment. In *Encyclopedia of Social Work*, ed. R. L. Edwards, 19th ed., pp 525–538. Silver Spring, MD: National Association of Social Workers.

——— (1996a). Challenging roles of the constructive therapist: expert and agent of social responsibility. *Constructivism in the Human Sciences* 1:16–21.

——— (1996b). Constructivist psychotherapy. *Families in Society: The Journal of Contemporary Human Services* 77(6):345–359.

——— (1997). Cognitive-behavioral therapy with adults. In *Theory and Practice in Clinical Social Work: A Handbook for the 1990s and Beyond*, ed. J. R. Brandell, pp. 164–201. New York: Free Press.

———, ed. (1994). *Cognitive and Behavioral Treatment: Methods and Applications*. Pacific Grove, CA: Brooks/Cole.

Granvold, D. K., and Jordan, C. (1994). The cognitive-behavioral treatment of marital distress. In *Cognitive and Behavioral Treatment: Methods and Applications*, ed. D. K. Granvold, pp. 174–201. Pacific Grove, CA: Brooks/Cole.

Greenberg, L. S., and Safran, J. D. (1987). *Emotion in Psychotherapy.* New York: Guilford.

—— (1989). Emotion in psychotherapy. *American Psychologist* 44:19–29.

Guidano, V. F. (1987). *Complexity of the Self: A Developmental Approach to Psychopathology and Therapy.* New York: Guilford.

—— (1988). A systems, process-oriented approach to cognitive therapy. In *Handbook of Cognitive-Behavioral Therapies*, ed. K. S. Dobson, pp. 307–354. New York: Guilford.

—— (1991). *The Self in Process.* New York: Guilford.

Guidano, V. F., and Liotti, G. A. (1983). *Cognitive Processes and Emotional Disorders.* New York: Guilford.

Hastie, R. (1981). Schematic principles in human memory. In *Social Cognition: the Ontario Symposium*, vol. 1, ed. E. T. Higgins, C. P. Herman, and M. P. Zanna, pp. 39–88. Hillsdale, NJ: Erlbaum.

Hayek, F. A. (1978). *New Studies in Philosophy, Politics, Economics, and the History of Ideas.* Chicago: University of Chicago Press.

Hazaleus, S. L., and Deffenbacher, J. L. (1986). Relaxation and cognitive treatment of anger. *Journal of Consulting and Clinical Psychology* 54:222–226.

Heimberg, R. G. (1990). Social phobia: cognitive behavior therapy. In *Handbook of Comparative Treatments for Adult Disorders*, ed. A. S. Bellack and M. Hersen, pp. 203–218. New York: Wiley.

Hollon, S. D., and Najavits, L. (1989). Review of empirical studies on cognitive therapy. In *Review of Psychiatry*, vol. 7, ed. A. Frances and R. Hales, pp. 643–667. New York: American Psychiatric Press.

Homme, L. E. (1965). Perspectives in psychology: XXIV. Control of coverants, the operants of the mind. *Psychological Record* 15:501–511.

Huber, C. H., and Baruth, L. G. (1989). *Rational-Emotive Family Therapy: A Systems Perspective.* New York: Springer.

Ingram, R. E., and Kendall, P. C. (1986). Cognitive clinical psychology: implications of an information processing perspective. In *Information Processing Approaches to Clinical Psychology*, ed. R. E. Ingram, pp. 3–21. New York: Academic Press.

Jay, S. M., Elliott, C. H., Katz, E., and Siegel, S. E. (1987). Cognitive behavioral and pharmacological interventions for children's distress during painful medical procedures. *Journal of Consulting and Clinical Psychology* 55:860–865.

Kaplan, R. M., Atkins, C. J., and Lenhard, L. (1982). Coping with a stressful sigmoidoscopy: evaluation of cognitive and relaxation preparations. *Journal of Behavioral Medicine* 5:67–82.

Keefe, F. J., Caldwell, D. S., Williams, D. A., et al. (1990). Pain coping skills training in the management of osteoarthritic knee pain: a comparative study. *Behavior Therapy* 21:49–62.

Kegan, R. (1982). *The Evolving Self*. Cambridge, MA: Harvard University Press.

——— (1994). *In Over Our Heads: The Mental Demands of Modern Life*. Cambridge, MA: Harvard University Press.

Kelly, G. A. (1955). *The Psychology of Personal Constructs*, vols. 1 and 2. New York: Norton.

Kendall, P. C., Williams, L., Pechacek, T. F., et al. (1979). Cognitive-behavioral and patient education interventions in cardiac catheterization procedures. *Journal of Consulting and Clinical Psychology* 47:49–58.

Kerns, R. D., Turk, D. C., Holzman, A. D., and Rudy, T. E. (1986). Comparison of cognitive-behavioral and behavioral approaches for the treatment of chronic pain. *Clinical Journal of Pain* 1:195–203.

Kiesler, D. J. (1966). Some myths of psychotherapy research and the search for a paradigm. In *Prescriptive Psychotherapies*, ed. A. P. Goldstein and N. Stein, pp. 102–126. New York: Pergamon.

Kingdon, D. G., and Turkington, D. (1991). The use of cognitive behavior therapy with a normalizing rationale in schizophrenia: preliminary report. *Journal of Nervous and Mental Disease* 179:207–211.

——— (1994). *Cognitive-Behavioral Therapy of Schizophrenia*. New York: Guilford.

Kuehlwein, K. T., and Rosen, H. (1993). *Cognitive Therapies in Action: Evolving Innovative Practice*. San Francisco: Jossey-Bass.

Laws, D. R., ed. (1989). *Relapse Prevention with Sex Offenders*. New York: Guilford.

Layden, M. A., Newman, C. F., Freeman, A., and Morse, S. B. (1993). *Cognitive Therapy of Borderline Personality Disorder*. Needham Heights, MA: Allyn & Bacon.

Lazarus, A. A. (1971). *Behavior Therapy and Beyond*. New York: McGraw-Hill.

Linehan, M. M. (1993). *Cognitive-Behavioral Treatment of Borderline Personality Disorder.* New York: Guilford.

Linehan, M. M., Armstrong, H. E., Suarez, A., et al. (1991). Cognitive-behavioral treatment of chronically parasuicidal borderline patients. *Archives of General Psychiatry* 48:1060–1064.

Linton, S. J., Bradley, L. A., Jensen, I., et al. (1989). The secondary prevention of low back pain: a controlled study with follow-up. *Pain* 36:197–207.

Lochman, J. E., Burch, P. R., Curry, J. F., and Lampron, L. B. (1984). Treatment and generalization effects of cognitive behavioral and goal setting interventions with aggressive boys. *Journal of Consulting and Clinical Psychology* 52:915–916.

Luborsky, L., Singer, B., and Luborsky, L. (1975). Comparative studies of psychotherapies: Is it true that everybody has won and all must have prizes? *Archives of General Psychiatry* 32:995–1008.

Lyddon, W. J. (1995). Forms and facets of constructivist psychology. In *Constructivism in Psychotherapy*, ed. R. A. Neimeyer and M. J. Mahoney, pp. 69–92. Washington, DC: American Psychological Association.

Mahoney, M. J. (1988). The cognitive sciences and psychotherapy: patterns in a developing relationship. In *Handbook of Cognitive Therapies*, ed. K. S. Dobson, pp. 357–386. New York: Guilford.

—— (1991). *Human Change Processes.* New York: Basic Books.

—— (1993). Introduction to special section: theoretical developments in the cognitive psychotherapies. *Journal of Consulting and Clinical Psychology* 61:187–193.

——, ed. (1995). *Cognitive and Constructive Psychotherapies.* New York: Springer.

Mahoney, M. J., and Lyddon, W. J. (1988). Recent developments in cognitive approaches to counseling and psychotherapy. *Counseling Psychologist* 16:190–234.

Mahoney, M. J., Miller, H. M., and Arciero, G. (1995). Constructive metatheory and the nature of mental representation. In *Cognitive and Constructive Psychotherapies: Theory, Research and Practice*, ed. M. J. Mahoney, pp. 103–120. New York: Springer.

Maslow, A. H. (1962). *Toward a Psychology of Being.* Princeton, NJ: Van Nostrand.

Mattick, R. P., Peters, L., and Clarke, J. C. (1989). Exposure and cognitive restructuring for social phobia: a controlled study. *Behavior Therapy* 20:3–23.

Maturana, H., and Varela, F. (1980). *Autopoiesis and Cognition*. Boston: Reidel.

McGinn, L. K., and Young, J. E. (1996). Schema-focused therapy. In *Frontiers of Cognitive Therapy*, ed. P. M. Salkovskis, pp. 182–207. New York: Guilford.

Meichenbaum, D. (1993). The "potential" contributions of cognitive behavior modification to the rehabilitation of individuals and traumatic brain injury. In *Seminars in Speech and Language*, ed. M. Ylvisaker, pp. 18–38. New York: Thieme Medical Publishers.

———— (1994). *A Clinical Handbook/Practical Therapist Manual: For Assessing and Treating Adults with PTSD*. Waterloo, Ontario, Canada: Institute Press.

Michelson, L., and Ascher, L. M., eds. (1987). *Anxiety and Stress Disorders: Cognitive-Behavioral Assessment and Treatment*. New York: Guilford.

Miller, P. C. (1991). The application of cognitive therapy to chronic pain. In *The Challenges of Cognitive Therapy: Applications to Nontraditional Populations*, ed. T. M. Vallis, J. L. Howes, and P. C. Miller, pp. 159–182. New York: Plenum.

Mitchell, J. E., Pyle, R. L., Eckert, E. D., et al. (1990). A comparison study of antidepressants and structural intensive group psychotherapy in the treatment of bulimia nervosa. *Archives of General Psychiatry* 47:149–157.

Munson, C. E. (1994). Cognitive family therapy. In *Cognitive and Behavioral Treatment: Methods and Applications*, ed. D. K. Granvold, pp. 202–221. Pacific Grove, CA: Brooks/Cole.

Neimeyer, G. J., ed. (1993). *Constructivist Assessment: A Casebook*. Newbury Park, CA: Sage.

Neimeyer, R. A. (1993a). An appraisal of constructivist psychotherapies. *Journal of Consulting and Clinical Psychology* 61:221–234.

———— (1993b). Constructivism and the cognitive psychotherapies: some conceptual and strategic contrasts. *Journal of Cognitive Psychotherapy* 7:159–171.

———— (1995). Constructivist psychotherapies: features, foundations, and future directions. In *Constructivism in Psychotherapy*, ed. R. A. Neimeyer and M. J. Mahoney, pp 11–38. Washington, DC: American Psychological Association.

Neimeyer, R. A., and Harter, S. (1988). Facilitating individual change in personal construct theory. In *Working with People*, ed. G. Dunnett, pp. 174–185. London: Routledge/Kegan Paul.

Neimeyer, R. A., and Mahoney, M. J., eds. (1995). *Constructivism in Psychotherapy*. Washington, DC: American Psychological Association.

Norcross, J. C. (1990). Commentary: eclecticism misrepresented and integration misunderstood. *Psychotherapy* 27:297–300.

Novaco, R. W. (1975). *Anger Control: The Development and Evaluation of an Experimental Treatment*. Lexington, MA: Heath.

—— (1977a). Stress-inoculation: a cognitive therapy for anger and its application to a case of depression. *Journal of Consulting and Clinical Psychology* 45:600–608.

—— (1977b). A stress-inoculation approach to anger management in the training of law enforcement officers. *American Journal of Community Psychology* 5:327–346.

Orwell, G. (1946). *Animal Farm*. New York: Harcourt Brace.

Parrott, C. A., and Howes, J. L. (1991). The application of cognitive therapy to posttraumatic stress disorder. In *The Challenge of Cognitive Therapy: Applications to Nontraditional Populations*, ed. T. M. Vallis, J. L. Howes, and P. C. Miller, pp 85–109. New York: Plenum.

Perris, C. (1989). *Cognitive Therapy with Schizophrenic Patients*. New York: Guilford.

Perris, C., Ingelson, U., and Johnson, D. (1993). Cognitive therapy as a general framework in the treatment of psychotic patients. In *Cognitive Therapy in Action: Evolving Innovative Practice*, ed. K. T. Kuehlwein and H. Rosen, pp 379–402. San Francisco: Jossey-Bass.

Perris, C., and Skagerlind, L. (1994). Schizophrenia. In *Cognitive-Behavioral Strategies in Crisis Intervention*, ed. F. M. Dattilio and A. Freeman, pp. 104–118. New York: Guilford.

Perry, S., Fishman, B., Jacobsberg, L., et al. (1991). Effectiveness of psychoeducational interventions in reducing emotional distress after human immunodeficiency virus antibody testing. *Archives of General Psychiatry* 48:143–147.

Piaget, J. (1926). *The Language and Thought of the Child*. New York: Harcourt Brace.

—— (1928). *Judgment and Reasoning in the Child*. New York: Harcourt Brace.

—— (1929). *The Child's Conception of the World*. New York: Harcourt Brace.

Popper, K. R. (1972). *Objective Knowledge: An Evolutionary Approach.* London: Oxford University Press.

Rosen, H. (1993). Developing themes in the field of cognitive therapy. In *Cognitive Therapies in Action: Evolving Innovative Practice,* ed. K. T. Kuehlwein and H. Rosen, pp. 403–434. San Francisco: Jossey-Bass.

Rosen, H., and Kuehlwein, K. T., eds. (1996). *Constructing Realities: Meaning-Making Perspectives for Psychotherapists.* San Francisco: Jossey-Bass.

Rothstein, M. M., and Vallis, T. M. (1991). The application of cognitive therapy to patients with personlaity disorders. In *The Challenges of Cognitive Therapy: Application to Non-Traditional Populations,* ed. T. M. Valis, J. L. Howes, and P. C. Miller, pp. 59–84. New York: Plenum.

Rush, A. J., and Beck, A. T. (1978). Adults with affective disorders. In *Behavioral Therapy in the Psychiatric Setting,* ed. M. Hersen and A. S. Bellack. Baltimore, MD: Williams & Wilkins.

Safran, J. D., Vallis, T. M., Segal, Z. V., and Shaw, B. F. (1986). Assessment of core cognitive processes in cognitive therapy. *Cognitive Therapy and Research* 10:509–526.

Saleebey, D. (1992). Introduction: power in the people. In *The Strengths Perspective in Social Work Practice,* ed. D. Saleebey, pp. 3–17. New York: Longman.

Salkovskis, P. M. (1989). Somatic problems. In *Cognitive Behavior Therapy for Psychiatric Problems,* ed. P. Hawton, P. Salkovskis, J. Kirk, and D. Clark, pp. 235–276. New York: Oxford University Press.

———, ed. (1996). *Frontiers of Cognitive Therapy.* New York: Guilford.

Sanchez-Craig, M., Annis, H. M., Bornet, A. R., and MacDonald, K. R. (1984). Random assignment to abstinence and controlled drinking: evaluation of a cognitive-behavioral program for problem disorders. *Journal of Consulting and Clinical Psychology* 52:390–403.

Sanders, M. R., Rebgetz, M., Morrison, M., et al. (1989). Cognitive-behavioral treatment of recurrent nonspecific abdominal pain in children: an analysis of generalization, maintenance, and side effects. *Journal of Consulting and Clinical Psychology* 57:294–300.

Schinke, S. P., and Singer, B. R. (1994). Prevention of health care problems. In *Cognitive and Behavioral Treatment: Methods and Ap-*

plications, ed. D. K. Granvold, pp 285–298. Pacific Grove, CA: Brooks/Cole.

Scott, J., Williams, J. M. G., and Beck, A. T. (1989). *Cognitive Therapy in Clinical Practice: An Illustrative Casebook*. New York: Routledge.

Sgroi, S. M. (1989). *Sexual Abuse Treatment for Childen, Adult Survivors, Offenders and Persons with Mental Retardation: Vol. 2. Vulnerable Populations*. Lexington, MA: Lexington Books.

Shorkey, C. T. (1994). Use of behavioral methods with individuals recovering from substance dependence. In *Cognitive and Behavioral Treatment: Methods and Applications*, ed. D. K. Granvold, pp. 135–158. Pacific Grove, CA: Brooks/Cole.

Smith, D., Marcus, M. D., and Kaye, W. (1992). Cognitive-behavioral treatment of obese binge eaters. *International Journal of Eating Disorders* 12:711–716.

Soldz, S. (1996). Psychoanalysis and constructivism. In *Constructing Realities*, ed. H. Rosen and K. T. Kuehlwein, pp. 277–306. San Francisco: Jossey-Bass.

Taylor, S. E., and Crocker, J. (1981). Schematic bases of social information processing. In *Social Cognition: The Ontario Symposium*, vol. 1, ed. E. T. Higgins, C. P. Herman, and M. P. Zanna, pp. 87–134. Hillsdale, NJ: Erlbaum.

Telch, C. F., Agras, W. S., Rossiter, E. M., et al. (1990). Group cognitive-behavioral treatment nor the nonpurging bulimic: an initial evaluation. *Journal of Consulting and Clinical Psychology* 58:629–635.

Telch, C. F., and Telch, M. J. (1986). Group coping skills instruction and supportive group therapy for cancer patients: a comparison of strategies. *Journal of Consulting and Clinical Psychology* 54:802–808.

Turk, D., Meichenbaum, D., and Genest, M. (1983). *Pain and Behavioral Medicine: A Cognitive-Behavioral Perspective*. New York: Guilford.

Turner, R. M., Becker, L., and DeLoach, C. (1994). Borderline personality. In *Cognitive-Behavioral Strategies in Crisis Intervention*, ed. F. M. Dattilio and A. Freeman, pp. 25–45. New York: Guilford.

Vallis, T. M., Howes, J. L., and Miller, P. C., eds. (1991). *The Challenge of Cognitive Therapy: Applications to Nontraditional Populations*. New York: Plenum.

von Glasersfeld, E. (1984). An introduction to radical constructivism. In *The Invented Reality*, ed. P. Watzlawick, pp 17–40. New York: Norton.

Wachtel, P. L. (1977). *Psychoanalysis and Behavior Therapy: Toward an Integration*. New York: Basic Books.

Wilson, G. T., and Fairburn, C. G. (1993). Cognitive treatment for eating disorders. *Journal of Consulting and Clinical Psychology* 61:261–269.

Wolpe, J. (1958). *Psychotherapy by Reciprocal Inhibition*. Stanford, CA: Stanford University Press.

——— (1969). *The Practice of Behavior Therapy*. New York: Pergamon.

Woody, G. E., Luborsky, L., McLellan, A. T., et al. (1983). Psychotherapy for opiate addiction? Does it help? *Archives of General Psychiatry* 40:639–645.

Young, J. (1990). *Cognitive Therapy for Personality Disorders: A Schema-Focused Approach*. Sarasota, FL: Professional Resource Press.

4

Clinical Assessment

Nina Rovinelli Heller and
Terry Brumley Northcut

INTRODUCTION

Client assessment has always been viewed as a critical component of clinical social work. As with any therapeutic intervention, the assessment reflects the philosophical and theoretical persuasion of the clinician. In this chapter we draw on our psychodynamic training and current practice knowledge to propose assessment guidelines that utilize clients' cognitive capabilities. Cognitive theory and research provide extensive literature supporting the efficacy of techniques potentially useful for assessment. But however beneficial these techniques can be, they do not preclude the need for a foundation in psychodynamic theory and technique.

We focus specifically on two contemporary and seminal concepts from the cognitive and social cognition literatures: schemas and attributions. A careful assessment of schemas and attributions, when completed as part of a general ego psychological assessment, engages the client, facilitates the integration of historical and current affects and events, and offers a means of systematically exploring and challenging motivating beliefs and assumptions about the operation of the world. The clinician's integrative assessment can point the way to change and modification in all spheres of the client's life in a way that is tangible, not mysterious or magical.

In addition to recent emphases in cognitive science, our perspective is also influenced by philosophical changes reflected by the postmodern movement. Thus we begin our discussion of assessment by identifying the contextual pieces that inform these assessment guidelines. First, we will briefly discuss *values* that guide assessment and foundational *beliefs* that are present in psychodynamically informed practice. These values and beliefs compel us to explore cognitive techniques available to both clients and clinicians that may enhance the outcome of clinical work. In revealing underlying values and beliefs, the limitations in our endeavor will be clear. It is helpful to begin by specifying these common values and articulating more clearly the hypotheses that form the foundation of our psychodynamic practice because of variation in the meaning of "clinical social work practice." Meaningful discourse can occur only in response to clarity about these values and guiding assumptions.

Second, we define the components of a *knowledge* base that are fundamental to psychodynamic assessment, and present relevant cognitive concepts that enhance traditional assessment tools. While we believe it is critical to assess clients' cognitions, affects, behaviors, and social systems, our purpose is to focus on the cognitive concepts that can enhance the psychodynamic clinician's repertoire. As noted, we focus on two particular cognitive concepts, schemas and attributions. Our assumption is that the assessment of affect (modulation, range, congruence with situation, cultural context) and behavior (impulsivity, vegetative symptoms, functioning) is routine for the psychodynamic clinician. Also, social work training prepares the clinician to assess the level of support or stress present in the client's social arena. While we are emphasizing cognition, we want to make clear that we understand the influence of the larger social environment, the impact of chance life events, and the existence of resiliency as particularly important in the understanding of cognition and related affect and behavior. For this reason one of our clinical examples demonstrates the relevance of the social system not just in the area of stressors/support, but in the formation of schemas and attributions. A clinical assessment is incomplete if any area is overlooked, whether it be cognition, affect, behavior, or social context.

Third, we demonstrate through the use of another clinical example how the clinician can use these cognitive concepts to refine his or her *skills* and arrive at treatment formulations that are more dynamic and reflect the idiosyncracies of individual client(s). With such a dynamic treatment formulation, clinicians will be better able to allow for the judicious selection of cognitive techniques over the course of treatment. The psychodynamic foundation, along with the therapeutic alliance, provides the context for both client and therapist to examine the ramifications of the shifting of technique in response to a client's fluctuating need. The cognitive intervention provides the scaffold needed to capitalize on the client's strengths and to build skills that are underdeveloped or impaired. Skill building may not be a concept often discussed in psychodynamic literature; we believe, however, that we implicitly practice skill building in a manner that is both reminiscent of the role of "the friendly visitor" and compatible with the deficit model (e.g., Blanck and Blanck 1974, Kohut 1971). Also, recent psychodynamic literature discusses Vygotsky's concept of the zone of proximal development (ZPD) (Vygotsky 1978). ZPD has been adapted to characterize the therapeutic task as one that not only fills in the gaps but ushers in new development (Wilson and Weinstein 1989, 1992) a position consistent with our approach to skill development.

While we are proposing integrative assessment guidelines, we are not attempting to provide an integrative model of human functioning. In a sense it is reassuring that a comprehensive model of human functioning and human change is not yet possible. The ever-developing knowledge bases in biology, genetics, sociology, philosophy, social work, and psychology require us to be integrative with the understanding that our information is changing and incomplete. Perhaps our greatest contribution to our clients and to our social work theories is our willingness and comfort in not having all the answers while continuing our search to find what can be known. Wachtel (1985) has stated, "If your theoretical perspective has remained constant throughout your career, it's a good sign that you've been looking at too narrow a range of data" (p. 16). Adaptability, however, does not mean "throwing the baby out with the bathwater" but determining what is worth preserving of psychoanalytic theory while trying to incorporate other effective approaches (Edmundson 1997, Stone 1997). We also do not provide a comprehensive literature review of psychoanalytic theory and cognitive-behavioral theory and technique. Such reviews are plentiful (see references).

VALUES THAT GUIDE ASSESSMENT

Attention to the social work values underlying practice has been a cornerstone of social work education and practice since its inception. Its inclusion in social work literature generally transcends theoretical differences, although some theories emphasize certain values over others. There are several familiar social work values that have relevance to the assessment phase of practice and in particular to our assessment guidelines. The first and foremost value is "starting where the client is." If we effectively start where the client is, we must be willing to suspend our dogmatic commitment to a particular theoretical orientation. For example, a prior bias against cognitive-behavioral theory and practice may prejudice the psychodynamic clinician in a way that precludes seeing all of a client's cognitive capabilities.

A second foundational value is the client's right to self-determination. This value when operationalized translates to using skills that encourage (1) collaboration between clinician and client, and (2) the client's active participation in developing and articulating hypotheses about his or her experience. Good treatment is collaborative treatment and treatment begins with the assessment. If, at the beginning of the assessment, the client is understood as the expert or potential authority on the clinical narrative, he or she will assume some sense of ownership of the therapeutic process. This ownership leads to increased self-efficacy. Also, when the therapist and client collaborate about the focus, process, and content of therapy, the client is socialized more effectively to the therapeutic process, which generally has been linked to good treatment outcome (Orlinsky et al. 1994).

Third, the systems perspective has enhanced the clinician's commitment to balancing the focus on the individual and the environment, a value historically unique to social work. While the profession has traditionally viewed this value as the dynamic interaction between the individual system and external ones (e.g., Bandura's [1986] triadic reciprocity), we suggest that the internal system has a similar interactive process, that is, intervention in cognition will influence affect and behavior, and vice versa. The clinician's challenge, however, is how to choose the most effective and efficient point to begin.

Finally, we are reminded of one of the profession's ethical prescriptions in the area of development of new knowledge. "The social worker should critically examine, and keep current with emerging knowledge relevant to social work" (National Association of Social Work [NASW], Code of ethics). It is easy to see that this ethical code is in the best interests of our clients. However, we also benefit if we can use this "new knowledge" to facilitate the process of critical analysis. One avenue to critical analysis is to continually examine our way of conducting treatment together with those approaches that may seem antithetical to our training and treatment experiences. In so doing we refine and purify our own weltanschauung (worldview) (Flax 1997).

KNOWLEDGE BASE

Psychodynamic Foundation

Psychodynamically informed social work practice rests on some common premises in addition to the values described above. Our clinical work has demonstrated to us the power and utility of the unconscious and its contributions to cognition, affect, and behavior. We value retaining each of the psychodynamic perspectives for their contributions in understanding motives (classical psychoanalysis), resources (ego psychology), and interpersonal functioning (object relations and self psychology) (Westen 1991). We would add to these perspectives the critical and historically overlooked (at least in traditional psychodynamic and cognitive theories) impact of class, gender, race, cohort, spiritual beliefs, and ethnicity on intrapsychic and interpersonal functioning.

Brenner (1955) discussed the two fundamental hypotheses underlying psychoanalysis: the principle of psychic determinism and the principle that consciousness is the exception rather than the rule. We agree with these fundamentals, but add a few clarifications. While there are times when the client's actions are shaped by psychic determinism, there are also times when transformative chance events and/or trauma are not related to preceding psychic processes. As clinicians we are aware of the need to understand the precursors of thoughts, feelings, and actions. We also understand the need for the client's interpretation of this process. For even if the critical events are not related to the client's thoughts, feelings, or actions, he or she may erroneously associate the two (as often seen with trauma survivors). For this client it is therapeutically beneficial to confirm the *lack* of psychic determinism at work.

The power of the unconscious is perhaps one of the greatest contributions of classical psychoanalysis, as Brenner has highlighted. There are many instances when it is critical to understand latent content of the client's narrative, affect, and behavior. It is equally clear, however, as in Freud's classic words, that "sometimes a cigar is just a cigar." Cognition plays an important role in both instances. By accepting this central role of cognition, we can sidestep "either/or" and "higher/lower" discussions about consciousness and maximize the power of thoughts to mobilize and/or effect affect and behavior. There seems to have been a historical bias that the clinician's primary task was to uncover the unconscious determinants in order to effect structural change. This task makes sense in terms of the client's unconscious being the area unknown to the client and perhaps most troublesome. However, when we appreciate that the unconscious has a role but not the only role in a client's life, we can consider alternative interventions. For example, at times interpretations are essential in finding and emphasizing connections. Sometimes, however, insight is valuable but not sufficient. What is missing are tools the client can use to maximize functioning while the process of "working through" can be accomplished (Heller and Northcut 1996). Skill building when constructed from a dynamic and comprehensive understanding of the client can enhance ego functioning and promote self-efficacy. The client's activity in the process of skill building does not necessarily preclude utilizing the transference and/or insight-oriented work. Results of empirical studies indicate that a variety of factors are consistently related to positive treatment outcome, including but not limited to therapeutic skill, the treatment relationship, client openness versus defensiveness, and so on (Orlinsky et al. 1994). Skill building offers tangible goals that can lower client defensiveness and enhance personal investment in therapy. The combination of insight, the treatment relationship, and skill building appears to maximize clinical wisdom and empirical results.

One other contribution from psychodynamic theory that is relevant to our discussion is the emphasis on verbalization in therapy. Verbalization is believed to enhance the ego's ability to delay action and to tolerate frustration. Katan (1961) proposed that verbalization leads to increased mastery of the ego over affects and drives. The ego is capable of processing affects by discharging them appropriately and not resorting to defensive action such as suppressing or repressing them. Language facilitates this processing by objectifying or distancing behavior, feelings, or experiences that may have been foreign or frightening. By giving the experience a name, the previously private nonobjective experience is rendered less frightening and isolating since the name itself implies connections to others' experience (Scharfenberg 1988). Once an experience is expressed, the observing aspect of the ego is strengthened as well as the capacity for object relationships (another important ego function), and psychological development can proceed (Northcut 1991). By using cognitive explanations and tools for organization of data, the client is able to use "names" for interpersonal processes and beliefs that powerfully influence his or her feelings and behavior and provide needed distance and perspective.

Contributions from Ego Psychology

Despite the influence of recent theoretical reformulations and biological discoveries, we continue to return to ego psychology for its utility in organizing assessments. Particularly compatible with social work practice, ego psychology emphasizes the capacity for human adaptation in a number of domains, including cognition, affect, and behavior. Hartmann's appreciation of the need for an average expectable environment, for example, allows us to integrate myriad contextual factors into the assessment configuration.

We have found Goldstein's (1995) text *Ego Psychology and Social Work Practice* to provide a concise and usable description of the primary ego functions and their application in assessment. The social work literature is replete with numerous descriptions of the development and structure of the ego (e.g., Berzoff et al. 1996, Mackey 1985, Turner 1984, Woods and Hollis 1990). For clarity and familiarity we will draw from Goldstein's framework. We assume the reader has a basic understanding of ego psychology, its place in psychoanalytic theory development, and experience in conducting traditional ego psychological assessments.

As a review, the ego functions critical for assessment include reality testing; judgment; sense of reality of the world and of the self; regulation and control of drives, affects, and impulses;

object relations; thought processes; adaptive regression in the service of the ego; defensive functioning; stimulus barrier; autonomous functioning; mastery; competence; and synthetic-integrative functioning (Goldstein 1995). All of these ego functions have aspects of cognition, affect, and behavior. Some are weighted more heavily in one domain than another, however. For example, judgment is influenced by complex cognitive processes. Defenses on the other hand are going to be called into action to cope with overwhelming affect/anxiety. Clearly, the regulation of impulses is demonstrated by behavior, though the impulses may be stimulated by affective states. We are using the organizing concepts of cognition, affect, and behavior as distinct but necessarily overlapping and interacting concepts. To some degree this distinction is an artificial one (Kelly 1955). Perhaps future theoretical refinements within the cognitive and social learning fields will find new ways to capture the ingredients of cognition, affect, and behavior. At this point, though, these terms are familiar and functional. Further, these three categories provide the clinician with a means of organizing a tremendous amount of data. They also identify potential areas for intervention as well as specific techniques that will be based on the assessment. Again, it is important to note the fourth aspect of assessment, which will not be discussed in detail in this chapter: the need to assess social context and systems.

COGNITION OVERVIEW

There are many overlapping and some contradictory definitions of cognition. Some focus on biological processes; others focus on complex informational processes or distortions. We have found several to be both clinically relevant and important to our beginning understanding of critical developments in the cognitive field. Many of these theorists and clinicians, such as Mahoney (1995) and Goldfried (1995), have participated in the Society for the Exploration of Psychotherapy Integration (SEPI) and have fostered lively debates about areas of convergence and divergence among a number of mainstream schools of thought. The work of Beck (e.g., 1976, Beck et al. 1990), a pioneer in the field of cognitive therapy, is particularly relevant to our own clinical interests. Although his writings are not psychodynamically oriented (he was trained in psychoanalytic theory and technique, however), his work lends itself well to integration with our psychodynamic view.

When we think about what is important in understanding and utilizing the client's cognitions, both to understand the presenting problem and to marshal his or her strengths in the service of the therapy, our definition of cognition is broad and flexible. When hearing the client's story, and focusing on cognitive functioning, we first listen for the gross disorders of thought—hallucinations, latency of response, perseveration (essentially typical measures on a mental status exam). This focus is important diagnostically, particularly with the more "disturbed" client who may be suffering from an acute mental illness. Likewise, critical cognitive issues for evaluation are the influences of intelligence/developmental functioning, organic dysfunction, and confounding nonnative language issues. Social and cultural factors that impinge on or affect the appearance of cognitive functioning must also be taken into account. In addition, we introduce several other areas for observation and exploration that probe more selectively for what we can term *cognitive style*. Specifically, we are listening for how the client thinks about him- or herself, others, the past, the present, and the future. By adding emphasis on others, past, present, and future, we elicit information that informs us more specifically about social cognition, object relations, developmental history, and current functioning. At this point in theory development in both psychodynamic and cognitive schools, it is understood that cognition is closely interwoven with affect (Greenberg and Safran 1987, Lazarus et al. 1980). We are attempting to broaden and deepen the application of cognitive techniques and concepts so as to reflect the complexity and depth of psychodynamic understanding.

While it is assumed that with further study and refinement many aspects of cognitive theory and technique can be adapted by the psychodynamic clinician, we are choosing to focus on only two concepts. The two that we believe show the greatest promise for organizing data regarding cognitive material are (1) schemas (Note: Both *schemas* and *schemata* are used in the literature as the plural of schema), and (2) attributions. These two concepts of cognition form the building blocks for understanding patterns of thinking, consistencies and contradictions, distortions and inaccuracies. Schemata and attributions have in common a basis in cognitive and social cognition theory; a utility for pointing toward clear, systematic assessment and intervention; a focus for hypothesis building and case formulation, thereby offering potential for empirical study, adaptability for idiosyncratic client application, and potential for tracking change over time. These building blocks form the foundation for the discernment and assessment of predominant cognitions that continually influence and are influenced by affect, behavior, and components of the client's social system.

Schemas

There has been considerable variation in defining schemas; however, there has been some consensus. Singer and Salovey (1991) have provided a historical outline of the conceptual definitions of the term. Historically, the concept described "the process of attaching meaning to events and the integration of meaning within the individual" (Granvold 1994a, p. 19). Currently, a schema generally refers to "a cognitive representation of one's past experiences with situations or people, which eventually serves to assist individuals in constructing their perception of events within that domain" (Goldfried 1995, p. 55). In layperson's terms, schemas organize and direct how we experience the world around us. They screen, discriminate, weigh, and code stimuli. We can have person schemas, role schemas, event schemas, and procedural schemas (Fiske and Taylor 1984).

These "basic rules of life" are developed relatively early and are reinforced by others and by experience in the world. Because schemas form as a result of our socialization, they are influenced by our familial, social, religious, cultural, ethnic, and gender systems. Once schemas are formed, they are then activated by various stimuli, but vary in their effect on the individual. Of particular interest to clinicians is the role schemas play in shaping how interpersonal interactions are categorized, evaluated, and often distorted (Granvold 1994a).

Schema structures vary considerably not only in content but in form. They can be rigid or flexible, discrete or global, and primitive or more highly conceptually developed. Because schemas can be conscious or unconscious, they are of particular interest to us in terms of the role they may play in motivation and conflict, two critical concepts in psychoanalytic theory. While psychoanalytic theory has relied traditionally on the technique of free association to elicit unconscious material, cognitive-behavioral theory uses systematic techniques such as deductive reasoning, laddering, and the repertory grid (Granvold 1994a,b, 1997) to elicit schema content. In combination, techniques from both theoretical schools can access and connect conscious and unconscious material.

In addition, schemas can be as grand and as far-reaching as a weltanschauung or as narrow and specific as the affective, sensory, and behavioral components that are evoked by a specific experience; for example, entering Wrigley Field for a baseball game. The "world view" schema can include the past experience of being told one would never amount to anything by a parent, subsequent school failures, recent job losses, learned helplessness regarding one's ability to effect change, awareness of the high unemployment in one's cultural group, and the perception that life will never improve. A schema associated with baseball can include the smell of peanuts and hot dogs, the roar of the crowd, the music associated with the seventh inning stretch, and the pleasure of attending past games with a parent.

Because schemas function as memory structures, they connect new situations to old information or experiences. In other words, current stimuli are connected to one's idiosyncratic psychosocial history. It should be clear that schemas are more complex than the psychodynamic term *object representation* because they include data and experiences not necessarily represented in a unidimensional developmental model. They include cognition, arouse affect, and prescribe stylized behavior in many spheres (e.g., expectations for a marriage versus appropriate behavior at a baseball game). The clinician, however, is most interested in the influence of schemas to distort thought processing, evoke maladaptive emotional episodes, and activate faulty, exaggerated, or unrealistic expectations of self, others, or environmental conditions (Granvold 1997). For example, Cindy, after months of frustration and weeks of deliberation, decided to leave her job. Her supervisor readily accepted her resignation. In the session following this, Cindy was upset and worried and said spontaneously, "You can't count on anybody" and "People just won't accept you as who you are." This brief case illustration is an example of how a schema relating to her expectations of the world and others was activated in the face of her recent job loss and the ongoing conflict with a demanding boss. These were themes that had been addressed with good effect early in treatment using standard psychodynamic technique. However, the current problem (job dissatisfaction) and the historical antecedents (aspects of her relationship with her mother and with peers during puberty) converged to reactivate the now dormant schema. Directing attention to the cognitive schema was useful in strengthening problem-solving skills, exploring affect, and in disconfirming the schema as it related to many areas of her life. Because both schemas (as represented by comments regarding the world and others) condensed a great deal of affective and historical data, the systematic exploration of each one was expedient and readily understandable to the client.

Certainly, clients and clinicians function on a daily basis with adaptive and maladaptive schemas. However, stress may activate a dormant maladaptive schema that would be inhibited during "normal" functioning. When a crisis occurs, the individual's maladaptive schema may bias information processing. This situation is of course not limited to the clinical realm as described in the case of Cindy, above. For example, an experienced teacher maintains a self-schema of competency in the classroom and with her professional role. In normal circumstances this schema would be enduring and consistent. If this instructor uncharacteristically receives negative student evaluations one semester, these data would not be compatible with the existing schema. Therefore the evaluations could be categorized as the result of a "difficult" class or perhaps some of the student comments could be assimilated into suggestions for another semester. The primary professional self-schema would not be altered. However, if these evaluations were received during a time of personal stress, a dormant schema of past recriminations could be activated. This dormant schema, out of the teacher's conscious awareness, might appear unrelated to her professional self-concept and reflect, rather, schemas built up around other, earlier aspects of her self-concept. The current stress, however, would lower the amount of stimulation needed to activate this punitive self-schema. Of concern when these maladaptive schema are activated is not only the tendency to demonstrate errors in perception, information, and self-efficacy, but the likelihood that more negative emotions will be experienced. Perhaps most critical is the fact that behavior may also be altered in a manner that reinforces additional dysfunction and reinforces the negative self-schema (Granvold 1994a).

Many theoreticians/practitioners have added greater specificity to the concept of schema. The literature is also full of alternative terms such as *personal constructs* (Kelly 1955), *irrational beliefs* (Ellis 1973), and *deep structures* (Guidano 1987, 1988, Guidano and Liotti 1983, 1985) (Granvold 1994a). J. Beck (1995) uses the term *core beliefs* to describe those schema that pertain most centrally to the self. A. Beck (in press) theorizes that there are two major categories of core beliefs: those organized around the theme of helplessness and those organized around unlovability. These core beliefs typically contain those beliefs with both positive and negative valences. Narrative material that conveys a sense of helplessness, weakness, vulnerability, inadequacy, ineffectiveness, disrespect, and incompetence indicates helpless core beliefs. Material that contains themes of unworthiness, feelings of being unwanted, unloved, bad, or different, suggests the category of unlovable core beliefs. Core beliefs are characterized by their globality, rigidness, and overgeneralization.

Several authors differentiate between these core beliefs and peripheral ones (Guidano and Liotti 1983, Kelly 1955, Mahoney 1982, Meichenbaum and Gilmore 1984). Core beliefs tend to be self-referent and activate a great deal of affect (Saffron et al. 1986), and unconditional rather than conditional (Young 1990). Because of their affect-laden or derived natures and their fixed content, these core beliefs tend to be harder to change. Safran and colleagues also note the existence of common themes across patient populations, reflected as core cognitions. They further identify the importance of using cognitive techniques such as vertical exploration and downward arrowing to separate core beliefs from those more peripheral ones concerning a specific situation. In so doing the clinician should be aware not only of content issues but process ones, as demonstrated in the client's expression of his or her difficulties.

Young (1990) on the other hand, identifies sixteen distinct schemas and three processes by which schemas work. The latter include schema maintenance, schema avoidance, and schema compensation. The descriptions offered by Young are not unlike familiar descriptions of defensive functioning and include affective, behavioral, and cognitive aspects. What these various authors have in common in their descriptions of schemas/ beliefs is the idea that schemas are psychological/cognitive structures that have two primary functions, the processing of information and the understanding of life experience (Dattilio and Freeman 1994).

Numerous other attempts have been made to identify cognitive styles associated with various mental disorders (e.g., depression, anxiety, personality disorders) and to develop treatment protocols based on these clusters of typical schema (e.g., Beck 1976, Beck and Emery 1985, Beck et al. 1990, Young 1990). However, it is in the client's and the clinician's best interest to remember one of the strengths of the schema concept: its idiosyncratic nature. For example, the schema "I am helpless" associated with dependent personalities (Beck et al. 1990) will have different antecedents, stimuli, and affective experiences for each client, which must be understood in order to reconstruct the self-schema. Psychodynamically oriented clinicians are particularly adept at identifying the unique cognitive, affective, behavioral, and social factors in the client's narrative that may constitute this kind of schema.

Perhaps most intriguing to clinicians struggling to determine what would indicate a "good" schema or a "healthy" schema is the literature that indicates that "persons with more differentiated and complex self-schemas generally show less day-to-day variability in mood" (Singer et al. 1989, p. 340). Compatible with Saari's idea of "identity complexity" (1993), there is evidence that suggests clients and clinicians with a complex self-schema may be less susceptible to fluctuations due to affective shifts (Linville 1982). This evidence raises clinical and research questions regarding Kohut's ideas of the degree of fragility in the self, that is, the degree to which it is vulnerable to empathic failures. Does the person with more complex self-schemas react with fewer fluctuations in self-esteem? The use of the empirical literature on schemas can enhance clinical psychodynamic research, as we have seen with research conducted by Horowitz and even Luborsky's concept of the Core Conflictual Relationship Theme (Horowitz 1991, Luborsky and Crits-Christoph 1990, Singer and Salovey 1991).

One other clinical ramification is the "perseverance of the schema even in the face of conflicting evidence" (Singer and Salovey 1991, p. 39). We see this situation in our everyday work with individuals, couples, families, and groups. Understanding the process by which persons screen stimuli in or out does much to enhance our clinical wisdom and entices clients to observe their own action during interactions. We can even see this tendency with clinicians who cling to a diagnosis of a client because their schema "looks" for confirmation and disregards confounding data.

Attributions

While schemas have been a primary emphasis in the cognitive school, attributions have been the subject of much study within the social cognition literature. Attributional style refers to "people's views about the cause of life events, including their own behavior and that of others . . . implied causality" (Granvold 1994a, p. 15). This concept is important for several reasons. First, the literature from social cognition has effectively demonstrated the usefulness of the concept in predicting and explaining behavior (Westen 1991). Second, it represents a normal cognitive function. We all make attributions about events, people, and so forth in our lives. Where attributions can be troublesome, however, are when they are faulty and insufficiently and erroneously explain the events and interpersonal interactions around them. The inaccurate explanation sets in motion a series of inaccurate patterns that perpetuate and exacerbate the faulty attribution. In contrast to the concept of projection, usually considered a primitive defense, attribution can be explained to the client in a way that emphasizes the normalcy of making attributions. By normalizing the process, the client can be freed to look at the content of the attribution and to consider alternative explanations. Focusing on attributions also allows us to focus on interpersonal expectations, experiences, and interactions in a more prescribed manner than with the concept of schema.

Certainly the clinician needs to understand the attributions clients have about the interpersonal world around them. An ex-

pedient attribution to be concerned with is related to the transference. Attributions actually are a part of, and consequently
influence, transference. Westen (1988) has delineated seven
phenomena that fall into the category of transference: person
schema/object representations, attachments, schema-triggered
affects, interpersonal expectancies, scripts, wishes, and defenses.
Although the concept of transference is immensely valuable, "it
is important to distinguish between these aspects, since the
degree to which they, or their eliciting events, covary is by no
means clear" (p. 173). Psychodynamic clinicians, while familiar with transference, are not always clear about what elicits,
provokes, and/or diminishes the transference with each individual client. Westen explains the complexity of the concept and
the utility of looking at the various distinctions. Our job here
is to focus on just one aspect that may move the psychodynamic
clinician to look at how cognitive-behavioral concepts can add
to his or her understanding during the assessment phase. Also,
by beginning to add this piece in the treatment formulation, the
clinician has at his or her disposal an understanding of a process that can be shared with the client, enhancing the client's
knowledge and control. Some clients are alarmed, frightened,
or angered by references to the transference too early in treatment (which does not preclude that transference is being
enacted). Such reactions may affect the treatment process adversely. Commenting on how attributions affect all relationships, even the therapeutic one, sets the stage for future interpretations. In addition, educating the client about attributions
allows for framing the treatment relationship in a manner that
normalizes talking about the transference even in the early
sessions.

How might attributions appear in the clinical narrative?

At the lowest levels, causality is illogical or alogical, with confused, inappropriate or highly unlikely attributions. At the middle levels, subjects make accurate attributions that are relatively
simple and concrete. At the highest levels, subjects manifest an
understanding of the way complex psychological processes, in-

cluding unconscious processes, are involved in the generation of thoughts, feelings and actions. [Westen 1990, p. 679]

For example, the bride who thinks "it's raining on my wedding day because I shouldn't be marrying this man" demonstrates a low level of attributions. Although it is unlikely that this woman's faulty attribution is an indication of psychosis, it does demonstrate errors that if left unchallenged contribute to a potentially enduring style that will negatively affect the marital relationship. It is erroneous in that it assumes egocentricity, that is, the rain is a result of something connected solely to her. It also demonstrates grandiosity that her decision to marry could provoke rain. Further, on the surface it defies logic. For one client it could reflect a religious belief about punishment from God. For another client it could represent a level of object relatedness, which is concrete and preoperational. Nothing precludes both explanations. The value for the clinician in making this observation and distinction is that it flags an area for discussion that can also direct the treatment in a way that enlists the client's assistance in checking out the validity of her attribution. As with any piece of assessment data or inference, it is critical that the clinician determine whether this attribution represents an isolated discrete area or is more pervasive.

At the middle level of attributional style a client could state, "I was fired because my boss didn't like me." Such a statement may be true, but chances are it reflects only a portion of the scenario around his termination. It is indeed a simple understanding of why he was fired. Here too, it is important to determine whether this attibution represents his general mode of understanding others' actions toward him. Also, it may point the way to a self-schema that reflects the belief "I am no good." This client may need the worker's assistance to elaborate and consider multiple possibilities. The worker and client considering together all possibilities is a common cognitive-behavioral intervention, such as the Socratic mode of questioning or cognitive restructuring techniques.

The higher range of attributions may be demonstrated by the

client who voices her concerns that "my paper was rejected by this professional journal for several reasons. I think maybe I didn't have the target audience pegged right. Maybe I wasn't as clear as I needed to be. I should have had others read it to help me. The topic also might not be politically palatable. The editors may have had trouble being unbiased given their belief systems." This client's opinion about the range of plausible explanations for the rejection demonstrates an ability to consider alternatives and to take into account reasons that may not be clearly stated by the editors. Such attributions may be representative of a general style of understanding disappointment or interpreting the behavior of others. If these attributions are characteristic of a general style, the clinician may search for ways to capitalize on this skill in resolving the identified presenting problem for treatment. As with the other levels of attributions, the clinician must intervene differentially, based on his or her understanding of both the level and content of the attribution.

COGNITIONS AND THE SOCIAL REALM: A NEGLECTED DIMENSION

While we have focused primarily on schemas and attributions that have their etiology in the intrapsychic and interpersonal worlds of the client, it is also important to assess the development and maintenance (confirmation or disconfirmation) of schemas and attributions from the larger social realm. This realm includes social, historical, and cultural influences and those derived from an individual's cohort. This domain has been largely neglected in the vast cognitive literature. Its exclusion is of critical importance to the clinical social worker who strives to balance understandings of the client with his or her environment and to maximize clinical effectiveness with the client that often has been marginalized. Without exploring and identifying these realms, the clinician risks misunderstanding etiological and reinforcing factors in the client's environment that are critical to the understanding of the client's cognitive style. These environmental factors become particularly important when the schemas and attributions derived from the larger social system provide necessary survival strategies. Without understanding the relationship between the client's belief system and the larger environment, the clinician might be tempted to see these beliefs as faulty or defensive. As always, the client's collaboration is essential and can strengthen his or her understanding of him- or herself in relation to the world. Together, the client and the clinician can more clearly identify when it is the environment, not the client, that is "faulty." Ultimately, the treatment goal is enhanced ego functioning that allows the client to have good reality testing regarding problem identification, the ability to make more informed choices, and an increase in the repertoire of effective transactions with the environment.

By considering social systems in our analysis of individual cognitive style, we acknowledge our belief that these constructs develop over the life cycle in response to changing events. This is in contrast to the view that schemas develop early and are relatively fixed, awaiting triggers to be activated. Just as we appreciate the value in cognitive-behavioral advances, we can appreciate the advances in writings related to adult development that indicate object relations are modified over time (i.e., Nemiroff and Colarusso 1990). Likewise, even relatively enduring patterns can be altered negatively or positively in the face of trauma, marginalization, economic deprivation, or within the context of a long-term relationship.

While life events may confirm or disconfirm already established schemas and attributions, they can also initiate the building of new constructs, perhaps most dramatically seen in the face of life-altering crisis events. In fact, many of our clients seek treatment following such a crisis, which is usually unexpected. It is these clients who may be experiencing a "crisis of faith" or an existential crisis. The client's predominant affect may be extreme anxiety or depression, perhaps in part because existing schemas/beliefs have been challenged. On the other hand, for the client with a history of, for example, abuse, a rape as an adult may confirm preexisting and maladaptive schemas. In either case, the client is struggling with either assimilating or accommodating a new world view. Typically, this client feels as if her life has turned upside down. This disequilibrium may also take the form of a spiritual crisis. The disequilibrium, although traumatic, allows for the ability to be transformed, a vital component in resiliency (Himelein and McElrath 1996). Perhaps it is clinically easier when the crisis is obvious. For some clients the "crisis" is hard to discern in an ongoing social environment where crises permeate everyday life.

Consider the 10-year-old African-American girl who lives in the inner city and is referred to treatment for alternately aggressive and depressed behaviors. In her play she reveals repetitive activity and verbalizations regarding shootings and funerals. The worker notices further that the child has newfound difficulty relating to the teenaged brother with whom she was always quite close, despite his repeated attempts to engage her. One could make several assumptions about this situation. If the clinician does not directly explore or specifically listen for cognitive material, one might begin to entertain the possibility that the brother had abused her or that she was reacting to the brother's exercising his age-appropriate separation maneuvers from the family. If, however, the worker is listening for and eliciting possible schemas and/or attributions, he or she may detect an underlying schema about the future, particularly the brother's future. In this community the brother has moved into an age group at risk for violent victimization. This 10-year-old girl may be making an unconscious assumption, based on multiple observations regarding the fate of young men in her family and community. Her distancing behavior can be understood as a defense against the confirmation of this belief. To simply conclude that this young girl was making faulty assumptions is to miss the complexity of the context from which she derives her assumptions.

In the assessment process, the cognitively informed clinician would inquire how this girl is thinking about her brother, whether this has changed over time, and about her views of both her and her brother's futures. Once the beliefs are determined and/ or understood, the clinician can make the choice about what interventions can alleviate the affects and behaviors resulting from the beliefs. This clinical example is not a situation requiring the cognitive intervention that tests out the validity of the belief. Given the reality of her social environment, the belief cannot be disproved. Rather, the clinician may need to reinforce the reality of the community in which she lives, while tending to her underlying despair. The cognitive intervention may appear in efforts to actively intervene to prevent this schema from generalizing to "the whole world is unsafe and we all (cohort) are at risk." Problem solving (a cognitive and an ego supportive technique) for her and her brother about how best to keep safe may address the realistic factors of her fear. Also, finding a way to allow for turning passive into active would be ego-enhancing for her. For example, becoming a peer mediator in one of a growing number of school-based programs across the country would allow her to develop some sense of power in what appears to be a powerless situation. Such action may reduce her acute anxiety while preserving those aspects of a discrete schema that serve a protective and predicting function. Likewise, cognitive techniques described by Seligman and colleagues (1995) in their work on the Penn Depression Prevention Project with latency-age children (role plays, "disputing and decatastrophizing," tracking automatic thoughts, etc.) offer a means to focus on learned helplessness and pessimism to help prevent further depression.

This example demonstrates both psychodynamic and cognitive understanding of complex etiologies and manifestations of multifaceted problems. The inclusion of perspectives and techniques from both schools of thought provide the clinician and ultimately the client with a clearer picture of the problem and of directions toward enhanced functioning. Here, this young client can be assisted in using already existing strengths (sup-

portive family, ability to verbalize and symbolize, reality testing, etc.) to learn concrete skills and gain a clearer understanding of herself and the world around her. Modified schemas and
attributions can potentially help her to mobilize internal and
external resources to change the realities of her environment,
rather than simply to adapt to the harsh realities around her.

FROM KNOWLEDGE TO SKILLS IN ASSESSMENT: CASE EXAMPLE

The following clinical vignette is used to demonstrate the development of a cognitive formulation. Again, it is important to
remember that this cognitive formulation constitutes one aspect
of an overall ego psychological assessment.

Case Example

In a first interview a 20-year-old single woman, Jane, tells
the social worker about her recent rape while walking home
to her dormitory from the campus library. She states that
her friends and family have urged her to seek treatment.
"They're worried about me but I'm not quite sure why. I dealt
with all that rape stuff with the crisis worker when it happened." However, she still expresses feelings of shame and
self-blame about the rape. Her narrative regarding the rape
centers around her belief that it was her fault, that she
"should not have walked home," that "I knew I shouldn't have
lost weight last year." She harbored the belief that if she'd
weighed twenty pounds more she would not have been raped:
"He wouldn't have wanted me then." She complains that since
the rape, six months ago, she is "eating everything in sight."
She also will not venture from her room after dark and had
become quite incensed when the intake worker offered her
an evening appointment. She further states that "it's no surprise this happened" and reveals a history of verbal abuse
by her father that began at puberty, manifested by his "pok-

ing fun at my body," saying, "I was a tease," and that "I'd better be careful or I'd end up pregnant." She reports a satisfactory and benevolent relationship with him prior to that time. She also reports her belief that her mother was uncomfortable about his behavior but "I guess she really didn't know what to do either."

In consideration of the cognitive assessment of this client, the worker ascertains that Jane is not psychotic, that there is neither latency of response nor paucity of speech and her articulations are sequential and generally coherent. The clinician assesses that Jane's cognitions are "intact," that she is of above average intelligence, and that there are no apparent organic limitations. For most psychodynamically oriented clinicians this information would suffice for the assessment of cognitive functioning. We are interested, here, in the potential yield of a more multidimensioned exploration of the client's cognitions. We utilize the following outline to identify and organize relevant areas for further exploration in preparation for the cognitive conceptualization. Clearly this material is greatly condensed and serves only as an organizational tool for the systematic consideration of the client's narrative material.

1. Presenting problem
   a. Recent rape
2. Behavioral sequelae
   a. Bingeing behavior with attendant weight gain
   b. Refusal to leave dorm after dark
3. Affective sequelae
   a. Fear
   b. Increased anxiety
   c. Shame
4. Historical antecedents
   a. Father's verbal abuse
   b. Vulnerability at puberty
5. Social/contextual issues
   a. Women's vulnerability to violence

  b. Victim blaming
  c. Societal norm/expectation of thinness

The outline reflects the underpinnings of the clinician's beginning hypotheses about likely schemas and attributions, based on the client's own words. Each of the terms listed under each category does not individually constitute the client's primary schemas or attributions. Each term does, however, provide a thematic "road map" that guides the clinician in identifying the areas that will need further exploration. In this case Jane is able to take an active role in considering her own cognitions. The degree of her distress (evident, but not incapacitating) and her innate cognitive strengths contribute to her ability to help identify both schemas and attributions.

The precipitating event is quite evident (Hoffman and Remmel 1975). It is a discrete event, as opposed to an existential crisis or affective state. In cases in which the presenting problem is not as clear, considerable effort is spent in clarifying this. Questions that address the timing and "Why now" aspects (Budman and Gurman 1988) are particularly useful in clarifying the presenting problem.

Schema Identification

Having reviewed the client's narrative material and identified the various sequelae, antecedents, and contextual factors, the worker identified the schemas listed below. We illustrate the use of fairly detailed schemas, which reflect the idiosyncratic features of the client's situation. Detailed schemas such as these vary from some of the more traditional examples of clinical schemas (e.g., Beck) that have typically grouped together more generalized schemas (e.g., "I am bad," "I am worthless," "People are malevolent") that are seen in particular groups of people (e.g., the depressed, anxious, narcissistic). We advocate the use of these lists of schemas to help the clinician consider possible core schemas for the client. However, we prefer to use more detailed schemas, gleaned from the details of the client's own narrative, as they more fully reflect the nature of this particular client's thoughts as they relate to this particular presenting problem.

Self
1. I'm vulnerable/helpless (core schema).
2. If I lose weight and look too attractive, then I will get into trouble (peripheral schema as it is conditional).

Other
1. Men are dangerous and powerless to resist attractive women (women end up pregnant and/or raped).
2. Other women are unable to protect me (which may be generalized to current peers and to a female therapist).

World
1. Sex and violence go together.
2. The world is not safe.

Present
1. It is unsafe to leave my dorm after dark. (Jane concretely equates danger and darkness. While it may well be prudent to travel across campus only with others after dark, Jane's belief about "the dangers of darkness" is concrete, rigid, and global, preempting the possibility of any accurate assessment of danger.)

Past
1. My past is my destiny. My father changed when my body did.

Future
1. I will be able to protect myself only by staying isolated and "unattractive."
2. I will always be "damaged" now.

Once the ongoing narrative is distilled to this schematic formulation, the worker and client can more readily and systematically address the content and nature of the various schemas. Because these schemas are derived directly from the client's own narrative, she will be able to affirm, disconfirm, or modify the list as needed in collaboration with the clincian. It also gives the client a very tangible means of exploring very affect-laden material. In this way affect can be contained and simultaneously explored while cognitions can be challenged and modes of behavior monitored and changed.

The clinician must also determine whether these schemas represent typical schemas for the client, or whether they are new schemas formed by a frightening, random event in her life. Without the category of historical antecedents, this would be a difficult distinction. The clinician will need to develop a style of questioning that will elicit specifically predominant schemas. In some instances these questions will be posed directly to the client; in others, the clinician finds a way to elicit material that answers the questions. The clinician's style in so doing will be determined by the sophistication and comfort level of the individual client, and whether it is clinically appropriate. In most cases the clincian might ask questions that will probe the following areas:

Have you ever felt before as you do now?
How early was this particular belief [the phrasing should reflect the idea of a schema, but belief may be more user friendly to client and clinician] reinforced and by whom?
Have you ever had beliefs that are in opposition to these?
Is there flexibility to these schemas or are they rigidly held?
Are these schemas operative under all conditions?
Are you [the client] surprised by any of these beliefs?
Are any of these schemas in direct opposition to your family's beliefs? To those of your religious affiliation or cultural group?
Are there alternative explanations for how you see yourself, others, the future and the past, and the presenting problems [addressing rigidity and globality of schemas]?

The clinician and client work together to determine which schemas seem most troublesome at this time. Listing the many possible schemas offers choices to intervene, not prescriptions that all must be covered during the initial assessment. A schema discussion should foster and solidify a therapeutic relationship, not derail the process or minimize the client's experience. Once there is some general agreement regarding the content of the relevant schemas, the therapist must determine with the client which are useful (adaptive) and which are detrimental (maladaptive). It is also important to identify which are enduring, active ones, and which are dormant, having been activated by certain events and associated affects. This task is similar to the examination of defensive functioning, familiar to psychodynamically oriented clinicians. However, this process of identifying and characterizing schemas is done with the client's full awareness and participation.

Attribution Identification

Attribution content appears to overlap with schema content. As noted earlier, attributions are active when we attribute meaning to others' actions, for example, "He hurt me because he hates me." The attribution is often preceded by "because." The self-schema can fuel or support the attribution. For example, assumed hatred by the other, as in the sentence above, fits with a self-schema that says, "I am worthless and unlovable." One effective way to ascertain attributions is to use the Socratic method. Very simply, the clinician will ask the client about his or her hypotheses about a given situation. This process can be as simple as asking, "What other explanations might there be?" which implants the idea with the client that there are different plausible explanations. As with the exploration of schemas, this information will yield clinically relevant material regarding the potential flexibility of the attribution.

In this case, Jane's attributions regarding the presenting problem might include:

1. He raped me because I was too attractive.
2. My father made fun of me because I was becoming too sexual/too attractive.

3. Women can't help me because they are weak.
4. Men rape because they are sexually excited.

These attributions can be conscious or unconscious. Psychodynamic training can be very useful in recognizing and eliciting the unconscious material. In this case, for example, the client's erroneous attributions regarding the rape are quite evident to the clinician but not to the client. Jane believes she was raped because she was attractive to the rapist. She further believes, as noted, that she was at greater risk because of her weight loss. These faulty attributions have their genesis both in general cultural beliefs about rape (that it is an expression of sexuality rather than violence) and in her own idiosyncratic history (her experience of her father's abusiveness to her at the time of the bodily changes of puberty). These attributions provide a pseudoprotective function; Jane mistakenly believes that if she "becomes fat" she can keep herself safe from rape and abuse. In this way she develops some semblance of control of a terrifying situation and of her affective life, particularly her fear and anxiety.

Brief treatments (e.g., Budman and Gurman 1988) place immediate and considerable importance on the client's presenting problem. Therefore we have organized our examination of this client's relevant cognitions around the presenting problem. Identification of the core presenting problem is critical in that it is likely this event, experience, or condition that triggers the operative schemas and attributions. This presenting problem can be expressed and understood in affective and/or behavioral terms. The emergent schemas and attributions are implicit in the client's narrative; it is the work of the clinician to elicit additional relevant material through careful questioning. Additionally, the client must ascertain the degree to which these cognitions are central and pervasive to the client's life and functioning.

Once the client and clinician agree on the primary, most immediate, and most damaging schemas and attributions, they have essentially prioritized their work on cognitions. At this point the clinician includes this material (which in fact reflects elements of the client's affect, behavior, history, and social system) in her overall ego psychological assessment. Further systematic exploration and modification of both schemas and attributions provides efficient and comprehensive means of modifying damaging and erroneous schemas and attributions. The cognitive literature is replete with techniques for the examination and modification of this material (see references). As the client and clinician work together to modify existing schemas and attributions, underlying psychological conflicts that contribute to or maintain erroneous thought content emerge. In this way the clinician's psychodynamic training is inordinately useful in understanding not only the "unconscious" material but "surface" content as well.

CONCLUSION

As is evident, we advocate the use of the cognitive aspects of the client's narrative as a window to conscious and unconscious styles of functioning that include but are not limited to self and object relations. The analysis of this material is initiated by the joint identification of operative schemas and attributions. Rather than relying on free association or the evocation or expression of affect, the client and worker purposefully extract the guiding structures (schemas) and assumptions (attributions) underlying cognition. For many clients, especially those in the briefer treatments, the systematic focus on eliciting and understanding cognitions and their underlying affects provides several advantages. First, it encourages a very active, directive approach that allows for purposeful exploration. Second, it may be a "safer" way of introducing difficult material. Third, the process of careful examination implicitly strengthens the client's own problem-solving skills (the identifying, considering, and choosing of alternative explanations), thereby enhancing the ego functions of insight, judgment, and the synthetic function of the ego. Further, the teaching of these skills enhances the client's behavioral functioning through increased impulse control. This approach is not unlike a goal of psychoanalytic treatment: "where id was, ego shall be" (Freud 1933, p. 81). Finally, and of particular importance in an age of limited treatment durations, the client becomes equipped with a structure for examination of thought, feelings, and behavior that can be continued independently beyond the point of termination.

REFERENCES

Bandura, A. (1986). *Social Foundations of Thoughts and Action: A Social Cognitive Theory*. Englewood Cliffs, NJ: Prentice Hall.

Bartlett, F. C. (1932). *Remembering*. Cambridge: Cambridge University Press.

———— (1958). *Thinking: An Experimental and Social Study*. New York: Basic Books.

Beck, A. T. (1976). *Cognitive Therapy and the Emotional Disorders*. New York: International Universities Press.

———— (In press). Cognitive aspects of personality disorders and their relation to syndromal disorders: a psychoevolutionary approach. In *Personality and Psychopathology*, ed. C. R. Cloninger. Washington, DC: American Psychiatric Press.

Beck, A. T., and Emery, G. (1985). *Anxiety Disorders and Phobias: A Cognitive Perspective*. New York: Basic Books.

Beck, A. T., Freeman, A., and Associates (1990). *Cognitive Therapy of Personality Disorders*. New York: Guilford.

Beck, J. S. (1995). *Cognitive Therapy: Basics and Beyond*. New York: Guilford.

Berzoff, J., Flanagan, L. M., and Hertz, P. (1996). *Inside Out and Outside In: Psychodynamic Clinical Theory and Practice in Contemporary Multicultural Contexts*. Northvale, NJ: Jason Aronson.

Blanck, G., and Blanck, R. (1974). *Ego Psychology in Theory and Practice*. New York: Columbia University Press.

Brenner, C. (1955). *An Elementary Textbook in Psychoanalysis*. New York: International Universities Press.

Budman, S. H., and Gurman, A. S. (1988). *Theory and Practice of Brief Therapy*. New York: Guilford.

Dattilio, F. M., and Freeman, A., eds. (1994). *Cognitive-Behavioral Strategies in Crisis Intervention*. New York: Guilford.

Edmundsen, M. (1997). Save Sigmund Freud: what we can still learn from a discredited, scientifically challenged misogynist. *The New York Times Magazine*, July 13, pp. 34–35.

Ellis, A. (1973). *Humanistic Psychotherapy*. New York: McGraw-Hill.

Fiske, S. T., and Taylor, S. E. (1984). *Social Cognition*. New York: Random.

Flax, J. (1997). *Taking multiplicity seriously*. Paper presented at the meeting of the Institute for Clinical Social Work, Chicago, June.

Freud, S. (1933). Anxiety and the instinctual life. *Standard Edition* 22:81–111.

Goldfried, M. R. (1995). *From Cognitive-Behavior Therapy to Psychotherapy Integration*. New York: Springer.

Goldstein, E. (1995). *Ego Psychology and Social Work Practice*. New York: Guilford.

Granvold, D. K., ed. (1994a). *Cognitive and Behavioral Treatment: Methods and Applications*. Pacific Grove, CA: Brooks/Cole.

——— (1994b). Cognitive therapy. In *The Encyclopedia of Social Work*, 19th ed., pp. 525–538. Washington, DC: National Association of Social Work.

——— (1997). Cognitive-behavioral therapy with adults. In *Theory and Practice in Clinical Social Work*, ed. J. R. Brandell, pp. 32–47. New York: Free Press.

Greenberg, L. S., and Safran, J. D. (1987). *Emotion in Psychotherapy: Affect, Cognition, and the Process of Change*. New York: Guilford.

Guidano, V. F. (1987). *Complexity of the Self*. New York: Guilford.

——— (1988). A systems, process-oriented approach to cognitive therapy. In *Handbook of Cognitive-Behavioral Therapies*, ed. K. S. Dobson, pp. 307–354. New York: Guilford.

Guidano, V., and Liotti, G. (1983). *Cognitive Processes and Emotional Disorders*. New York: Guilford.

——— (1985). A constructivist foundation for cognitive therapy. In *Cognition and Psychotherapy*, ed. M. J. Mahoney and A. Freeman, pp. 101–142. New York: Plenum.

Heller, N. R., and Northcut, T. B. (1996). Utilizing cognitive-behavioral techniques in psychodynamic practice with clients diagnosed as borderline. *Clinical Social Work Journal* 24(2):203–215.

Himelein, M., and McElrath, J. (1996). Resilient child sexual abuse survivors: cognitive coping and illusion. *Child Abuse and Neglect* 20(8):747–758.

Hoffman, D., and Remmel, M. (1975). Uncovering the precipitant in crisis intervention. *Social Casework* 56(5):259–267.

Horowitz, M. J. (1991). States, schemas, and control: general theories for psychotherapy integration. *Journal of Psychotherapy Integration*, 1:85–102.

Katan, A. (1961). Some thoughts about the role of verbalization in early childhood. *Psychoanalytic Study of the Child* 16:184–188. New York: International Universities Press.

Kelly, G. A. (1955). *The Psychology of Personal Constructs*. New York: Norton.

Kohut, H. (1971). *The Analysis of the Self*. New York: International Universities Press.

Lazarus, R., Kanner, A., and Folkman, S. (1980). Emotions: a cognitive-phenomenological analysis. In *Theories of Emotion*, ed. R. Plutchik and H. Kellerman, pp. 189–217. New York: Academic Press.

Linville, P. W. (1982). Affective consequence of complexity regarding the self and others. In *Affect and Cognition: 17th Annual Carnegie Symposium*, ed. M. S. Clarke and S. T. Fiske, pp. 79–95. Hillsdale, NJ: Erlbaum.

Luborsky, L., and Crits-Christoph, P. (1990). *Understanding Transference: The CCRT Method*. New York: Basic Books.

Mackey, R. A. (1985). *Ego Psychology and Clinical Practice*. New York: Gardner.

Mahoney, M. J. (1982). Psychotherapy and human change processes. In *Psychotherapy Research and Behavior Change*, vol. 2, ed. J. H. Harvey and M. M. Parks, pp. 689–721. Washington, DC: American Psychological Association.

———, ed. (1995). *Cognitive and Constructive Psychotherapies: Theory, Research and Practice*. New York: Springer.

Meichenbaum, D., and Gilmore, B. (1984). The nature of unconscious processes: a cognitive-behavioral perspective. In *The Unconscious Reconsidered*, ed. K. S. Bowers and D. Meichenbaum, pp. 273–298. New York: Wiley.

Nemiroff, R. A., and Colarusso, C. A. (1990). *New Dimensions in Adult Development*. New York: Basic Books.

Northcut, T. (1991). *The level of referential activity in time-limited dynamic psychotherapy*. Unpublished doctoral dissertation, Smith College, Northampton, MA.

Orlinsky, D. E., Grawe, K., and Parks, B. K. (1994). Process and outcome in psychotherapy—Noch Einmal. In *Handbook of Psychotherapy and Behavior Change*, ed. A. E. Bergin and S. L. Garfield, 4th ed., pp. 311–338. New York: Wiley.

Piaget, J. (1926). *The Language and Thought of a Child*. New York: Harcourt, Brace.

Saari, C. (1993). Identity complexity as an indicator of health. *Clinical Social Work Journal* 21(1):11–24.

Safran, J. D., Vallis, T. M., Segal, Z. V., and Shaw, B. F. (1986). Assessment of core cognitive processes in cognitive therapy. *Cognitive Therapy and Research* 10:509–526.

Scharfenberg, J. (1988). The therapy: healing through language. In *Sigmund Freud and His Critique of Religion*, trans. O. C. Dean, Jr., pp. 76–106. Philadelphia: Fortress.

Seligman, M. E., Reivich, K., Jaycox, L., and Gillham, J. (1995). *The Optimistic Child: A Revolutionary Program that Safeguards Children against Depression and Builds Lifelong Resilience*. Boston: Houghton Mifflin.

Singer, J. L., and Salovey, P. (1991). Organized knowledge structures and personality: person schemas, self schemas, prototypes, and scripts. In *Person Schemas and Maladaptive Interpersonal Patterns*, ed. M. J. Horowitz, pp. 33–79. Chicago: University of Chicago Press.

Singer, J. L., Sincoff, J. B., and Kolligan, J. (1989). Countertransference and cognition: the psychotherapist's distortions as consequences of normal information processing. *Psychotherapy* 26(3):344–355.

Stone, A. A. (1997). Where will psychoanalysis survive? *Harvard Magazine*, Jan/Feb, pp. 35–39.

Turner, F. (1984). *Social Work Treatment: Interlocking Theoretical Approaches*. New York: Free Press.

Vygotsky, L. S. (1978). *Mind and Society*, ed. M. Cole, V. John-Steiner, S. Scribner, and E. Souberman. Cambridge, MA: Harvard University Press.

Wachtel, P. L. (1985). Need for theory. *International Newsletter of Paradigmatic Psychology* I:15–17.

Westen, D. (1988). Transference and information processing. *Clinical Psychology Review* 8:161–179.

———— (1990). Towards a revised theory of borderline object relations: contributions of empirical research. *International Journal of Psycho-Analysis* 71:661–693.

———— (1991). Social cognition and object relations. *Psychological Bulletin* 109:429–455.

Wilson, A., and Weinstein, L. (1989). *Freud and Vygotsky: an investigation into the implications for psychoanalysis of the Vygotskian perspective on the origins of mind.* Unpublished manuscript.

———— (1992). An investigation into some implications for psychoanalysis of Vygotsky's perspective on the origins of mind. *Journal of the American Psychoanalytic Association* 2:349–380.

Woods, M. E., and Hollis, F. (1990). *Casework: A Psychosocial Therapy.* New York: McGraw-Hill.

Young, J. (1990). *Cognitive Therapy for Personality Disorders: A Schema-Focused Approach.* Sarasota, FL: Professional Resource Exchange.

II

APPLICATIONS TO PRACTICE POPULATIONS IN DIVERSE SETTINGS

5

A Synthesis of Theory in Couple Therapy: No Longer an Unlikely Coupling

Kathryn Basham

INTRODUCTION

Allegiance to one particular theoretical approach in couple therapy may temper anxiety for clinicians and in fact provide a predictable, organizing frame for a planful treatment course. However, such a unidimensional loyalty could lead to dismissal of ideas and interventions from other theoretical frameworks that might be useful to a distressed couple. In our contemporary practice climate, with constant pressures to manage crises rapidly and to provide symptom relief, clinicians often wonder if and how cognitive behavioral interventions might be useful in the context of a psychodynamic understanding of the case.

This chapter argues that a thorough biopsychosocial assessment based on a psychodynamic conceptualization—in this case, object relations theory—provides wisdom and clarity in designing a treatment plan that includes the selection of particular cognitive-behavioral interventions useful to a particular couple. Features of solution-focused, intergenerational, and narrative approaches to couple therapy are very important; however, for the sake of brevity, this chapter will maintain a focus on the interface between psychodynamic theory and cognitive behavioral interventions (Chasin et al. 1990, Freedman and Combs 1996, Hudson and O'Hanlon 1991). Even with the acknowledgment of fundamental differences between these models regard-

ing the role and meaning of development, the unconscious, and
motivation, there is still room for mutual compatibility. Rather
than assuming that this connection makes for an unlikely coupling, I will demonstrate the congruence and mutually reinforcing nature of reliance on both object relations *and* cognitive-
behavioral theoretical frames.

To provide a rationale for such an integrative practice model,
the editors of this text have already offered several reasons to
support this synthesis, that is, theoretical controversies; practice characteristics and constraints, including managed care;
and treatment issues related to trauma histories—all factors
that call for greater attempts to find a "meeting of the minds"
and using the best of each framework (Heller and Northcut
1996, p. 206). Girded by a biopsychosocial assessment that is
informed by psychodynamic formulations, a clinician can better understand a couple's receptivity to various treatment approaches (e.g., insight-oriented, solution-oriented, and/or cognitive-behavioral). They may also be more effective in dealing with
certain themes that surface regularly in couple therapy: domes-
tic violence, addictions, aftermath of trauma, and parenting,
issues that call for skills in crisis intervention, cognitive-behavioral, and/or psychoeducational approaches. Although many clinicians in the real world of practice actually use several theoretical models, either alternately or simultaneously, there is
virtually nothing written about the linkages between theoretical
models and selection of interventions for particular populations
with specific issues.

In response to this gap, this chapter presents a social constructionist meta lens that recognizes the inherent value and
liabilities of each theoretical model without privileging a particular model. Based on a historical legacy of marital therapy
and marriage counseling, social work practice with couples has
broadened beyond the original focus of work primarily with
married couples. To this day, the majority of outcome studies
evaluating the efficacy of couple therapy explores practice with
heterosexual white couples (Zachs et al. 1988). In reality, so-

cial work practice with couples deals with considerable diversity in terms of race, ethnicity, socioeconomic class, sexual orientation, age, religion, and disability. Although these variables cannot be considered all at once, it is nevertheless imperative to hold onto the tension and complexity of these diverse themes within a conceptual framework while attending to one or more of them that enter the foreground at any given time.

Given this heterogeneity in our client population, it seems clear that clinicians should not only work with a wide range of practice models, but also be capable of assuming a critical stance to evaluate the helpfulness of different theory and practice models for any given population. In summary, this chapter aims to present a synthetic practice model that is attuned to a diverse range of clients.

LITERATURE REVIEW

The following literature review addresses outcome research on the efficacy of couple theory based on integrative, object relations, cognitive, and behavioral models. In general, the research on couple therapy does not suggest that any one particular model is more effective than others. In fact, several of the approaches reported seem to be comparably effective with couples (Baucom and Epstein 1990, Kayser 1997).

Although a review of the literature in couple therapy provides some limited support for the efficacy of an integrative approach, unipolarity of theoretical choice is still very prevalent within professional circles. A four-year follow-up study developed by Snyder and colleagues (1991) found that the effects of an insight-oriented treatment were significantly more durable than the outcome of behavioral marital treatment. The investigators discovered a 3 percent divorce rate for those couples treated with an insight-oriented approach as compared with a 38 percent divorce rate for the couples treated with behavioral therapy. Needless to say, these findings support the notion of an insight-oriented model as more effective. However, a major critique of this project offered by Jacobson (1991) suggested that many of the research subjects had actually participated in insight-oriented couple therapy that included cognitive-behavioral interventions. In fact, it appears that what the authors report to be a more effective unitheoretical treatment model is actually an integrative model combining insight and cognitive-behavioral components (Kayser 1997).

Although outcome and practice evaluation research is fairly scanty in the arena of integrative couple therapy, valuation of integrative models in couple therapy in the world of practice has moved more rapidly into working with multitheoretical, integrative, and/or synthetic practice models (Burch 1993, Dym and Glenn 1993, Weeks and Hof 1995, Weeks and Treat 1992). The limited research findings on integrative models of couple therapy should be placed in the context of outcome research in the general area of couple therapy. For example, Kayser (1997) presents an excellent comprehensive overview of the outcome studies in object relations, cognitive, behavioral, and integrative couple therapy. Clearly, object relations couple therapy has received the least attention in terms of empirical research studies; however, many clinical studies have been reported that document ongoing clinical processes (Basham 1992, Lachkar 1992, Lewis 1997, Scharff 1995, Scharff and Scharff 1991, Sussal 1992). There are two noteworthy exceptions where the insight-oriented model appears to be more effective than others (Johnson and Greenberg 1985, Snyder et al. 1991). Again, Kayser (1997) reviews the research thoroughly in the realm of cognitive approaches. She suggests that several studies reviewed the effectiveness of cognitive restructuring as adjunctive to traditional behavioral marital therapy (Baucom et al. 1990, Halford et al. 1993) while three other studies compared the effectiveness of cognitive restructuring alone to behavioral marital therapy (Emmelkamp et al. 1988). Overall, the studies reveal that cognitive restructuring helps to increase marital satisfaction and facilitate major cognitive changes for couples (Baucom et al. 1995). There is evidence, however, that a combination of cognitive restructuring and behavioral therapy is equally effective in improving marital satisfaction as compared with behavioral therapy alone (Kayser 1997).

In the field of couple therapy, behavioral couple therapy has always received the greatest attention in terms of outcome studies (Beck 1988, Fincham and Beach 1988, Holtzworth-Munroe and Jacobson 1991, Jacobson and Margolin 1979, Snyder and Wills 1989). This model focuses primarily on improvements in relationship through reinforcement of positive exchanges and extinction of maladaptive behavior. Jacobson (1989) reports that two thirds of the couples receiving behavioral marital therapy improve substantially, and half recover to the point where they are in the happily married range on measures of marital satisfaction. Results from the Holtzworth-Munroe and Jacobson study reveal that behavior exchange or communication and problem-solving training alone may be sufficient to produce the same short-term outcome to treatment that combines both components (Kayser 1997). Generally, it appears that outcomes that persist over time are associated with a combination of interventions rather than only one approach. Although there are outcome data based on empirical investigations in cognitive and behavioral practice models and to a lesser degree with object relations models, virtually no outcome studies that evaluate integrative couple therapy approaches were discovered.

In summary, after exploring the breadth of research and clinical data addressing an interface of psychodynamic and cognitive-behavioral theories in couple therapy, I found the paucity of research and clinical literature in integrative couple therapy fairly obvious. Even more striking is the absence among these theory models of any discussion of linkages with assessment and selection of interventions and attunement to diversity.

MAJOR FEATURES IN OBJECT RELATIONS AND COGNITIVE-BEHAVIORAL MODELS

Before the integration of object relations and cognitive-behavioral theories in couple therapy is addressed and illustrated with clinical examples, it seems valuable to spend a little time reviewing the major features of each model as well as commonalities and differences.

Object Relations Couple Therapy

An object relations couple therapy model, as one example of a psychodynamic perspective, focuses on the importance of relationship as a motivating force. More specifically, the early relationship with a mother (or primary caregiver) is vitally influential in affecting relationships in adult life. The following features are central in understanding an object relations approach: (1) the unconscious plays a central role; (2) choices in coupling are affected by conscious and unconscious determinants; (3) mutual complementarity is a major feature; (4) conflict is related to projected intrapsychic conflicts through the process of projective identification; (5) the development of insight is a primary treatment goal; and (6) the meaning and use of transference–countertransference phenomena are important.

The construct of *projective identification* is fundamental to this approach and is the organizing principle for this chapter (Ogden 1982, Scharff 1992, Zinner 1989). Initially, the construct was first introduced by Melanie Klein (1946). The term was used to describe the splitting of the ego during infancy, followed by the projection of split-off parts into the other, and ultimate identification with the disowned split-off "bad parts" of the self, now situated in the other. Although the construct has been redefined and reinterpreted in recent decades, the clarification offered by Ogden (1982) will be the definition used here. He views projective identification as a group of fantasies and accompanying object relations involving three phases that make up a single psychological unit. First, the projector unconsciously fantasizes getting rid of an aspect of the self and putting that aspect into another person in a controlling way. Second, via the interpersonal interaction, the projector exerts pressure onto the recipient to experience feelings that are congruent with the projection. Third, the recipient processes the projections and makes a modified version of it available for reinternalization by the projector (Ogden 1982).

Couples vary greatly in their capacities to recognize the unconscious or conscious nature of this projective identification process. Given the complexity of shared projective systems, it is not surprising why cognitive and affective distortions prevail. The mental image of the significant person and the relevant conflict in early life is projected onto the partner. In other words, the individual unconsciously perceives the partner to be similar to the person in the early relationship. When exploring in some depth, it is evident that the projection usually involves dynamic conflictual themes. When the partner is invited unconsciously to enter into this historical drama, it does not require imagination to envision where the distortions and misunderstandings prevail. The extent to which the couple is conscious of this process will determine the therapy course for the clinician in promoting insight or engaging in cognitive-behavioral interventions to unearth faulty attributions or polarized thinking.

Cognitive-Behavioral Couple Therapy

Since cognitive and behavioral approaches are often interrelated in practice, I will present these models together. Integration of cognitive therapy into couple therapy has been gaining in popularity, specifically among the behavior therapists who have been practicing for decades improving the behaviors in the relationship. Research in the area of cognition and attribution has enhanced this study area with some focus on the role of cognition in marital distress (Baucom et al. 1989, 1995).

The fundamental goal of this cognitive approach is to discover how partners think about each other and the relationship with the underlying beliefs and basic assumptions as the focus. Several key factors are of importance: (1) a partner's perception and interpretation of the other's actions is central; (2) partners de-

velop their own belief systems about relationships that consist
of attributions regarding individuals and cognitive explanations
of behaviors; (3) assumptions, standards, and values are central to a relationship; and (4) since couples in turmoil often use
cognitive distortions and negative generalizations, a major goal
of the work is to identify cognitive distortions by helping clients to evaluate the appropriateness of their cognitions and
challenge their thoughts. An example of this process is offered
by Baucom and colleagues (1995) who discuss interventions that
aim to modify attributions. Techniques include reattribution and
planned experimentation.

Behavioral couple therapy has a lengthy history, distinguished by the germinal work of Richard Stuart (1980), a social
work researcher, first discussing the application of behavior
therapy to troubled couples. The major tenets of a behavioral
approach are that (1) partners mutually reinforce each other's
behavior through reinforcement or extinction, (2) adaptive and
maladaptive behavior is learned and therefore can be unlearned
and replaced by new behavior patterns, and (3) the focus is on
problem resolution without any historical reconstruction. Interventions include the reinforcement and enhancement of positive exchanges and the development of communication and conflict resolution skills.

A more recent advance in the field relates to the notion of
"acceptance," in what is called integrative behavioral couple
therapy (Christensen et al. 1995). This shift involves the recognition that each partner might possess unchangeable attributes
that require acceptance rather than efforts toward change.

In summary, although many practitioners practice with integrative models and speak eloquently of the value of this work,
there is a distinct dearth of research data on outcomes in integrative couple therapy. A review of the existing data in the field
of couple therapy thus far reveals insignificant differences in
efficacy of different treatment models with the exception of a
few studies that support the greater effectiveness of a synthetic
model.

CLINICAL ILLUSTRATIONS

Now that I have presented the unique features of the respective theoretical models in couple therapy, I am returning to projective identification and its interface with cognitive-behavioral interventions as demonstrated in several clinical vignettes. Assessment of the nature and degree of projective identification occurring within the couple helps to determine the appropriate recommendations for treatment course. The following case material will present the ways in which projective identification can be understood in terms of faulty attributions, polarized thinking, cognitive and affective splitting, and troubled communication patterns.

Faulty Attributions and Projective Identification

The vignettes from the following case of John and Jeannie highlight the interface between projective identification and faulty attributions.

> John, age 48, and Jeannie, age 42, initiated couple therapy following Jeannie's discharge from a two-week psychiatric hospitalization in response to her serious suicide attempt. The couple wished to reduce their level of acrimonious fighting, get relief from Jeannie's depression, and try to avert another crisis, especially since they experienced the many players in the care plan as divisive, contradictory, and undermining. Jeannie's recent history of relapse from polysubstance abuse and intensified depression was compounded by historical issues of severe neglect and physical abuse during toddlerhood and sexual abuse by a stepfather from ages 7 to 14. John's childhood history was comparable in terms of the enormity of childhood abuses. Having been reared by a violent alcoholic father, John deals with the aftermath of trauma from his childhood and the Vietnam War by burying his feelings and zealously caring for Jeannie. After exploration of the recent issues and historical key events, it

became apparent to me that mutual projective identification
processes were entrenched. For example, John's perception
of Jeannie as fragile and dependent is fueled by his unresolved conflicts of overresponsibility and rage toward his
alcoholic father. On the one hand, John unconsciously invites
Jeannie to behave like a fragile victim while also resenting
her lack of cooperation with his alleged protective and caring stance. Jeannie in turn responds in a critical, rejecting
manner, not dissimilar to the hurtful responses of John's
father. Jeannie anticipates criticism and abuse at the hands
of other people. Her experience of John's protectiveness is
that he dominates and coerces her into compliance. She reacts alternately with submission and intermittent outrage,
characterized by yelling, or leaving the house to engage in
dangerous activities with former drug liaisons. Jeannie, as
a resilient survivor of horrendous childhood trauma, experiences certain people in the world as perpetrators. John, although intending to be benignly parental, starts to lose control of his temper to the extent of yelling abusively at Jeannie,
once again reenacting her historical abuses. However, he does
not strike her. Neither Jeannie nor John has any awareness
of these projections, nor is either interested in talking about
his or her family of origin. Understandably, at this stage of
crisis, neither wants to talk about the uncovering of traumatic memories from childhood abuses or the Vietnam War.
Nevertheless, they are suffering bitterly in the face of these
distortions.

At this point a question arises: What interventions will
help this couple to accomplish their stated goals of improved
communication, reduction of acrimony, and lessening of suicidal depression? Several factors should be considered: (1) the
degree of unconsciousness of projective identifications, (2) receptivity to family of origin clarifications, and (3) level of stability in personal, work, and family lives. John and Jeannie
were living in the midst of chaos with Jeannie's loss of employment, financial stresses, recovery from her suicide at-

tempt, and family dissension. Projective identifications were rampant and completely unconscious.

Since the likelihood of promoting insight with this couple in a nondirective, reflective manner did not seem appropriate or helpful given the level of crisis, resistance to family-of-origin themes, and pervasiveness of unconsciousness involved in their mutual projective identificatory process, what then was the direction? How does the couple and the clinician grapple with the damaging effects of these mutual projections?

The first goal in treatment was to establish a therapeutic holding environment by structuring meetings, arranging for telephone accessibility, and coordinating the vast array of argumentative, fragmented, and contradictory mental health professionals, which was no easy task. Providing an external structure that allowed for greater cooperation about the competing split-off objects allowed the focus to be paid to the actual couple.

Second, the pervasive projective identification needed to be addressed, but since it was completely unconscious, a more directive, cognitive approach seemed indicated. In this case the notion of faulty attribution based on cognitive theory seemed useful here. Both John and Jeannie needed help in recognizing their distorted cognitions and challenging their respective thinking. The first step was for each of them to recognize signals that denoted either suffocation for Jeannie or escalating anger for John in response to Jeannie's challenging words and behavior. For each of them to interrupt the cycle of emotional escalation was vitally important. At this time each partner was encouraged to explore the objectivity of the situation by asking a series of questions. For example, questions are posed that search for data that support or challenge one's interpretation. Does it appear logically based on the partner's actions that he or she may actually have the motive or attribute assigned? Could there be alternative explanations for this behavior or attitude?

If there could be another explanation for these behaviors, then could the faulty attributions be challenged? Although both partners were reluctant to explore family-of-origin patterns, they were quite responsive to a psychoeducational approach, which is congruent with a cognitive model. Since both are survivors of trauma, I shared information regarding the symptomatology and phenenoma of PTSD, the tendency toward sensitivity to issues of power, control, and subjugation of will, and the necessity for biopsychosocial self-care to enable healing. Along the same lines, much material was shared about the psychological, social, and biological impact of addictions, the role of family members in terms of responsibility, and the power of addictions to erode the soul of the family.

When faulty attributions signaled escalating anxiety and emotion, both Jeannie and John were able to call upon their increased understanding of these topics to adjust their thinking. As a result, the reduction of faulty attributions was associated with less reliance on mutual projective identification patterns, reduced acrimony and fighting, and abatement of depression for Jeannie.

The next case vignette will illustrate the ways that projective identification can be understood in terms of dichotomizing splitting and disowning of part-objects manifest in the polarization of affect and cognition.

Projective Identification and Cognitive/Affective Splitting

Rod, age 43, and Yolanda, age 41, are a middle-income African-American couple referred by a friend to couple therapy with presenting concerns of continuous arguments, threats of divorce, and general unhappiness. They had recently adopted, through an informal process, a little 2-year-old girl, after unsuccessfully battling with infertility and many years of frustration and failed pregnancies. Yolanda, the eldest of six children, was reared in relative financial comfort by her mother and abusive father, who left home when she was 6 years old. Rod's early childhood, as the fifth of seven children reared in a poor rural community, was characterized by physical abuse from an alcoholic father and general chaos at home.

Yolanda criticized Rod relentlessly in response to her profound frustrations with what she perceived as his incompetence and lack of care; in turn, Rod felt powerless, frustrated, and distanced, replicating Yolanda's earlier family-of-origin experience of abandonment by her father. Rod on the other hand felt angry and ashamed when criticized by Yolanda, but responded indirectly and passively by distancing and failing to follow through on agreed-upon chores. He behaved irresponsibly at times and provoked censure from Yolanda, a pattern reminiscent of the historical wrath Rod received from his father. Needless to say, these projective identifications were hurtful to this couple, with each partner only partially conscious of how their histories of abuse affected their attitudes toward power, control, and intimacy. Both Rod and Yolanda hoped to reduce the number of continuous "verbal battles" and reach some decision regarding staying together or divorce.

What then is the basis for selection of interventions to help this couple accomplish their goals? Although it appears that this couple is capable of some self-reflection regarding their mutual projective identification processes, there are several contraindications for an insight-oriented approach at this time. First, the couple is experiencing a crisis of possible divorce. Second, Rod, in particular, is wary about psychotherapy and tentative about working with a white therapist. Third, neither partner is receptive to talking about families of origin. Fourth, both Rod and Yolanda present rigid, polarized depictions of the other, which immobilize most discussions. To provide some stabilization of the crisis and relief from the destructive exchanges of polarized thoughts and feelings, specific cognitive-behavioral interventions were selected.

First, efforts were made to establish a positive therapeutic alliance and a workable holding environment. A structured plan to meet for ten sessions to review the strengths and vulnerabilities in the relationship was offered as a way for them to arrive at a decision to work on issues, to separate, or to remain together without working on issues.

The second intervention aimed to address rigid polarized thinking and affect. This couple regularly presented fixed polarities in their attributions toward the other. For example, Yolanda and Rod were viewed as overresponsible versus underresponsible, uptight versus carefree, unhappy versus happy, competent versus incompetent, and productive versus lazy. To address these fixed polarizations the couple was taught to identity uncomfortable disturbing emotions by acknowledging their feelings as well as the automatic thoughts that entered their minds. (A written automatic thought record may be useful in self-monitoring reactions; this couple, however, preferred to work the process through in their minds.) Rod and Yolanda discussed the possibilities for cognitive distortions, including polarized thinking, overgeneralizations, and mind reading. Again, they were introduced to tools that helped them to challenge their own thinking. To slow down the escalating process of debate, each partner had to ask, What information supports or challenges my interpretation? Is there logic that supports my perception of what I've assigned to him or her? Could there be any other explanation for this behavior?

During this process of challenging nonproductive cognitive and affective distortions, Yolanda was able to recognize that her perception of Rod as lazy and incompetent did not hold up given Rod's fifteen-year history of reliability and responsibility on the job. Rod also saw that Yolanda was, in fact, very capable, but tired and yearning to depend more on him for support. Over time, Rod and Yolanda were able to challenge these projective identifications through cognitive processes without necessarily gaining insight early on.

In the process, however, Rod noticed that the critical denigrating attributions that Yolanda hurled against him reflected racist stereotypes about many African-American men. Transference phenomena fueled this situation as Rod experienced me, in one particular session, as siding with Yolanda and less supportive of him. The combination of Rod's awareness and the transferential challenge to me raised issues related to cross-racial therapy. Did I, in fact, see Rod as incompetent? In fact, my countertransferential feelings were more empathic toward Rod and more annoyed with Yolanda for her critical harangues. What surfaced in the crossfire of these multiple projective systems was that Yolanda was horrified that her attitudes were demeaning and disrespectful; Rod recognized his own battle with internalized racism by putting up with this erosion from Yolanda; and I recognized that Rod's wariness about race matters interfered with my dealing with this topic early in the sessions. Once the racial themes entered the realm of therapeutic discussions, the notions of right or wrong, black or white, power versus powerlessness took on added meaning. Rod and Yolanda recognized that, as survivors of abuse and pervasive racism, they struggled regularly with real issues of oppression and racism in everyday life as well as with the ghosts of family-of-origin projections that have haunted the relationship. Although the projections of polarized feelings and thoughts had set the stage for mutual criticism, disappointment, and disrespect, this couple was able to emerge from the hurtful force of these projective processes and directly challenge distortions.

Throughout the work, although Yolanda and Rod spoke openly and articulately, they were habituated to speak in blaming and condemning tones most of the time. When such an unrelenting destructive communication pattern surfaces, it is often helpful to specifically teach couples how to communicate more effectively by assuming "I" statements, avoiding "You" blaming messages, and learning empathic listening (Guerney 1987).

In conclusion, cognitive distortions occur not only in the assignment of faulty attributions, but also on a much more fundamental level regarding value assumptions. After Yolanda and Rod were able to interrupt blaming discussions and enter the realm of nuance and balance in their discussions, they talked openly about their value assumptions about family, gender roles, and parenting styles. Since their relationship had never allowed room for direct expression of feelings, this couple had never grieved the profound losses of three failed pregnancies. When the acrimony diminished, Rod and Yolanda were able to cry together; plan a memorial service for the lost children; discuss the meaning of family, intimacy, and ritual; and orchestrate a celebration party for their new daughter. Once Yolanda and Rod decided to continue to work on their relationship, arguments diminished, communication improved, and both partners were then able to draw connections between their relationship issues with earlier family-of-origin themes. In the midst of chaos and destructive undermining, there was less room for the emergence of insight; however, after a period of sustained progress, insight started to augment the positive changes for Rod and Yolanda.

CONCLUSIONS

Although the clinical world often echoes with criticisms of incompatibility toward practice that integrates psychodynamic and cognitive-behavioral models, I have attempted to describe the value and coherence of a synthetic model that relies on both theoretical frames. Several criteria are introduced in the biopsychosocial assessment to determine a treatment course, including (1) presence or absence of crisis, (2) degree of consciousness of projective identification, and (3) receptivity to discussion of family-of-origin issues. Consideration of these factors helps to determine what goals and interventions seem most useful to a couple at a given moment. In an effort to describe the interface between psychodynamic and cognitive-behavioral models, I have selected two case vignettes to express how projective identification can be addressed and understood both in terms of faulty attributions and cognitive/affective splitting. The use of cognitive-behavioral interventions with these couples also demonstrates how the affective and cognitive distortions involved in projective identification can be challenged and altered.

REFERENCES

Basham, K. K. (1992). Resistance and couple therapy. *Smith College Studies in Social Work* 62(3):245–264.

Baucom, D. H., and Epstein, N. (1990). *Cognitive-Behavioral Marital Therapy*. Prospect Heights, IL: Waveland.

Baucom, D. H., Epstein, N., and Rankin, L. A. (1995). Cognitive aspects of cognitive-behavioral therapy. In *Clinical Handbook of Couple Therapy*, ed. N. S. Jacobson and A. S. Gurman, pp. 65–90. New York: Guilford.

Baucom, D. H., Epstein, N., Sayers, S., and Sher, T. G. (1989). The role of cognitions in marital relationships: definitional, methodological, and conceptual issues. *Journal of Consulting and Clinical Psychology* 57:31–38.

Baucom, D. H., Sayers, S. L., and Sher, T. G. (1990). Supplementing behavioral marital therapy with cognitive restructuring and emotional expressiveness training: an outcome investigation. *Journal of Consulting and Clinical Psychology* 58:636–645.

Beck, A. T. (1988). *Love Is Never Enough*. New York: Harper & Row.

Burch, B. (1993). *On Intimate Terms: The Psychology of Difference in Lesbian Relationships*. Chicago: University of Illinois Press.

Chasin, R., Grunebaum, H., and Herzig, M., eds. (1990). *One Couple Four Realities: Multiple Perspectives on Couple Therapy*. New York: Guilford.

Christensen, A., Jacobson, N. S., and Babcock, J. C. (1995). Integrative behavioral couple therapy. In *Clinical Handbook of Couple*

Therapy, ed. N. S. Jacobson and A. S. Gurman, pp. 274–291. New York: Guilford.

Dym, B., and Glenn, M. L. (1993). *Couples: Exploring and Understanding the Cycles of Intimate Relationships*. New York: HarperCollins.

Emmelkamp, P. M. G., Van Linden Vanden Henvel, C., Ruphan, M., et al. (1988). Cognitive and behavioral intervention: a comparative evaluation of clinically distressed couples. *Journal of Family Psychology* 4:365–377.

Fincham, F. D., and Beach, S. R. (1988). Attribution processes in distressed and nondistressed couples: real vs. hypothetical events. *Cognitive Therapy and Research* 12:505–514.

Freedman, J., and Combs, G. (1996) *Narrative Therapy: The Social Construction of Preferred Realities*. New York: Norton.

Guerney, B. (1987). *Relationship Enhancement Manual*. State College, PA: Ideals.

Halford, W. K., Sanders, M. R., and Behrens, B. C. (1993). A comparison of the generalization of behavioral marital therapy and enhanced behavioral marital therapy. *Journal of Consulting and Clinical Psychology* 61:51–60.

Heller, N. R., and Northcut, T. B. (1996). Utilizing cognitive-behavioral techniques in psychodynamic practice with clients diagnosed as borderline. *Clinical Social Work Journal* 24(2):203–215.

Holtzworth-Munroe, A., and Jacobson, N. S. (1991). Behavioral marital therapy. In *Handbook of Family Therapy*, ed. A. S. Gurman and D. P. Kniskern, pp. 96–113. New York: Brunner/Mazel.

Hudson, P. O., and O'Hanlon, W. H. (1991). *Rewriting Love Stories: Brief Marital Therapy*. New York: Norton.

Jacobson, N. S. (1989). The maintenance of treatment gains following social learning based marital therapy. *Behavior Therapy* 20:325–336.

——— (1991). Toward enhancing the efficacy of marital therapy and marital therapy research. *Journal of Family Psychology* 4:373–393.

Jacobson, N. S., and Margolin, G. (1979). *Marital Therapy*. New York: Brunner/Mazel.

Johnson, S. M., and Greenberg, L. S. (1985). Differential effects of experiential and problem-solving interventions in resolving marital conflicts. *Journal of Consulting and Clinical Psychology* 53:175–184.

Kayser, K. (1997). Couples therapy. In *Theory and Practice in Clinical Social Work*, ed. J. R. Brandell. New York: Free Press.

Klein, M. (1946). *Envy and Gratitude and Other Works 1946–1963*. London: Hogarth.

Lachkar, J. (1992). *The Narcissistic/Borderline Couple: A Psychoanalytic Perspective on Marital Treatment*. New York: Brunner/Mazel.

Lewis, J. M. (1997). *Marriage as a Search for Healing: Assessment and Therapy*. New York: Brunner/Mazel.

Ogden, T. H. (1982). *Projective Identification and Psychotherapeutic Technique*. New York: Jason Aronson.

Scharff, D. E., and Scharff, J. S. (1991). *Object Relations Couple Therapy*. Northvale, NJ: Jason Aronson.

Scharff, J. S. (1992). *Projective and Introjective Identification and the Use of the Therapist's Self*. Northvale, NJ: Jason Aronson.

—— (1995). Psychoanalytic marital therapy. In *Clinical Handbook of Couple Therapy*, ed. N. S. Jacobson and A. S. Gurman, pp. 164–193. New York: Guilford.

Snyder, D. K., and Wills, R. M. (1989). Behavioral vs. insight oriented marital therapy: effects on individual and interspousal functioning. *Journal of Consulting and Clinical Psychology* 57:39–46.

Snyder, D. K., Wills, R. M., and Grady-Fletcher, A. (1991). Long-term effectiveness of behavioral versus insight-oriented marital therapy. *Journal of Consulting and Clinical Psychology* 59:138–141.

Stuart, R. (1980). *Helping Couples Change: A Social Learning Approach to Marital Therapy*. New York: Guilford.

Sussal, C. M. (1992). Object relations family therapy as a model for practice. *Clinical Social Work Journal* 20(3):313–331.

Weeks, G. R., and Hof, G. R., eds. (1995). *Integrative Solutions: Treating Common Problems in Couples Therapy*. New York: Brunner/Mazel.

Weeks, G. R., and Treat, S. (1992). *Couples in Treatment: Techniques and Approaches for Effective Practice*. New York: Brunner/Mazel.

Zachs, E., Green, R-J., and Marrow, J. (1988). Comparing lesbian and heterosexual couples on the circumplex model: an initial investigation. *Family Process* 27:471–484.

Zinner, J. (1989). The implications of projective identification for marital interaction. In *Foundations of Object Relations Family Therapy*, ed. J. Scharff, pp. 155–173. Northvale, NJ: Jason Aronson.

6

Clinical Work with Mistrusting, Aggressive, Latency-Age Children

James W. Drisko

This chapter addresses how a developmental psychoanalytic approach to child psychotherapy can incorporate cognitive-behavioral treatment techniques to the benefit of both the child and those in the child's world. The clientele under study are mistrusting, aggressive, latency-age children: an increasingly frequent population served by clinical social workers (Ronen 1994). This population initially lacks the capacity to cooperate and collaborate with adults, communicates via action more than words, and may evoke strong responses from adults. As such, it is a challenging population for therapists of any theoretical orientation. With their focus on relationship, psychodynamic theories help us conceptualize the development and use of a working alliance. In this process and during the "middle" phases of therapy, cognitive-behavioral techniques can further enhance the therapy with child and collaterals. Using a case illustration, the strengths in combining treatments are described, as are some areas of difference.

RATIONALE

There are several reasons to examine the strengths and limitations of integrating cognitive behavioral techniques into psychodynamic therapy with children. First, surveys of mental health professionals (Jensen et al. 1990), and specifically of social workers (Jayaratne 1978), document that most practitioners consider themselves eclectic. If we already integrate aspects of more than one approach we need to carefully assess the purposes and potential hazards of doing so (Heller and Northcut 1996). Recent work also shows practitioners draw eclectically to orient what they *do* in therapy, rather than applying a consistent theoretical approach (Hensley 1996).

Further, a significant body of psychotherapy research suggests relationship is a key factor in therapeutic change across approaches based on different theories. That is, some common factors, such as relationship and treatment alliance, appear to be the active ingredients of therapeutic change rather than particular techniques. For example, Castonguay and colleagues (1996) found symptomatic improvement through cognitive-behavioral therapy among depressed clients. However, improvement occurred only where there was a strong therapeutic alliance and strong emotional involvement by the client. Improvement was not necessarily associated with the therapist's focus on the interpersonal consequences of cognitions and behaviors; indeed, such a focus was found counterproductive without a solid working alliance. Thus exploration of the potential integration of psychodynamic and cognitive theories may help us clarify the active therapeutic components of treatment more fully.

Second, child therapy always involves parties other than the child client who inform, support, enhance, or hinder the work. Some aspects of this indirect or collateral work are inherently instructional and psychoeducational. For many adults, such as teachers and protective services staff, a cognitive, instructional approach is consistent with their training and expected from mental health professionals (Caplan 1970, Drisko 1993). Integrated within a psychodynamic understanding, psychoeducation can be part of building a collaborative relationship, can offer insight and perspective, and can provide norms for the feelings and behaviors of child and adult alike. Psychoeducation can also be a vehicle used for achieving other goals as well as a goal in its own right.

Third, child therapy with many challenging children begins with a period of active intervention. Mistrusting, aggressive children lack the ego skills and interpersonal capacities needed to negotiate the start of treatment. Necessary tasks during this initial period include building a relationship and a therapeutic alliance, framing the boundaries and purposes of therapy, setting expectations, ensuring safety, and developing ego skills such as identifying and labeling both affects and behaviors (Chethik 1989, Katz 1992, Redl and Wineman 1952). With certain mistrusting, aggressive, and traumatized populations, following only the child's lead is often ineffective and anxiety producing for the child. Active intervention is needed to develop an alliance while assuring the safety of the client and others (Katz 1992, Redl 1966). This initial relationship work is well conceptualized and described in the psychodynamic child literature. It is rarely addressed in the cognitive-behavioral literature, however, which assumes some capacity for cooperation and some self-awareness in the child client (see Kendall and Braswell 1982, Lantz 1996). As such, the integration of perspectives may be especially useful to cognitive-behavioral practitioners.

Where children have trauma histories (Brandell 1992, Monahon 1993) or changing living situations (Pilowsky 1992), helping the child understand the actions of others may be crucial to developing trust and lessening problematic behavior. Yet here too, active, educational techniques may be integrated within a relationship-based therapy (Forehand and Wierson 1993). The techniques employed in this work may be conceptualized with merit from either a psychodynamic or a cognitive-behavioral perspective. Relationship, developing inner ego structure, improving affect awareness and regulation, and building conscious, cognitive understanding all matter.

Fourth, therapists from both cognitive-behavioral and psychodynamic perspectives seek to help children better understand themselves and others. Being dependent, children expect and require adult direction and guidance, even when their behavior and words suggest otherwise. This directive/directing work takes a variety of direct and indirect forms. At some point in assessment or therapy, therapists must articulate (give voice to) the child's concerns in an empathic manner. Therapists must also articulate the child's strengths. They must often provide perspective on the actions, anxieties, and likely goals of adults in the child's life. This may be done directly or in displaced fashion. Not surprisingly, therapists from both psychodynamic and cognitive-behavioral perspectives report the use of storytelling in child therapy. Why, how, and when stories are told in therapy may provide another bridge between psychodynamic and cognitive-behavioral perspectives. At the same time, care must be taken not to speak for the child. Lacking a sense of agency and autonomy leads many mistrusting children to be keenly sensitive to coercion or manipulation. Thus directive techniques must be employed thoughtfully.

Adult guidance and direction, empathically provided, fits with the purpose of fostering development common to child therapy. Ego-supportive and ego-building work with children is a central part of treatment. In supporting normal development and helping the child address ego distortions or deficits, an active approach is often employed in child treatment. This is analogous to Heller and Northcut's (1996) recommendation for the use of cognitive-behavioral ego-building and ego-supportive techniques with traumatized and personality-disordered adults in crisis.

Cognitive-behavioral techniques can be used to help children identify affects and related cognitive distortions such as "all or nothing" thinking. Indeed, many cognitive "educational" games and group exercises employed by therapists, guidance, counselors, and special education teachers specifically target these issues (Forehand and Wierson 1993). Coupled with an adult therapist's ability to tolerate and talk about painful affects, these techniques improve affect awareness, clarify mental representations of self and others, and thus contribute to ego development. In turn, these new skills can be used to support further growth and progress (Indoe 1995).

Finally, the current economic climate promotes problem- and

symptom-oriented treatment of brief duration to reduce cost. The language used by case managers/payer representatives is symptom-focused and appears to assume an engaged, modestly self-aware client with some interest in changing. "Unmotivated" clients may be refused treatment. Children who are mistrusting (typically with justification), are developmentally unlike adults in self-awareness and modes of cognition, and who see others as the cause of their problems (again, often with justification) fit this model poorly. The need to develop preliminary skills necessary for therapy, which are often impaired as the legacy of interpersonal or affective experiences with a variety of adults, is not emphasized under current payer models. Such work can be cost effective only when economic benefits are assessed over a lifetime. Further, as public sector services follow private models of managed care, key contextual issues may become disconnected from therapy. These include the safety and permanency of the child's living situation, medical and medication needs, the ability of parents and other caregivers to meet the child's developmental and remedial needs, and the thoroughness of educational services. It is also possible to address attention to these contextual issues using problem-focused cognitive techniques within a broader psychodynamic understanding of the child in family and systems contexts. Cognitive-behavioral approaches provide a way to identify the contextual antecedents and consequences of many problematic cognitions and behaviors in the language of payers—so long as we understand them broadly and choose to look at the child in an interpersonal context. In this task a contextual psychodynamic understanding integrated with a cognitive-behavioral perspective works very well.

THE NEED FOR WORK WITH PARENTS AND COLLATERALS

Child psychotherapy with mistrusting, aggressive children is typically a "set" of related therapeutic encounters with different purposes, composition, and membership all serving a common purpose. This is because child psychotherapy always involves the concerns, fears, and perspectives of the child, parents, and others in the community. These nonfamily caregivers include teachers, school administrators, child protective staff, and court personnel. They are key initial referral sources. They are also sources of support for, or resistance to, therapeutic change by the mistrusting, aggressive child.

While direct, in-office work with the child is most often the focus taken in the practice literature, the impact of adult supports and challenges is pivotal to effecting and sustaining change. Yet the adults in the child's life are typically ambivalent about therapy. To some a need for outside help is clear. Even so, most adults perceive the need for mental health intervention as a narcissistic failure. Some see therapeutic services as an opportunity to abdicate their responsibilities to the child. Psychotherapists must engage these adults as collaborators in service to the child. This engagement process is not well detailed in the literature. What literature does exist often takes a supportive, instructional, psychoeducational approach that appears to blend psychodynamic and cognitive-behavioral components. Such a psychoeducational approach may be used to increase adult understanding of the child and empathy for the child's views and needs. Using cognitive-behavioral techniques fits adult expectations and can be a tool in forming and maintaining a working alliance.

It is also important to note that most adults refer a child to therapy in order to have the child change. That is, they locate the problem exclusively within the child. It is therefore important that the therapist assess the ability of the child's support system to permit change and support further development. Where limitations exist, both psychodynamic and cognitive-behavioral therapists must work with parents and collaterals. Parents must be helped to permit therapy to continue and support its progress. They must be helped to become more understanding and empathic to the child. Helping them observe their reactions to the child and alter their responses is often required. Normalizing psychoeducation is often employed as one part of this process. More explicit use of "conscious techniques" (Westen 1991) is rarely reported in the child treatment literature, but can be used to increase understanding and empathy. The process of enacting such techniques also provides an opportunity for relationship growth between therapist and adults.

JERRY: A CASE ILLUSTRATION

I will use my work with Jerry as an illustration of some techniques joining psychodynamic and cognitive-behavioral approaches to the therapy of a mistrustful, aggressive boy.

Jerry is a 9-year-old Latino male. He was referred for psychotherapy by his child protective worker after several fights with his foster brother of similar age. Protective services had custody of Jerry, with reunification as a continuing goal. His Latina foster mother described him as moody, oppositional, and quick to anger at simple directions ("Come for dinner") or everyday comments he interprets as insults. This change in behavior followed a "fine start" of about six weeks. For Jerry, this was his fourth placement in four years, mainly due to parental neglect by his substance-abusing mother and her boyfriends. No physical or sexual abuse of the children was substantiated, but several lengthy periods of minimal adult attention to physical and emotional needs was clear. Extended family frequently provided child care, but the biological mother had moved away from them more than a year earlier. Protective services provided supervised visits with his mother on a monthly basis, when she appeared. Though he lived in an area with a large Latino population, he resided between cultures in largely white schools and social institutions. Jerry generally did fairly well in school but got into fights occasionally during less structured periods (recess, lunch, transitions). He had no peer friends.

Jerry, his foster parents, his protective worker, his teacher, and by extension his biological family, are all clients within this web of child therapy.

Getting Started: Parents

Sloves and Peterlin (1986) suggest predicting for parents some challenges that are likely to occur as even brief psychotherapy progresses. This may be viewed as a psychoeducational approach to preparing parents about some pivotal issues within a larger relationship context. Spurlock (1985) notes that careful preparation of parents for time-limited psychotherapy may fit well with the concerns of African-American parents about psychotherapeutic services. I have found careful preparation to be extremely useful with families of several different races and ethnicities, especially where the family has had no prior exposure to therapy.

Initial work with Jerry's foster family centered around gaining their support for therapy on Jerry's goals in light of their wish to have Jerry stay with them permanently. I explained that I could clearly see they cared deeply for Jerry and very much wanted him to grow and be happier. I also allowed that connections to family, including extended family, would be important for Jerry as in any Latino family. This led to valuable discussions about Jerry's ties to his family of origin and some beginning appreciation by the foster parents of his connection and appropriate loyalty despite his poor care by his biological mother. As I had no clear contract with Jerry, I told the foster parents that I imagined our work would center on issues of Jerry's personal worth, which adults are trustworthy, and how they would show this. I said I imagined that feeling more able to understand his situation and to have some say in it would likely allow Jerry to let his foster parents care for him with less sense of shame and disloyalty on Jerry's part. They too thought this was likely. I added that our work together would have ups and downs, and that their support of the therapy was crucial to its success. I predicted that Jerry might improve initially, then later ask permission to leave therapy when more painful issues emerged. I also predicted that the foster parents might doubt I was helping if symptoms returned later on during therapy, and that they might wish to end the therapy prematurely. I noted that as Jerry had so little power over the moves in his life, this would repeat the changes and losses that he had already suffered. They appeared surprised, more open to thinking about how his moves may have impacted Jerry. Psychoeducation and prediction helped to frame the role in support of the therapy and also enhance their empathy for Jerry.

Such psychoeducation helps parents understand the nature of psychotherapeutic change while simultaneously clarifying roles. It makes clear that therapy is a process that changes over time and evokes many different feelings. It also emphasizes the centrality of the parents to their child's life without minimizing the importance of the therapist and the therapy. The therapist's knowledge is clear and addresses parents' concerns helpfully. Sharing such information in the context of understanding the parents' goals for therapy and likely ambivalence about change can be a way to help parents make changes. This information also frames the interaction between parents and therapist as an active, ongoing exchange that is compatible with the emphasis in cognitive-behavioral therapy. Such information also helps encourage parents to ask questions and to communicate worries and doubts directly to the therapist.

Getting Started: Collateral Adult Caregivers

The need for consultation with a range of collaterals is another way in which child therapy differs from adult work. Work with school personnel and child protective services staff, like work with parents, is a necessary part of the assessment and therapy with mistrusting, aggressive children. Both schools and child protective agencies have clear goals for the child. School staff have the mission of improving the child's education while protective service staff focus on ensuring the safety of the child and quality of care provided by adults to the child. Both share a focus on behavior and compliance. Both may see affective development and self-awareness as secondary to their missions. As a result, one role of the therapist is to improve the quality of adult empathy to the child while addressing behavioral improvement. Both cognitive-behavioral and relationship approaches can help meet this goal.

Like parents, teachers often experience their inability to help a child succeed in school as a narcissistic insult. Some are quite directly "blamed" for the child's difficulties by administrators. When mental health consultants arrive, some teachers are at wit's end, frustrated and helpless to achieve change (Caplan 1970, Drisko 1993). In such circumstances it is useful to sympathize fully with the teacher's view of the situation and to normalize the teacher's responses through generalization. This is a form of externalizing the teacher's problem with the child. It also includes affect clarification.

Jerry's protective services worker felt very frustrated about her inability to get Jerry's biological mother to comply with the treatment plan they had established. Further, she told me (spilled out) that she had been questioned by her supervisor about why Jerry had not made it in his prior placement. It appeared the worker interpreted the supervisor's comments to be a highly critical evaluation of her performance. She wanted this placement to work, but seemed to have lost track of Jerry's needs in light of her own concerns. We entered into a discussion of how troubling Jerry's behavior could be to these apparently "good-enough" parents who wanted only to care for him, and how hard it was to stay focused on what Jerry's behavior communicated and meant when their feelings got in the way. I told her I found Jerry to be very frustrating as he sat silently making me feel like a police interrogator. She said: "Yeah, me too!" I asked her what he might be seeking by such behavior. The discussion shifted to Jerry's world and Jerry's need.

The child is (initially) the "problem," not the feelings or performance of the protective service worker or the classroom teacher. The problem is temporarily externalized as we work to understand the child and find ways to enhance the worker's or teacher's empathy for the child. Another goal is to make it clear that any affect is acceptable and open for discussion. Occasionally, protective workers and teachers chuckle upon hearing me articulate my feelings about a difficult child. When these words are spoken by another concerned adult, they begin to understand that their feelings are acceptable but insufficient to help the child. We then move into trying to define and understand the behavior more fully. This increases the teacher's sense of adult mastery and control while providing a way to expand empathy for the child's needs. Such work gradually moves from the external back to an empathic understanding of the child's motives in context. Attitudes change and new ways of acting emerge.

In addition, I have developed three structured behavioral devices useful in providing ongoing consultation to school and child protective staff (Drisko 1993): (1) an emotional-behavioral profile, (2) a time-on-task profile, and (3) a group-functioning profile. Each includes a range of questions about the child's behaviors and their likely meaning. Each provides information vital to prevention and each serves to clarify the child's needs and motivations. This helps the teacher feel more in control and more empathic to the child as a unique individual.

These three profiles fit neatly within the theoretical orientation of many teachers, and especially those with special education training. They seek to help teachers more clearly define what students do and why they might do it. Attention is directed to defining antecedents and consequences to problematic behaviors, which may allow for preventive interventions. Attention is also directed to understanding what needs may be met by such behavior. The cognitive component emerges as teachers begin to hear student comments more fully. A student's comment, "No one ever helps me," may be better understood, leading to a contract for routine "checking in" by the teacher as well as discussion of the accuracy of this automatic thought in the school setting. Sharing of information between teacher and therapist allows a more complete picture of the child in different contexts to emerge, which may be brought into the therapy. Teachers feel more in control and more able to see the child's needs in a helpful manner. Space for change is created.

Helping the Child Understand Therapy and Its Purposes

How we help children understand the nature and boundaries of therapy deserves clarification. Anna Freud (1946) noted that a period of "treatment training" is needed to help (even neurotic) children understand the role of therapy and the therapist. While we typically clarify the routine of treatment, confidentiality, and fees to adults, the child therapy literature does not detail how we do this with children. We also expect adults to present with a complaint, while children are brought to therapy with a presenting problem generally constructed by others. Yet how we understand and support children's agency and autonomy is defined in this early work of therapy. Both the structure and focus of therapy should be a part of the initial relationship building work with child client and therapist. Children, like adults, should be afforded a chance to hear about, and question, the structure, roles, and purposes of therapy.

I have found it useful to give children the same information about therapy that we give to adults. Times for sessions, their duration, and my best estimate of the length of therapy are all stated. Sometime during assessment or in the earliest treatment sessions I talk about my role as therapist in the child's language. This will always focus on helping to clarify worries and problems defined by the child, but will also always include clear mention of the concerns of important others. Finding a way to start with the child's concerns while joining these with the views of others is part of the art of child therapy. It is not always a quick process with mistrusting, aggressive children who need attention to their needs front and center. It also helps clarify my role in relation to other adults.

In our first interview Jerry sat passively and morosely. Invitations to draw or play evoked grunts, but not tantrums. He appeared scared. When I told him about the purposes of therapy he had no noticeable reaction. However, when I told him I would keep what we talked about private, and that children often didn't believe I would keep our talk private, he turned and looked at me. I told him I wanted him to tell me if he ever thought I did not follow these rules. I moved into telling him a bit about what I knew about why protective services and his foster family wanted him in therapy. He gradually warmed to a low-key approach in which I wondered aloud how confusing it would be for "a boy" to be moved from his family by people he did not know and placed in a new family. I also imagined such a boy might wonder how he could stay a part of his biological family. Jerry's response was to become more alert and slightly more active. A gentle cognitive overview coupled with concern and appreciation of affect provided a starting point for longer work on trust, differences, pleasure in cooperation, and the inevitable disappointments of relationships.

Such psychoeducation about the purposes and processes of therapy help distinguish this new experience from others the child has known. They build relationship, enhance dignity and respect, and show that dialogue in words is expected within this relationship. Frank (1997) describes a similar process in her psychodynamic treatment of children as recognizing that this new relationship will be a different object experience, and one in which the therapist may not seem fully believable to the child.

She highlights the object relations understanding of this preliminary alliance building. I concur fully with her view and would add only that the cognitive, psychoeducational dimension is also crucial to help convey our therapeutic purposes and processes. It begins ego building, through the exercising of cognitive capacities.

Building Ego or Building Cognitive Capacity: Two Labels for Similar Ideas

In the treatment of mistrusting, aggressive children, many ego skills must be strengthened or developed. By definition these children's skills are not at age-appropriate levels. A good deal of the therapeutic work centers on the observation and identification of affects, cognitions, and patterns of behavior within an empathic relationship context. The psychodynamic literature tends to underemphasize this ego-building work, framing it instead as part of relationship-based work with a focus on core anxieties and affect. Such ego-building work may be described as having a modeling, instructional aspect as well. Successful ego building involves changes in cognitions along with their associated affects.

The cognitive-behavioral literature, in contrast, emphasizes the identification and clarification of cognitive beliefs (Lantz 1996, Spence 1994). The cognitive-behavioral literature assumes the child client has the ability to enter into a collaborative, cooperative relationship with the adult therapist. The challenges of connecting with mistrusting, action-oriented children who perceive connection as a threat is not addressed. Mistrusting, aggressive child clients appear to lack the capacities needed to engage in cooperative work. Further, latency-age children's thinking is concrete and egocentric. Self-reflection is not a typical skill, especially of mistrusting children. An adult may quickly fall into "telling" children about their problems when the child holds a quite different view. Cognitive-behavioral literature also often overlooks how therapists can bridge the gap between the perspectives of adults and that of the child (who may communicate through symbolic action).

Despite these differences, therapists from either approach must help mistrusting, aggressive latency-age children identify patterns of thought, feeling, and behavior. These patterns include the antecedents and consequences of behavior as well as cognitions and affects. To achieve this goal, therapists will help the child observe, or become aware of, patterns they have noticed.

In therapy Jerry often spoke of his biological mother and other adult caregivers in split, all-or-nothing terms. I'd often say: "I notice your mother seems all good in your story today. Last week she was all bad. I think you called her a 'horrible witch.' She seems to go back and forth from good to bad as your feelings change."

The work within the therapeutic relationship also provides (or models) different consequences for problematic behaviors. That is, the therapist's exploratory, less-reactive, nonpunitive stance provides a different consequence for the child's behavior than provided in more management-focused settings. Even if the child client angrily devalues the therapist's statement, the therapist's reaction (words and actions) supports new skills while not reinforcing old ways with strong, familiar responses. Again, room for change is created.

At one point I gently wonder if caring for his foster parents sometimes made Jerry feel like he was not being loyal to his biological mother. Jerry yelled back: "Jim, you are so stupid. I would never let my mother down. I don't care about my stupid foster parents. They just care for me for the money." After a moment of recovery I softly stated that I must have misunderstood him, and that his feelings for his mother were clear in the power of his answer. Jerry seemed happy, full of himself, and continued talking in a conversational voice.

Developing some capacity to slow down, to self-observe, and to put experience into symbols builds the ego needed to improve self-control (in psychodynamic language). These achievements are nonetheless largely cognitive in nature. Once capacity to reflect is present, cognitive-behavioral techniques of identifying automatic thoughts can then be successfully employed (Lantz 1996). Self-instructional methods, modeling, and changing behavioral contingencies all can expand self-regulation (Kendall and Braswell 1982). Instructional techniques to improve social awareness and perceptions of others can also be successfully employed (Spence 1994).

Storytelling: Cognitive and Affective Restructuring in Displacements

As mentioned earlier, storytelling is a technique employed by both psychodynamic (Brandell 1985) and cognitive-behavioral practitioners (Friedberg 1994). It is also offered as a culturally sensitive approach to the treatment of Puerto Rican children (Costantino et al. 1985) and has a long history among African-American families (Canino and Spurlock 1994). Storytelling has a special and respected place in parent–child relationships. It may serve several purposes. First is enhancing the production of clinical material from hesitant or actively resistant clients. The displacement afforded by placing discussion in other times or realms may increase symbolic communication (assuming the capacity to invest symbols with meaning is present). Psychodynamic approaches to child treatment purposefully sustain this displacement to avoid confronting defenses and rupturing a tentative empathic connection (Mishne 1996). Symbols, affects, and omissions may be as meaningful as what is stated in the here and now. Psychodynamic practitioners assume the "message" pertains to the child's own situation, which may be more directly addressed as relationship deepens and ego skills develop.

Cognitive-behavioral therapists also use storytelling to get at automatic thoughts and distortions of attribution by child clients who will not, or cannot, engage in direct discussion (Friedberg 1994, Indoe 1995). Stories are also used as a vehicle to convey alternative coping strategies to the child client (Indoe 1995). The protagonists of the story often face overwhelming odds with few resources but always find redeeming strengths that are applied to successful change. Periods of bewilderment and puzzled thought precede action. Happy reunions often follow. Thus stories convey the possibility of change via the use of one's own resources in a new and different manner. Stories convey hope and new cognitive strategies. They support mastery of unpleasant feelings via thought and creativity. They are a map for change with positive consequences.

Given Jerry's cultural background, I had thought about introducing some Puerto Rican folktales into our sessions to bridge his periods of lengthy silence. Jerry's connection to these cultural pathways was limited, however. From storyboards on my wall and books in the office Jerry found the story of Rapunzel. Two parts of the story held him in rapt attention: first was how the parents' own neediness led them to take cabbage from the witch's garden, and how the witch required their child as punishment. I wondered aloud how weak these parents must be to give up their child, but Jerry noted they had no choice and the witch's powers were incredible. The second part Jerry adored was how the Prince found Rapunzel, was blinded by the witch, and finally was reunited with Rapunzel, whose tears brought him sight and her perfect love. He identified with the Prince who was so strong and tried so hard but suffered so much. While he listened repeatedly and with great interest to the ending, he never responded to any of my queries about how much the Prince gained from the care of others. Clearly, both the story and the opportunity to displace his situation into a fantasy with a happy ending was meaningful and inspiring.

From a broad psychoeducational perspective, storytelling allows teaching about potentially different images of self and others, about self-regulation and affect regulation (Brandell 1992), about cultural and social expectations (Costantino et al. 1985), and about new ways to handle problematic feelings or interactions. Storytelling may also be used to gently articulate the core anxiety or immediate challenge for the child client. It can be used to help children understand the experiences and reactions of others to specific situations and behaviors (Friedberg 1994). Storytelling can model the therapist's role as facilitator in finding solutions to frightening and complex problems.

When the therapist tells a story to the child client, great care must be taken to avoid evoking in the child feelings of being coerced, controlled, or manipulated. Mistrusting, aggressive children are extraordinarily sensitive to such control and manipulation by others. This may occur despite the potential displacement offered by the story. (Psychodynamic child therapists also face this challenge when clarifying or interpreting core conflictual issues to child clients and parents.) Many psychodynamic therapists offer stories (or interpretations) in a very tentative, exploratory manner, allowing the child considerable room to ignore off-target or ill-timed remarks without appearing to insult the therapist directly. Cognitive-behavioral therapists also face this challenge when using stories to identify focal problems for treatment. Since a shared problem focus is required in cognitive work, the risk of coercion and manipulation must be carefully assessed by the cognitive-behavioral therapist. From either theoretical perspective, providing supportive guidance with some assurance is typically understood, correctly, as positive and caring when well timed in a good-enough therapeutic alliance.

Termination

Child psychotherapy is inevitably about doing a "piece of work." With the increasing impact of managed care, determining which "piece" to address now has even greater prominence. Child psychotherapy can be central to creating new possibilities for the child's images of self and others, valuable for freeing up energy used unproductively, and adaptive in offering improved ways to interact with others. Yet given the child's ongoing development, the work is never fully finished and done. With mistrusting, aggressive latency-age children, termination of the psychotherapeutic relationship can solidify gains already made and model new ways to manage the thoughts and affects associated with loss and change. Done well, the termination can help the child apply new capacities to understanding both current and past losses and leave-takings (Fox et al. 1969).

Jerry initially denied termination and would talk over me to keep me from talking about ending. We ended at a point of good symptomatic improvement but unfortunately while his living situation was unresolved. (A hearing was scheduled to terminate his biological mother's parental rights, and though she said she would contest it, she ultimately did not.) Jerry's foster parents were able to support him in maintaining contact with his biological mother on a regular but infrequent basis, and hope to be able to adopt him. It was easy for me to identify and praise his growth and progress, as well as his power and passion, which had become more evident and focused during our work together, even now evident in his strong wish to keep me and evade ending.

The cognitive-behavioral literature on child psychotherapy tends to minimize the importance of termination as a process. Improvement on the tightly focused goals of therapy is seen as propelling the ending of therapy on a positive note (Ronen 1994). During the ending phase, a summary of changes made is typically articulated by the therapist to the child. Considerable modeling of new and different ways of thinking and acting occurs within the therapeutic relationship. Direct reinforcement of changes by the therapist helps sustain the changes and improvement the child has made. Work with parents and collaterals to change reinforcement contingencies may be an aspect of cognitive-behavioral therapy. However, explicit planning with parents and collaterals to reinforce and sustain change is not emphasized in the cognitive-behavioral literature.

Psychodynamic authors also tend to emphasize termination directly within the therapeutic dyad (Chethik 1989, Fox et al. 1969, Sloves and Peterlin 1986). This termination work typically employs the new capacities developed by the child to hold and articulate experience. Discussion of ending, and the loss of the therapeutic relationship, aims to help the child internalize change as fully as possible. This work may be alternatively viewed as both summarizing and reinforcing changes made by the child client, parallel to the cognitive-behavioral approach. There is, however, very little psychodynamic literature describing termination practices with parents and collaterals who are part of the larger "child therapy." Greater attention to encouraging support for the child by significant others may lead to a more optimal ending of the therapy. It might also provide a source of follow-up support for the child after the loss of the therapist's support. Integrating cognitive-behavioral techniques into the termination of psychodynamic child therapy with child client, parents, and collaterals could improve the effectiveness of the work.

SUMMARY

Therapeutic work with mistrusting, aggressive latency-age children demonstrates the merit of integrating cognitive-behavioral techniques into relationship-based psychodynamic therapy. This integration has merit for work with the child, parents, and collaterals. The psychodynamic work has strengths in engaging the child and helping the therapist understand symbolic and enacted communication. Cognitive-behavioral techniques are important tools to build relationships with parents and collaterals who can impede or expedite and sustain the child's progress. As an alliance is established, cognitive-behavioral techniques focus on building self-awareness and self-regulation in a manner that may be employed effectively within an empathic relationship. Attention to the strengths of both approaches in context suggests useful ways to enhance our therapeutic effectiveness with these challenging children.

REFERENCES

Brandell, J. (1985). Using children's autogenic stories in dynamic clinical assessment. *Child and Adolescent Social Work Journal* 2:181–190.

——— (1992). Psychotherapy of a traumatized 10-year-old boy: theoretical issues and clinical considerations. *Smith College Studies in Social Work* 62:123–138.

Canino, I., and Spurlock, J. (1994). *Culturally Diverse Children and Adolescents: Assessment, Diagnosis and Treatment.* New York: Guilford.

Caplan, G. (1970). *The Theory and Practice of Mental Health Consultation.* New York: Basic Books.

Castonguay, L., Goldfried, M., Wiser, S., et al. (1996). Predicting the effect of cognitive therapy for depression: a study of unique and common factors. *Journal of Consulting and Clinical Psychology* 64(3):497–504.

Chethik, M. (1989) *Techniques of Child Therapy: Psychodynamic Strategies.* New York: Guilford.

Costantino, G., Malgady, R., and Rogler, L. (1985). *Cuento Therapy: Folktales as a Culturally Sensitive Psychotherapy for Puerto Rican Children.* (Fordham University Hispanic Research Center Monograph #12.) Maplewood, NJ: Waterfront Press.

Drisko, J. (1993). Special education teacher consultation: a student-focused, skill-defining approach. *Social Work in Education* 15(1):19–28.

Forehand, R., and Wierson, M. (1993). The role of developmental factors in planning behavioral interventions for children: disruptive behavior as an example. *Behavior Therapy* 24(1):117–141.

Fox, E., Nelson, M., and Bolman, W. (1969). The termination process: a neglected dimension in social work. *Social Work* 14:53–63.

Frank, M. (1997). Clinical practice with children. In *Clinical Social Work: Theory and Practice,* ed. J. Brandell, pp. 83–100. New York: Free Press.

Freud, A. (1946). *The Psychoanalytic Treatment of Children*. New York: Schocken, 1964.

Friedberg, R. (1994). Storytelling and cognitive therapy with children. *Journal of Cognitive Psychotherapy* 8(3):209–217.

Heller, N., and Northcut, T. (1996). Utilizing cognitive-behavioral techniques in psychodynamic practice with clients diagnosed as borderline. *Clinical Social Work Journal* 24(2):203–215.

Hensley, P. (1996). *Clinical social worker's theories of cure: a qualitative study*. Unpublished doctoral dissertation, Smith College School for Social Work, Northampton, MA.

Indoe, D. (1995). Cognitive behavioral therapy and children of the code. *Educational and Child Psychology* 12(4):71–81.

Jayaratne, S. (1978). A study of clinical eclecticism. *Social Service Review* 52(4):621–631.

Jensen, J., Bergin, A., and Greaves, D. (1990). The meaning of eclecticism: new survey and analysis of components. *Professional Psychology Research and Practice* 21(2):124–130.

Katz, C. (1992). Aggressive children. In *Psychotherapy with Children and Adolescents: Adapting the Psychodynamic Process*, ed. J. O'Brien, D. Pilowsky, and O. Lewis, pp. 91–108. Washington, DC: American Psychiatric Press.

Kendall, P., and Braswell, L. (1982). Cognitive behavioral self-control therapy for children: a components analysis. *Journal of Consulting and Clinical Psychology* 50(5):672–689.

Lantz, J. (1996). Cognitive therapy and social work treatment. In *Social Work Treatment: Interlocking Theoretical Approaches*, ed. F. Turner, 4th ed., pp. 94–115. New York: Free Press.

Mishne, J. (1996). The therapeutic challenge in clinical work with adolescents. *Clinical Social Work Journal* 24(2):137–152.

Monahon, C. (1993). *Children and Trauma: A Parent's Guide to Helping Children Heal*. New York: Lexington.

Pilowsky, D. (1992). Short-term psychotherapy with children in foster care. In *Psychotherapy with Children and Adolescents: Adapting the Psychodynamic Process*, ed. J. O'Brien, D. Pilowsky, and O. Lewis, pp. 291–312. Washington, DC: American Psychiatric Press.

Redl, F. (1966). *When We Deal with Children*. New York: Free Press.

Redl, F., and Wineman, D. (1952). *Controls from Within*. Glencoe, IL: Free Press.

Ronen, T. (1994). Cognitive behavioral social work with children. *British Journal of Social Work* 24(3):273–285.

Sloves, R., and Peterlin, K. (1986). The process of time-limited psychotherapy with latency-aged children. *Journal of the American Academy of Child Psychiatry* 25(6):847–851.

Spence, S. (1994). Practitioner review: cognitive therapy with children and adolescents: from theory to practice. *Journal of Child Psychology and Psychiatry and Allied Disciplines* 35(7):1191–1228.

Spurlock, J. (1985). Assessment and therapeutic intervention of black children. *Journal of the American Academy of Child Psychiatry* 24:168–174.

Westen, D. (1991). Cognitive-behavioral interventions in the psychoanalytic psychotherapy of borderline personality disorders. *Clinical Psychology Review* 11:211–230.

7

"No Way!" "You Know?" "Whatever": Clinical Work with Adolescents

Cheryl Springer

A 16-year-old female adolescent, Tessa, sits silently staring at some point on the wall as her mother and father take turns recounting the events of the previous weekend. In short, without parental permission, Tessa and a few friends drove three hours to her family's summer cottage for an afternoon. Shortly after their arrival, several more male and female friends appeared, equipped with substantial amounts of beer and liquor. According to neighbors, the party became a "public nuisance," the local sheriff was called, and Tessa's parents were summoned to the country in the middle of the night. As their description draws to a close, the father demands Tessa's attention and angrily exclaims, "And I want to know what you were *thinking*. *What* the hell was going on inside your head?"

Tessa looks at her father, looks away, and shrugs her shoulders. Her father responds with more anger, "No! I want to know what you were thinking while all that shit was going on. You *have* to tell us."

Tessa shrugs her shoulders again and meekly replies, "I don't know. I don't know what I was thinking."

Incredulous, her father looks at me, then his wife, back to his daughter, and announces, "Young lady, *that* is *not* an acceptable answer."

Clinicians who integrate psychodynamic and cognitive-behavioral perspectives in their work with adolescents understand and concur with both Tessa and her dad. Her behavior is likely to be best understood by combining its association with "thinking" and "not thinking." The overall goal of clinical work with adolescents often includes the prevention of risk-taking behaviors as well as the establishment (or reestablishment) of healthy physical, emotional, and social development. In reaching such goals, the clinician needs to consider the adolescent's affective *and* cognitive motivations and abilities in addition to the sociocultural context and meaning of her behaviors. An integration of psychodynamic and cognitive-behavioral perspectives, as opposed to just one or the other, provides for a fuller understanding of the adolescent and enriches the treatment process.

This chapter will first summarize the principles and techniques from cognitive-behavioral and psychodynamic perspectives that are particularly relevant to social work practice with adolescents. Then a case application will be presented to illustrate the integration of such principles and techniques. Finally, the strengths of using an integrative perspective in social work practice with adolescents will be discussed. It should be noted that throughout this chapter the focus is on time-limited outpatient services for adolescents. Addressing the integration of psychodynamic and cognitive-behavioral perspectives in residential and inpatient treatment settings is a worthwhile endeavor but one that is beyond the scope of this chapter. Nonetheless, it is anticipated that social workers who are based in such settings will find useful contributions here.

COGNITIVE-BEHAVIORAL PRINCIPLES AND TECHNIQUES

Functional and dysfunctional behaviors and, to some extent, cognitive processes have a relatively long history as topics of research and theorizing with regard to adolescent development, adolescent–parent relationships, and psychopathology among adolescents. However, reports of cognitive-behavioral therapy with adolescents along with empirical studies of its effectiveness with adolescents have emerged primarily over the past decade (Finch et al. 1993, Kendall 1991, 1993, Reinecke et al. 1996, Shirk 1988, Spence 1994, Zarb 1992). Specific reports and studies have addressed the following presenting problems among adolescents: *depression* (Carey 1993, Clarke et al. 1992, Lewinsohn et al. 1990, Mufson et al. 1993, Safran 1988, Wilkes et al. 1994), *anxiety* (Kendall 1992, Kendall and Chansky 1991), *behavioral and antisocial disorders* (Ager and Cole 1991, Hunter and Santos 1990, Kearney and Silverman 1990, Larson 1990, Polyson and Kimball 1993), *chemical dependence* (Nay and Ross 1993, O'Connell and Patterson 1996), *suicidology* (Rotheram-Borus et al. 1994), *and trauma in association with a history of childhood sexual abuse* (Heflin and Deblinger 1996), and *eating disorders* (Bowers et al. 1996, Vitousek and Ewald 1993, Wilson and Fairburn 1993).

Cognitive-behavioral theory and therapy emphasize the following principles: the centrality of the "here and now"; the adaptive nature of beliefs or attitudes; the significance of problem solving, coping strategies, and interpersonal skills (DuBois and Felner 1996, Goldfried 1995, Reinecke et al. 1996). All of these principles are clearly in keeping with some of the central tenets of both social work practice in general and clinical work with adolescents in particular (Allen-Meares 1995). For example, in presenting their "Quadripartite Model of Social Competence," DuBois and Felner (1996) note that cognitive-behavioral approaches have emphasized "concepts such as resiliency, protective factors, coping, life skills, social skills, mastery, hardiness, empowerment, self-esteem, and social competence" (pp. 124–125). DuBois and Felner also argue that proponents of cognitive-behavioral practice need to pay increased attention to "a person-environment, transactional perspective" (p. 147). Such attention is not new to either past or present students of social work (e.g., Hollis and Woods 1964, Longres 1995, Woods and Hollis 1990).

There are two central advantages to including a cognitive-behavioral perspective in social work practice with adolescents. First, it underscores the importance as well as the realities and complexities of clinical social work's transactional biopsychosocial orientation. Second, a cognitive-behavioral perspective has led to the development of specific techniques and interventions that enhance psychodynamically oriented work with adolescents. Following is a brief elaboration of each of these advantages.

COGNITIVE-BEHAVIORAL PRINCIPLES AND THE BIOPSYCHOSOCIAL PERSPECTIVE

The biopsychosocial orientation is especially critical in social work practice with adolescents. At adolescence, each domain of human functioning—the biological, the psychological, and the social—proclaims its eminence and demands attention. For this reason it is easy for social work practitioners (as well as parental figures and adolescents themselves) to lose sight of the interdependence of biological, psychological, and social realms. Attending to adolescents' behaviors and cognitions keeps clinicians in tune with two major elements of maturation and psychosocial development: (1) the status or absence of physical and intellectual abilities; and (2) the powerful influence of social and cultural constructs on adolescents' behaviors and ways of thinking. Adolescents' behaviors and cognitions reflect and shape the meaning that is being made of environmental, social, and cultural realities associated with gender, ethnicity, race, age, class, sexuality, sexual orientation, and physical abilities.

Social workers' articulation of the transactional nature of a biopsychosocial orientation is greatly enhanced by an increased awareness of the relationship between adolescents' cognition and social behaviors. Just as we have come to know the importance of identifying the norms of adolescents' psychological and social development, we must also appreciate cognition as developmental in nature. Clinicians who are inattentive to the developmental norms of adolescent cognition are likely to either overestimate or underestimate an individual teenager's health or psychopathology. In short, psychotherapeutic modalities and strategies are most effective when they are in keeping with the adolescent's level of cognitive development and skills (Holmbeck and Updegrove 1995).

For example, in the brief vignette described above, Tessa states that she doesn't know what she was thinking in the midst of a social situation that placed her and others at risk. To adequately understand Tessa's behavior, it is important to assess the maturational status of her cognitive development and skills. It is, of course, quite possible that Tessa's psychological needs or conflicts interfere with her ability "to think." At the same time, however, her ability to recognize danger or to value her autonomy and social connectedness is directly related to her overall cognitive development as well as the development of social cognition—her ability to think about herself, others, and social relations (Guerra 1993). The clinician will be able to intervene more effectively when he or she attends to what Tessa is able to do, not to what she should do. Moreover, accessing Tessa's awareness of her psychological motivations and the influence of her sociocultural environment involves a willingness to travel her way of thinking.

Of particular interest would be Tessa's cognitive development with regard to concrete and formal operational thinking (Piaget 1932) as well as the associated capacity for social perspective taking (Levitt et al. 1991, Selman 1980, Selman and Schultz 1988). Is she able to think about her own thoughts? Many adolescents, particularly young ones and those under immediate or prolonged stress, are unable to do this. Tessa's father is asking her to engage in formal operational thinking. Tessa may hear his questions as related to a demand she is simply unable to meet. A more productive strategy might include asking Tessa to trace, in very concrete terms, the various decision-making processes related to getting to the cabin and inviting friends. In so doing the clinician might also ask whether Tessa can imagine how other people (friends, neighbors, her own or others' parents) viewed the events in question. In this manner one learns whether Tessa is able to consider multiple perspectives. Such an ability (or absence thereof) is related to being able to anticipate the consequences of her behavior (i.e., the ego function of judgment). Thus Tessa's status with regard to cognitive maturation, development, and abilities has enormous ramifications for her physical, psychological, and social well-being.

An interest in adolescents' social cognitions provides social work practitioners with concepts that integrate biological, psychological, and social functioning. Social cognition is evident in psychological functioning as well as the social behaviors and beliefs that are shaped by, and reinforce, cognitive development, cognitive abilities, distortions, or deficiencies (Reinecke et al. 1996). For example, cognitive distortions are often readily apparent in how and what adolescents "think about" some of the most important aspects of their lives: physical appearance and competence, sex and sexuality, academic and social competence, and gender and sexual identity, as well as parental care and control (Zarb 1992). Guerra (1993) has described several areas of social cognition that have particular relevance to clinical work with adolescents: moral reasoning, social perspective taking, and self-understanding, as well as interpersonal cognitive problem solving and cognitive self-control.

The point here is to underscore the importance of appreciating cognition as a dynamic aspect in the biopsychosocial perspective. The individual adolescent's cognitive substrate is not necessarily a feature of adolescent functioning that is set in stone. It may be limited or damaged as a result of biological, psychological, and social forces, but it may also be accessed to enhance psychological and social health. The following section describes some of the intervention techniques developed by cognitive-behavioral therapists. These techniques often provide creative means by which social workers can assess and access adolescent cognition and use it as a "royal road" to affect, insight, social awareness, adaptation, change, or simply different ways of thinking and behaving.

INTERVENTION TECHNIQUES FROM A COGNITIVE-BEHAVIORAL PERSPECTIVE

One of the most frustrating experiences in clinical work arises when the practitioner has evolved a solid, carefully considered understanding and explanation for an adolescent's difficulties, but is unable to bring the client along for the ride, or even interest him or her in getting on the bus! Cognitive-behavioral methods provide a means of inquiry and understanding that is experienced by most adolescents (but not all) as less intrusive than direct explorations of affect, motivations, or internal conflict.

This is not to say that such explorations should not occur. Some adolescents benefit from the identification, awareness, or appreciation of affect, motivations or internal conflicts. Some adolescents, particularly older ones, are ready and able to engage in insight-oriented psychotherapy; however, even with these adolescents it is worthwhile to periodically explore their social behaviors and thinking processes in order to evaluate their functioning in the real world. For most adolescents a focus on social behavior and cognitive processes is experienced as tolerable, safe, and indeed helpful. The clinician bears the weight of selecting and guiding the use of techniques that consider the adolescent's cognitive abilities and allow space for optimum psychological safety and psychosocial development.

Several clinicians have outlined and described cognitive-behavioral strategies that have been used with adolescents. Zarb's (1992) work is by far the most comprehensive presentation of cognitive-behavioral techniques and interventions that have been adapted specifically to the assessment and treatment of adolescents. However, within the social work literature, clinical reports of the direct application of cognitive-behavioral techniques with adolescents have been limited and the focus has been primarily on children, parents, families, or adults and not on the individual adolescent. Exceptions to this are the contributions of Barth (1986) and Allen-Meares (1995), whose practice-focused integrations of cognitive-behavioral techniques with social or ecological perspectives include work with adolescents. The interested reader is referred to these bodies of work for detailed descriptions of various cognitive-behavioral techniques.

Of interest here is a brief delineation of a few techniques and interventions that are viewed as most readily integrated and compatible with a psychodynamic perspective. The treatment context in which the author has found the technique to be most effective or useful will also be identified. The focus here is on the techniques that Zarb (1992) refers to as "cognitive-behavioral coping skills interventions" (p. 51)—interventions that are valuable components of work with adolescents who are unable or uninterested, temporarily or permanently, in self-reflection or introspection.

Teaching

One of the unique aspects of a cognitive-behavioral perspective with regard to treatment is the use of distinct educational approaches. These approaches may include direct teaching, homework assignments, and video or audio presentations. While these techniques are often used in psychoeducational groups designed to address a range of social issues, they also have their place in individual work with adolescents as well as in family work and groups that are not necessarily conceptualized as psychoeducational. In clinical work with adolescents there are times in which "teaching" is not only appropriate but critical. For example, in discussions about sex and sexuality it is often critical for the clinician to be prepared not only to discuss but to teach about safer sex, sexual practices, masturbation, reproductive anatomy, and birth control methods. In collaboration with parents, specific readings, videos, or movies may be recommended as homework assignments and then discussed (or brought into the clinical hour).

Assertiveness Training

Assertiveness training was developed for use with adults yet can be particularly useful in work with adolescents (see Zarb 1992 for a full description of the technique as used with adolescents). This is an especially valuable technique in group therapy where peer support and feedback make it more likely that the individual adolescent will be able to make use of the assertiveness training skills in other, more difficult, circumstances. Assertiveness training involves a distinction between the interpersonal behavioral styles of aggression, passivity, and assertiveness. It is important to be clear that the focus is on aggressive and passive behaviors, not feelings. Thus assertiveness training also becomes an arena in which to distinguish between actions and feelings. Another aspect of assertiveness training is the individual's own identification of situations in which he or she wants to be more assertive, rather than passive or aggressive.

It is critical to recognize the limits of assertiveness training for adolescents who live in highly conflictual communities or families. It is also important to recognize that assertiveness training itself may reveal environmental dangers and stressors that are beyond the adolescent's control or any degree of assertiveness. The absence of agency may be particularly felt by female adolescents in unsafe as well as in apparently "safe" circumstances. It is then the clinician's responsibility to help adolescents see the constraints, dangers, and limitations of their own efforts as well as to advocate on behalf of young people who live under such circumstances.

Self-Monitoring Techniques

There are several cognitive-behavioral techniques that involve efforts to help adolescents observe, and as a result change, their own dysfunctional behaviors. From a psychodynamic perspective, self-monitoring is related to the existence of a "self-observing ego." Self-monitoring techniques can be used to assess the adolescent's self-observing capacities or to develop them. For many adolescents, there are spheres in which their self-monitoring skills are quite strong and others in which they are weak

or nonexistent. While self-monitoring techniques focus on behaviors, it is essential to recognize their cognitive, psychological, and social aspects. Self-monitoring, by definition, requires
a "self" that is cognitively able to objectify one's social or behavioral "self" and then tolerate the affect that emerges in the
process.

Self-monitoring is a component of other techniques such as
activity or time management techniques as well as goal planning and self-control training. Self-monitoring involves obtaining (usually in writing) detailed reports of the adolescent's daily
routine or of "undesirable" behaviors (Zarb 1992). It is not especially necessary, or productive, to ask adolescents to record
their undesirable behaviors. However, many young people are
willing to report on daily activities for the sake of acquiring more
information about who they are and the external events that
affect them. Some adolescents are more responsive than others
to the keeping of a "diary," journal, or daily activity sheet. Other
adolescents may be more interested in using tape recorders or
a beeper as a reminder for record keeping (see Csikszentmihalyi
and Larson 1984 for the use of such a method in research that
can be adapted to clinical work). The acquired "data" are then
used to identify strengths or skills that need to be developed.
The record can also be used to explore events, thoughts, or feelings that lead to behaviors. Regardless of the specific technique,
the clinician's interest in an adolescent's record keeping can be
a valuable assessment instrument as well as a powerful means
of engaging the adolescent in a collaborative treatment relationship. Only then can the clinician and the adolescent together
establish a reward system that reinforces positive behaviors.

Role-Playing

One of the major contributions of cognitive-behavioral researchers, theoreticians, and practitioners pertains to the function of
social competence in the lives of adolescents and its associations
and interactions with mental health (DuBois and Felner 1996).

Role-playing is often an effective clinical method for assessing and enhancing an adolescent's social competence. It is a technique that can be used in group, family, and individual work, keeping in mind the power-related adolescent–adult dynamics that vary in each of these modalities. Several different areas pertinent to social competence are effectively addressed through role playing: the development of conversational skills, identification of the pros and cons of different forms of social coping, the resolution of interpersonal dilemmas. Role-playing is an integral part of other cognitive-behavioral techniques (e.g., assertiveness training) and is also used, as noted above, to identify areas of concern that might benefit from self-monitoring.

Effective role-playing involves the therapist's ability to clearly communicate, in and outside of the role play, an empathic and maximally accurate understanding of the adolescent's social struggle or situation. Adolescents are typically on the lookout for clues that the therapist "gets it," and role playing provides them a unique opportunity to evaluate the clinician's knowledge and empathy. Unless the adolescent is confident that the clinician is at least trying to accurately understand, suggestions regarding alternative approaches to interpersonal or social situations may not be heard. Teenagers are unlikely to state directly, or even realize, the weight being placed on their confidence in the therapist's understanding. For this reason role playing with adolescent clients requires that the clinician be simultaneously self-observing, flexible, and observant of content and process.

PSYCHODYNAMIC PRINCIPLES AND TECHNIQUES

The principles of social work practice with adolescents has a long historical association with psychodynamic theories. The work, and sometimes the very presence, of Anna Freud (1936, 1958), Erik Erikson (1968), August Aichhorn (1925), and Peter Blos, Sr. (1962, 1967, 1968), infused much of the agency-based training of social workers in the U.S. during the 1950s and 1960s. In turn, social workers themselves, such as Shirley Cooper, Selma Fraiberg, and Judith Mishne have articulated the application of psychodynamic principles to the unique and diverse aspects of social workers' clinical experiences with adolescents. The reader is directed to their contributions for a full delineation of the psychodynamic principles that inform clinical work with adolescents (Cooper and Wanerman 1977, 1984, Fraiberg 1955, Mishne 1986). The intent here is only to highlight those principles that most readily complement a cognitive-behavioral perspective.

One of the most valuable contributions of psychodynamic theories (e.g., ego psychology, object relations theories, and self psychology) to clinical work with adolescents is their developmental orientation. A developmental orientation considers the interplay between maturation and specific psychological processes that build on one another to allow for continuing psychological growth and mastery. An emphasis on maturation draws clinical attention to the adolescents' psychological and social responses to puberty and its concomitant body-based changes. Thus a psychodynamic perspective provides the clinician with a way of thinking about the complex affective and relational aspects of adolescent sexuality. This is not to say that a psychodynamic perspective, more so than any other one, has always done justice by adolescents with regard to their developing sexual identity. This is especially true with regard to sexual orientation and gender role identity as well as the gendered sociocultural and political constructions of pregnancy and sexual agency. But a theoretical or clinical framework that does not acknowledge the emotional significance of adolescent sexuality is ignoring a critical realm in human development.

With regard to the distinct psychodynamic processes of adolescence, individuation has undoubtedly received the most attention. Blos (1967) proposed that the process of individuation assumed a normative centrality in adolescents' object relations—their internal representations of self and other—thus replaying its importance in early childhood. A psychodynamic perspective specifically recognizes individuation as a psychological process and not necessarily a behavioral one. An autonomous, well-functioning, and articulate young person does not necessarily experience him- or herself as an individuated person. Moreover, recent psychological perspectives that explore the salience of relationships in female development have come to recognize the dialectic nature of connectedness and psychological individuation (Benjamin 1995, Stern 1989). The conflict, deficits, or guilt associated with individuation may partially account for the behavior of adolescents who are not perceived by others as "troubled" youth.

A psychodynamic perspective emphasizes psychic development and the mediation of psychic conflict as well as discontinuities between internal wishes and external demands or realities. Cognitive maturation allows adolescents more or fewer apparatuses with which to contemplate psychic functioning and environmental factors. At the same time, however, unconscious needs, wishes, and conflicts tax the adolescent's ego and developing sense of self. The concepts of ego, superego, ego ideal, defense mechanisms, and object relations are particularly useful in theorizing adolescent development and engaging in clinical work. These concepts create a framework for clinical understanding of the affective meanings assigned to social and cultural experiences as well as trauma and loss. This understanding can then be applied to adolescents as a group and to the unique character structure of an individual adolescent.

There are, in fact, two cognitive concepts that already have been particularly well integrated with psychodynamic perspectives on work with adolescents: the personal fable and the imaginary audience (Elkind 1967). However, these concepts have not been used fully in the clinical milieu to understand adolescents' unique means of constructing and integrating past and present experiences. In brief, the personal fable refers to teenagers' conceptions of themselves as unique and original, especially with regard to thoughts and feelings. The imaginary audience refers to adolescents' conviction that other people are focused on them—especially on their appearance and behaviors. The personal fable and imaginary audience are characteristic of adolescents' cognitive and affective egocentrism. At the same time, they also reflect specific past as well as present internal and external object relations. Exploring the narrative content of a personal fable or detailing the membership and sightlines of an imaginary audience reveals an adolescent's past and current object relations as well as his or her psychological vulnerabilities and strengths. In turn, the connections and distinctions between inner and outer realms of experience and points of view can be appreciated and used to establish an ego, a self, or a sense of personal agency that is neither alienated from nor subjugated by others.

For adolescents who have suffered multiple losses, physical or sexual trauma, and social or cultural alienation, a sole focus on cognitive or behavioral reformulations is likely to be inadequate. Psychic representations of the self as unworthy, unlovable, and expendable are not easily relinquished. On the one hand, maturational and cognitive forces often combine to make adolescence the optimal time to address excessive stressors and hardships of childhood. On the other hand, clinicians need adequate time with their adolescent clients in order to help them access, bear, and place in perspective the nature and consequences of exceptionally difficult childhood and adolescent experiences. Thus time and timing become essential and critical elements in the treatment process. The contemporary U.S. mental health care system, by virtue of its emphasis on short-term treatment, is leaving in its wake an entire cohort of adolescents whose clinicians are not allowed the time and resources we know it takes to help them establish or reestablish a normative developmental trajectory. A high emotional as well as social and financial price is paid and will continue to be paid by current and future citizens.

This examination of the features of a psychodynamic perspective on clinical work with adolescents that potentially complement a cognitive-behavioral perspective is not complete without a discussion of transference and countertransference. There is a relatively small but growing literature on the singular features of transference and countertransference in clinical work with adolescents. This literature has contributed significantly to an understanding of the relationship between clinician and adolescent as well as between the clinician and the adolescent's significant others. In generic and idiosyncratic ways, adolescent clients present a wish to connect with, or at least have an impact on, the clinician. Concomitant with this wish is an overt or covert fear of adult power. Transference and countertransference are concepts that can serve several therapeutic purposes, but they are particularly useful in reminding clinicians of the ever-present valence of adolescents' wishes and fears vis-à-vis the person who is both an adult and a clinician. An awareness of this reality does not guarantee success with adolescent clients. But any clinical perspective that does not take such wishes and fears into account in working with adolescents is doomed to pretense or failure.

The primary foci of contemporary psychodynamic theories are the psychic representations of self and others and the childhood experiences that contributed to their formation. However, in their exploration of the past and the present, psychodynamically oriented clinicians do not necessarily assume a direct translation from past to present. One of the most intriguing aspects of the human psyche is our capacity to make individual meaning of our experiences. Psychotherapy pursues an understanding of the unique meaning assigned to past experiences of self and other as well as the impact of this meaning on the client's current relationships. Both cognition and affect are central to the translation being made between actual experience and representation. This interest in translation and the "making of meaning" is usually referred to as *constructivism*. This perspective is currently being aptly explored with regard to its applicability to social work practice and theory (Berlin 1996, Granvold 1996, Saari 1991). Such work represents an exciting integration of psychodynamic, cognitive-behavioral, *and* social work perspectives. Unfortunately, to date the clinical application of social work's interest in constructivism has centered on work with adults and has not included children or adolescents.

APPLICATION OF AN INTEGRATIVE PERSPECTIVE

The case application presented here centers on a male adolescent whose healthy development is threatened with derailment by the psychological and cognitive meaning he attributes to circumstances surrounding his parents' separation. The young man attributes his anger to what he perceives as his father's immoral behavior. The clinician's efforts at remaining "neutral" with regard to the question of morality, while understanding the adolescent's anger and fears, are facilitated by an integrative perspective.

Case Application

Sam, age 16½, agreed to be seen by a clinical social worker but for "one time and one time only." Sam and his family were referred for psychotherapy by the guidance counselor at Sam's school. Sam was one of a few Asian-American students in his high school and, until recently, was an outgoing student who was involved in several sports and performed exceptionally well academically. In the previous two months Sam had been truant twice and his grades had dropped dramatically. The school guidance counselor initiated the referral after hearing the rumor that Sam had passed out from drinking at a party. When the counselor spoke to Sam about the rumor, he readily admitted drinking excessively but "doubted the story about passing out."

Sam's parents (Mr. and Mrs. W.), who were relatively well-known in the community, had separated eight months prior to being referred, along with Sam, for treatment. They were in the midst of a bitter divorce process that involved the father's petition for joint physical custody of both Sam and his daughter, age 14 years. Because Mrs. W. refused to consider joint physical custody, the parents were also currently participating in court-ordered mediation. In brief, each parent blamed the other for Sam's "getting in trouble." While Mr. and Mrs. W. agreed that their past parenting relationship had been compatible and effective, a major shift occurred when Mrs. W. learned of her husband's beginning a relationship with another woman shortly after the separation. Within minutes of learning about this relationship, Mrs. W. told her children that their father was in love with someone else. She agreed that Sam had subsequently withdrawn from his father but saw this as related to Mr. W.'s having "destroyed the family" and pressuring Sam to "want to live with him." Psychotherapy with Sam was short-term (ten sessions) and included separate work with both parents. The focus here is on the individual work with Sam.

Sam presented as an adolescent who seemed socially at ease, articulate, and forthright. It quickly became clear that his intense negative beliefs about his father were activated anytime his father made an effort to see him, or any time he felt "forced" to think about his father. At those times his cognitive style was characterized by dichotomous thinking (he's right, his father is wrong), loss of perspective (focusing entirely on his father's behavior and losing sight of his own wishes or goals), overgeneralization (his current beliefs do not incorporate past realities), and control fallacies (others could force him to see his father). These particular cognitive "distortions" are, in fact, normative for many adolescents, especially those whose cognitive development is characterized by concrete operational thinking. However, through collaborative contacts with his parents, sister, and guidance counselor, the clinician concluded that such cognitive distortions were not typical for Sam. Prior to the parental separation, Sam's overall cognitive development included an exceptional ability to think about his own thinking, to consider multiple perspectives on a situation, and to tolerate differences of opinion.

Sam's anger with his father was fueled by reality-based cognition and unconscious defense mechanisms. His thinking was reality-based in that, from his point of view, his father had betrayed the values and the sense of loyalty on which his family's life had been built. Sam had once regarded his father as a man of integrity and honor and such regard had been violated by his becoming involved with another woman. Sam saw no difference between his father's having a girlfriend before or after the separation. As he put it, "He was still married to my mother—he shouldn't have done it."

Sam's current cognitive style was likely reactive—a response to the stress of dramatic changes in a father (and a family system) that sustained and supported his world view (Janoff-Bulman 1992). The clinician hypothesized that Sam's awareness of the discontinuity between his past and current cognitive abilities heightened his anxiety and sense of powerlessness. Cutting classes and drinking represented dramatic efforts to distract himself from "thinking about his thinking as well as his feelings." The clinician was aware that contact with her likely stimulated Sam's negative thoughts about his father— thoughts that he was trying hard to avoid or control.

Sam's anger with his father also reflected unconscious defense mechanisms. Reversal of affect and reaction formation protected him from experiencing an intense sense of loss and fended off any awareness of the significance of his attachment to his father. Directing all of his anger toward his father (displacement) served to shield Sam from the realities of the divorce, knowledge of difficulties between his parents to which his mother might have contributed, and feelings he might have about his mother's emotional behaviors. It was also possible that his at-risk behaviors represented an identification with the aggressor and turning passive into active. He engaged in behavior that he himself would perceive as wrong or immoral, in keeping with his judgment of his father's behavior. His doing so may have been motivated by a desire to create in his father the same sense of loss and disappointment that Sam was experiencing.

Taken together, Sam's behaviors, cognitive style, and defense mechanisms expressed both risk and coping. To some extent his coping efforts placed him at risk. Thus the clinician needed to simultaneously respect his coping and address what placed him most at risk. Sam was at risk on several counts: an interference with his ability to concentrate and continue to do well in school, the impaired development of an ego ideal and of his own identity as a person of integrity, an unhealthy alignment with his mother whom he perceived as the victim but from whom he would gradually need to separate, and the loss of a relationship with his father.

In discussing Sam's anger toward his father, the clinician was walking a thin line. On one side was her acknowledgment of his anger as "understandable," on the other was her awareness of the danger of buttressing the consolidation of this anger. The strategy with Sam was based on the conviction that Sam needed to have his sense of moral integrity validated by someone who had no emotional investment in his father or mother being right or wrong. The goal was to free Sam from acting out in a manner that was potentially self-destructive and possibly reflective of a negative identification with his father. The clinician hoped to achieve this goal by addressing Sam's thinking or cognitive structuring of his experiences and feelings. Cognitive-behavioral clinicians refer to this as "cognitive restructuring." Thus the clinician's understanding of the risks in this case was based primarily on a psychodynamic formulation but the intervention focused on cognition, cognitive style, and cognitive distortions. It was anticipated that in the context of a structured relationship with a "neutral" other, Sam would feel safe enough to "think about his thinking," and in so doing gain some sense of control and perspective about his own life. It was hypothesized that this process in turn would reduce his anxiety and acting out. Following is an excerpt from the third session with Sam.

SAM: My dad and I got into a big fight about the weekend. (*Pause*) He calls at the last minute to play tennis with him and some of his friends. (*Pause*) I told him I had something else to do and he says I'm lying! (*The final comment is said with contempt and anger.*)

CLIN: What did you think about his saying you were lying? (*The clinician picks up on an issue pertaining to morality.*)

SAM: I think he's paranoid, that's what I think! (*Pause*) And he accuses me of lying—what about him and all the lies he's told! (*Sam's anger becomes more intense. His overt focus is on his father, complete with a "diagnosis." He also draws a defensive distinction between himself and his father's morality, thus revealing possible fears about his own identity or identification with his dad.*)

CLIN: What did you mean when you said your father was "paranoid"? (*If the clinician is going to pursue Sam's fears about his identification with his father, she needs to know how serious Sam is about this diagnosis.*)

SAM: (*Sam looks at the clinician as if she should know the answer to this question, but he withholds comment and politely answers.*) It's when someone is afraid of something and there's no rational reason to be afraid—it's irrational.

CLIN: What's your father afraid of?

SAM: He's afraid I don't want to have anything to do with him. (*Sam hesitates, appears uncertain and confused, but quickly recovers.*) He's paranoid because he thinks I'm lying when I'm not—he thinks my mother is telling me not to see him and she's not doing that! He's the one who's lied. He lied to me. He lied to my mother. He lied to my sister. He went out with someone else while he was still married to my mother. That's wrong! (*Sam appears to regain cognitive and affective clarity when he focuses on his father's moral transgressions, albeit his affect is one of intense righteous anger.*)

The clinician is aware of the need to move carefully at this point. She surmises that Sam became uncertain and confused because he recognized that the fear he attributed to his father is not irrational—Sam told the clinician directly that he does not want anything to do with his father. So father is "right." Sam had momentarily exposed his own cognitive distortions, and in response he loses perspective and his thinking becomes dichotomous and overgeneralized. The clinician decides not to address Sam's cognitive distortions or their defensive purpose directly. Instead she chooses to affirm Sam's moral perspective, follow his own thinking processes, and reformulate the accompanying emotions as understandable and manageable.

CLIN: I understand what you're saying. I understand why you feel your dad is wrong and why you might not trust him. (*She pauses to see if Sam says anything about the qualifying nature of "might not." Sam says nothing so she proceeds.*) Can you tell me what went through your mind when your father asked you to play tennis with him and some friends?

SAM: (*Pauses and sighs heavily*) Well, first I wondered if his girlfriend was going to be there, but right away he named the people—I guess so I would know she wasn't going to be there. (*Said with cynicism*)

CLIN: What did you think about when you heard who the other players were? Do you know them?

SAM: Oh yeah. (*He goes on to note that the other players are also a father–son team, the son is a college freshman and someone Sam clearly admires. He also describes in some detail his father's long-standing relationship with the other father as well as a camping trip that the four of them had taken shortly before the parental separation.*)

CLIN: Do you think it's possible that some of these memories came to mind when your father mentioned their names?

SAM: Yeah, I guess so.

CLIN: I would guess that might be kind of confusing. (*Pause*) In your mind, there might be two very different pictures of your father—the father you don't respect right now and the father of your past who sounds like a pretty good guy.

SAM: He *used* to be a good guy.

Sam's acknowledgment of the past as different from the present (however careful) opened a door for the exploration of different perspectives, different time frames, different moralities, and different capabilities. In future sessions this cognitively based exploration uncovered the ideas and feelings that frequently accompany the recognition of difference. Uncovering his own sense of betrayal (as opposed to identifying with his mother's) and having the clinician's support in accepting it as "understandable" reduced Sam's anxiety. His diminished anxiety did not restore the father–son relationship immediately, for that needed to include the father's willingness to regain Sam's trust and respect by admitting the impact his choices had upon his son. For his part, Sam eventually resumed a focus on his academic goals and reportedly stopped drinking, yet declared his "right" to go out with friends every weekend.

In a brief intervention it is not possible to help an adolescent come to a full resolution and integration of his or her positive and negative images of a parent. But the processes of resolution and integration can begin in a therapeutic context in which cognitive awareness and the intensity of emotions associated with loss are simultaneously respected. In such an arena, the adolescent is free to mourn the partial loss of previously held ideals and object relationships while holding onto those that still benefit the youngster's development and well-being.

SUMMARY: THE STRENGTHS OF AN INTEGRATIVE PERSPECTIVE

One of the primary strengths of an integrative perspective is the foundation it provides for the use of here-and-now interventions most likely to fit the operative dimensions of an adolescent's developmental history, character structure, intrapsychic conflicts, affective patterns, cognitive and physical abilities, sociocultural environment, and response to treatment. These dimensions may or may not be directly articulated with the teenager, but the clinician's recognition of their combined nature and power actively informs treatment goals and processes.

Such recognition is especially valuable as social work practitioners strive to ameliorate the psychological impact of society's gravest social problems while simultaneously addressing their differential effects according to age, ethnicity, race, sexual orientation, and gender.

For example, exposure to intense and chronic violence disproportionately affects North American teenagers. Its presence in schools and communities of black, African-American, and Latino youth who live in economically impoverished urban settings has been well documented (Aber 1994, DuRant et al. 1993, Gustavsson and Balgopal 1990, Prothrow-Stith 1991, Schwab-Stone et al. 1995). Lesbian and gay adolescents are also likely to be directly exposed to violence or threats of violence that are based on gender and sexual orientation as well as race or ethnicity (Berk 1990, Berrill 1990). While adolescent males, in general, are far more likely than females to be victims of homicide, robbery, and nonsexual assault, adolescent females are more than twice as likely to report being sexually abused (Children Now/Kaiser Permanente 1995, Schoen et al. 1997, Snyder and Sickmund 1995). Within this context of direct, indirect, as well as insidious violence (Root 1992), it is not surprising to discover exceedingly high rates of posttraumatic stress disorder (PTSD) symptomatology among contemporary adolescents (Giaconia et al. 1995, Singer et al. 1995, Springer et al. 1998).

The social problem that has been constructed as "youth violence" demands our most sophisticated understanding of the interaction of psychological, cognitive, social, economic, and cultural forces. At the present time, however, "youth violence" programs focus on male perpetrators and center primarily on cognitive-behavioral approaches. Such approaches tend to overlook the experience of direct and indirect victimization as well as the physical and affective experiences associated with PTSD symptoms. Pynoos and colleagues (1996) specifically endorse intervention strategies that incorporate our clinical knowledge of the affective and subjective experience of violence as well as its cognitive components. An illustration of such an incorporation has been presented by Dutton and Yamini (1995), who linked aversive self awareness (a social cognition process) and the affective projective-introjective cycling of aggression (psychodynamic defense mechanisms) to explain how adolescent parricide may emerge from an abusive environment. This model of integrating cognitive-behavioral and psychodynamic perspectives holds promise for understanding and addressing the combined affective, cognitive, and behavioral effects of violence exposure, PTSD symptomatology, and psychological, social, or economic deprivation.

Following an adolescent's cognitive pathways and noting cognitive deficiencies or distortions yield valuable information about behaviors, emotions, and psychological abilities. Under certain circumstances with some adolescents, addressing cognitive patterns and belief systems and offering alternative ways of thinking and behaving serve as optimum interventions. Yet for many troubled adolescents this is not enough because they need to know that there are places and people who can understand and withstand the expression of their most monstrous feelings—emotions that the adolescents themselves can barely tolerate. It is unfortunate but true that in contemporary society adolescents can readily find places and people who not only tolerate but encourage or profit from their self-destructive acting out. In order to redirect self-destructive behaviors, the adolescent may especially need an adult who has the courage and patience to withstand the verbal expression of uncontrollable impulses or unacceptable feelings.

The treatment of adolescents in contemporary American society is a particularly challenging endeavor. Social and cultural forces combine with economic realities and place many of our young people at risk. The relational, psychological, cognitive, or physical demands and possibilities of adolescence itself are often overwhelming. Moreover, these demands and possibilities are experienced both in the intrapersonal and interpersonal worlds of the adolescents. When the understanding and treatment of adolescents are informed by attention to only one realm of experience, an opportunity is lost. This is, of course, true for all individuals but it is particularly true in work with adolescents who, for distinct developmental reasons, do not give us many openings. For such limited openings, an integration of psychodynamic and cognitive-behavioral perspectives optimizes clinical understanding and the availability of a wide range of techniques.

REFERENCES

Aber, J. L. (1994). Poverty, violence, and child development: untangling family and community effects. In *Threats to Optimal Development: Integrating Biological, Psychological, and Social Factors*, ed. C. A. Nelson. Hillsdale, NJ: Erlbaum.

Ager, C. L., and Cole, C. K. (1991). A review of cognitive-behavioral interventions for children and adolescents with behavior disorders. *Behavioral Disorders* 16:276–287.

Aichhorn, A. (1925). *Wayward Youth*. New York: Viking. (Original work published in 1963.)

Allen-Meares, P. (1995). *Social Work with Children and Adolescents*. New York: Longman.

Barth, R. (1986). *Social and Cognitive Treatment of Children and Adolescents*. San Francisco: Jossey-Bass.

Benjamin, J. (1995). Sameness and difference: an "overinclusive" view of gender constitution. *Psychoanalytic Inquiry* 15:125–142.

Berk, R. A. (1990). Thinking about hate-motivated crimes. *Journal of Interpersonal Violence* 5:334–349.

Berlin, S. B. (1996). Constructivism and the environment: a cognitive-integrative perspective for social work practice. *Families in Society* 77(6):326–335.

Berrill, K. T. (1990). Anti-gay violence and victimization in the United States: an overview. *Journal of Interpersonal Violence* 5:224–294.

Blos, P. (1962). *On Adolescence*. New York: Free Press.

——— (1967). The second individuation process of adolescence. *Psychoanalytic Study of the Child* 22:162–186. New York: International Universities Press.

——— (1968). Character formation in adolescence. *Psychoanalytic Study of the Child* 23:245–263. New York: International Universities Press.

Bowers, W. A., Evans, K., and Van Cleve, L. (1996). Treatment of adolescent eating disorders. In *Cognitive Therapy with Children and Adolescents: A Casebook for Clinical Practice*, ed. M. A. Reinecke, F. M. Dattilio, and A. Freeman, pp. 227–250. New York: Guilford.

Carey, M. (1993). Child and adolescent depression: cognitive-behavioral strategies and interventions. In *Cognitive-Behavioral Procedures with Children and Adolescents*, ed. A. J. Finch, Jr., W. N. Nelson III, and E. S. Ott, pp. 289–314. Boston: Allyn & Bacon.

Children Now/Kaiser Permanente (1995). Campaign for Children's Health and Safety. Oakland, CA: Author.

Clarke, G., Hops, H., Lewinsohn, P. M., et al. (1992). Cognitive-behavioral group treatment of adolescent depression: predictors of outcome. *Behavior Therapy* 23(3):341–354.

Cooper, S., and Wanerman, L. (1977). *Children in Treatment: A Primer for Beginning Psychotherapists*. New York: Brunner/Mazel.

——— (1984). *A Casebook of Child Psychotherapy: Strategies and Technique*. New York: Brunner/Mazel.

Csikszentmihalyi, M., and Larson, R. (1984). *Being Adolescent: Conflict and Growth in the Teenage Years*. New York: Basic Books.

DuBois, D. L., and Felner, R. D. (1996). The quadripartite model of social competence: theory and applications to clinical intervention. In *Cognitive Therapy with Children and Adolescents*, ed. M. A. Reinecke, F. M. Dattilio, and A. Freeman, pp. 124–152. New York: Guilford.

DuRant, R. H., Cadenhead, C., Pendergrast, R. A., et al. (1993). Factors associated with the use of violence among urban black adolescents. *American Journal of Public Health* 84(4):612–617.

Dutton, D. G., and Yamini, S. (1995). Adolescent parricide: an integration of social cognitive and clinical views of projective-introjective cycling. *American Journal of Orthopsychiatry* 65(1):39–47.

Elkind, D. (1967). Egocentrism in adolescence. *Child Development* 38:1025–1034.

Erikson, E. H. (1968). *Identity: Youth and Crisis*. New York: Norton.

Finch, A. J., Jr., Nelson, W. M., III, and Ott, E. S., eds. (1993). *Cognitive-Behavioral Procedures with Children and Adolescents: A Practical Guide*. Boston: Allyn & Bacon.

Fraiberg, S. (1955). Some considerations in the introduction to therapy in puberty. *Psychoanalytic Study of the Child* 10:264–286. New York: International Universities Press.

Freud, A. (1936). *The Ego and the Mechanisms of Defense.* New York: International Universities Press, 1966.

———— (1958). Adolescence. *Psychoanalytic Study of the Child* 13:255–278. New York: International Universities Press.

Giaconia, R. M., Reinherz, H. Z., Silverman, A. B., et al. (1995). Trauma and posttraumatic stress disorder in a community population of older adolescents. *Journal of the Academy of Child and Adolescent Psychiatry* 34(10):1369–1380.

Goldfried, M. R. (1995). *From Cognitive-Behavior Therapy to Psychotherapy Integration.* New York: Springer.

Granvold, D. K. (1996). Constructivist psychotherapy. *Families in Society* 77(6):345–359.

Guerra, N. G. (1993). Cognitive development. In *Handbook of Clinical Research and Practice with Adolescents,* ed. P. H. Tolan and B. T. Cohler, pp. 45–62. New York: Wiley.

Gustavsson, N. S., and Balgopal, P. R. (1990). Violence and minority youth: an ecological perspective. In *Ethnic Issues in Adolescent Mental Health,* ed. A. R. Stiffman and L. E. Davis, pp. 115–130. Newbury Park, CA: Sage.

Heflin, A. H., and Deblinger, E. (1996). Treatment of an adolescent survivor of child sexual abuse. In *Cognitive Therapy with Children and Adolescents: A Casebook for Clinical Practice,* ed. M. A. Reinecke, F. M. Dattilio, and A. Freeman, pp. 199–226. New York: Guilford.

Hollis, F., and Woods, M. E. (1964). *Casework: A Psychosocial Therapy.* New York: Random House.

Holmbeck, G. N., and Updegrove, A. L. (1995). Clinical-developmental interface: implications of developmental research for adolescent psychotherapy. *Psychotherapy* 32(1):16–33.

Hunter, J. A., Jr., and Santos, D. R. (1990). The use of specialized cognitive-behavioral therapies in the treatment of adolescent sexual offenders. *International Journal of Offender Therapy and Comparative Criminology* 34(3):239–247.

Janoff-Bulman, R. (1992). *Shattered Assumptions: Towards a New Psychology of Trauma.* New York: Free Press.

Kearney, C. A., and Silverman, W. K. (1990). Treatment of an adolescent with obsessive-compulsive disorder by alternating response prevention and cognitive therapy: an empirical analysis. *Journal of Behavior Therapy and Experimental Psychiatry* 21(1):39–47.

Kendall, P. C. (1992). *Anxiety Disorders in Youth: Cognitive-Behavioral Interventions*. Boston: Allyn & Bacon.

—— (1993). Cognitive-behavioral therapies with youth: guiding theory, current status and emerging developments. *Journal of Consulting and Clinical Psychology* 61:235–247.

——, ed. (1991). *Child and Adolescent Therapy: Cognitive-Behavioral Procedures*. New York: Guilford.

Kendall, P. C., and Chansky, T. E. (1991). Considering cognition in anxiety disordered youth. *Journal of Anxiety Disorders* 5:167–185.

Larson, J. D. (1990). Cognitive-behavioral group therapy with delinquent adolescents: a cooperative approach with the juvenile court. *Journal of Offender Rehabilitation* 16(1,2):7–64.

Levitt, M. Z., Selman, R. L., and Richmond, J. (1991). The psychological foundations of early adolescents' high-risk behavior: implications for research and practice. *Journal of Research on Adolescence* 1(4):349–378.

Lewinsohn, P. M., Clarke, G. N., Hops, H., and Andrews, J. (1990). Cognitive-behavioral treatment for depressed adolescents. *Behavior Therapy* 21(4):385–401.

Longres, J. F. (1995). *Human Behavior in the Social Environment*, 2nd ed. Itasca, IL: Peacock.

Mishne, J. M. (1986). *Clinical Work with Adolescents*. New York: Free Press.

Mufson, L., Moreau, D., Weissman, M. M., and Klerman, G. L. (1993). *Interpersonal Psychotherapy for Depressed Adolescents*. New York: Free Press.

Nay, W. R., and Ross, G. R. (1993). Cognitive-behavioral intervention for adolescent drug abuse. In *Cognitive-Behavioral Procedures with Children and Adolescents*, ed. A. J. Finch, Jr., W. M. Nelson III, and E. S. Ott, pp. 315–343. Boston: Allyn & Bacon.

O'Connell, D. F., and Patterson, H. O. (1996). Recovery maintenance and relapse prevention with chemically dependent adolescents. In *Cognitive Therapy with Children and Adolescents: A Casebook for Clinical Practice*, ed. M. A. Reinecke, F. M. Dattilio and A. Freeman, pp. 79–102. New York: Guilford.

Piaget, J. (1932). *The Moral Judgment of the Child*. New York: Free Press, 1965.

Polyson, J., and Kimball, W. (1993). Social skills training with physically aggressive children. In *Cognitive-Behavioral Procedures with*

Children and Adolescents, ed. A. J. Finch, Jr., W. M. Nelson III, and E. S. Ott, pp. 206–232. Boston: Allyn & Bacon.

Powell, K. E., and Hawkins, D. F., eds. (1996). Youth violence prevention: descriptions and baseline data from 13 evaluation projects [Special issue]. *American Journal of Preventive Medicine* 12(5).

Prothrow-Stith, D. (1991). *Deadly Consequences*. New York: Harper-Collins.

Pynoos, R. S., Steinberg, A. M., and Goenjian, A. (1996). Traumatic stress in childhood and adolescence: recent developments and current controversies. In *Traumatic Stress: The Effects of Overwhelming Experience on Mind, Body, and Society*, ed. B. A. Vander Kolk, A. C. McFarlane, and L. Weisaeth, pp. 351–358. New York: Guilford.

Reinecke, M. A., Dattilio, F. M., and Freeman, A., eds. (1996). *Cognitive Therapy with Children and Adolescents: A Casebook for Clinical Practice*. New York: Guilford.

Root, M. P. P. (1992). Reconstructing the impact of trauma on personality. In *Personality and Psychopathology: Feminist Reappraisals*, ed. L. S., Brown and M. Ballou, pp. 229–265. New York: Guilford.

Rotheram-Borus, M. J., Piacentini, J., Miller, S., et al. (1994). Brief cognitive-behavioral treatment for adolescent suicide attempters and their families. *Journal of the American Academy of Child and Adolescent Psychiatry* 33:508–517.

Saari, C. (1991). *The Creation of Meaning in Clinical Social Work*. New York: Guilford.

Safran, J. D. (1988). Feeling, thinking, and acting: a cognitive-behavioral therapy and relaxation training for the treatment of depression in adolescents. *Journal of Consulting and Clinical Psychology* 2:109–130.

Schoen, C., Davis, K., Collins, K. S., et al. (1997). *The Commonwealth Fund Survey of the Health of Adolescent Girls*. New York: The Commonwealth Fund.

Schwab-Stone, M. E., Ayers, T. S., Kasprow, W., et al. (1995). No safe haven: a study of violence exposure in an urban community. *Journal of the American Academy of Child and Adolescent Psychiatry* 34(10):1343–1352.

Selman, R. L. (1980). *The Growth of Interpersonal Understanding: Developmental and Clinical Analysis*. New York: Academic Press.

Selman, R. L., and Schultz, L. H. (1988). Interpersonal thought and action in the case of a troubled early adolescent: towards a developmental model of the gap. In *Cognitive Development and Child Psychotherapy*, ed. S. R. Shirk, pp. 207–246. New York: Plenum.

Shirk, S. R., ed. (1988). *Cognitive Development and Child Psychotherapy*. New York: Plenum.

Singer, M. I., Anglin, T. M., Song, L. Y., and Lunghofer, L. (1995). Adolescents' exposure to violence and associated symptoms of psychological trauma. *Journal of the American Medical Association* 273(6):477–482.

Snyder, H. N., and Sickmund, M. (1995). *Juvenile Offenders and Victims: A National Report*. Washington, DC: Office of Juvenile Justice Delinquency Prevention.

Spence, S. H. (1994). Practitioner review: cognitive therapy with children and adolescents: from theory to practice. *Journal of Child Psychology and Psychiatry* 35(7):1191–1228.

Springer, C., Padgett, D., Spellman, M., and Landsberg, G. (1998). *Clinical and research perspectives on young adolescents' experience of violence and PTSD symptomatology*. Paper presented at the American Orthopsychiatric Association's 75th annual meeting, Washington, DC, April.

Stern, L. (1989). Conceptions of separation and connection in female adolescents. In *Making Connections: The Relational Worlds of Adolescent Girls at Emma Willard School*, ed. C. Gilligan, N. P. Lyons, and T. J. Hanmer, pp. 73–87. Troy, NY: Emma Willard School.

Vitousek, K., and Ewald, L. (1993). Self-representation in eating disorders: a cognitive perspective. In *The Self in Emotional Distress: Cognitive and Psychodynamic Perspectives*, ed. Z. Segal and S. Blatt, pp. 221–257. New York: Guilford.

Wilkes, T. C. R., Belsher, G. Rush, A. J., et al. (1994). *Cognitive Therapy for Depressed Adolescents*. New York: Guilford.

Wilson, G. T., and Fairburn, C. G. (1993). Cognitive treatments for eating disorders. *Journal of Consulting and Clinical Psychology* 61:261–269.

Woods, M. E., and Hollis, F. (1990). *Casework: A Psychosocial Therapy*, 4th ed. New York: McGraw-Hill.

Zarb, J. (1992). *Cognitive-Behavioral Assessment and Therapy with Adolescents*. New York: Brunner/Mazel.

8

Treating Women Survivors of Childhood Abuse

Emily Lyon Gray

INTRODUCTION

Trauma-related mental illness is unique because it is the only disorder created by real, outside events in a woman's life as a child. Other clients' neurotic difficulties may include reactions to environmental influences. However, the impact of abuse trauma on a child's development is rather like that of a train that has run off its rails into the delicate patterns of a formal garden. Normal growth and development does not proceed as planned.

Women restore themselves when they struggle through the enormously complex and painful damage inflicted by the trauma, transform the nightmare memories into a digestible narrative, and assign responsibility for the trauma where it belongs. They may then begin to replant their own hedges and flower beds.

Cognitive treatment approaches are an essential part of this recovery. Survivors must learn to separate present-day reality from the jumbled abuse memories, old terrors, experiences of betrayal, impulses to self-abuse, and intense, ongoing psychic and, often, physical pain. The trauma always seems present for abuse survivors (van der Kolk et al. 1996), so they continue to use the distorted assumptions and perceptions and the old defenses that helped them survive their childhoods. While the treatment of abuse requires many different approaches, cognitive therapy is essential in reorienting survivors to the present-day world beyond their trauma.

LITERATURE REVIEW AND THEORETICAL FRAMEWORK

There have been two historic sources of cognitive theories as they relate to very disturbed patients: the theories about trauma and consciousness of Pierre Janet, and theories about ego structure and ego processes derived from the work of Freud.

Pierre Janet in his *L'Automatisme Psychologique* (1889) indicated that he saw his traumatized patients as suffering primarily from a disorder of consciousness (van der Kolk et al. 1989). Janet suggested that when traumatic events overwhelm the mind's ability to organize and categorize experience, the mind uses dissociation as a way to remove the indigestible experience from conscious memory. Dissociation then becomes a habitual way to manage stress so that ongoing experience fragments, at the same time as the stored trauma, return as bits of emotions, images, or somatic states. Thus Janet saw the traumatized patient as constantly living with physiological hyperarousal, intrusive memories alternating with numbing dissociation and cognitive confusion so that there was no way to make sense of contemporary reality (van der Kolk et al. 1989). Like many contemporary trauma therapists, he saw recovery as the cognitive work of remembering traumatic memories and reintegrating them as meaningful narratives.

In his early work Freud was influenced by the work of Janet and his teacher, Charcot, to consider traumatic experience as a basis for the pathology of his patients. However, he later made his well-known decision to explain psychopathology as an outcome of childhood intrapsychic conflict between instinctual drives and the environment (Herman 1992, van der Kolk et al. 1989). After that time, most psychoanalytic thinking was focused on internalized conflict.

Some within the psychoanalytic school of thought were still interested in cognitive functioning. Psychiatrists predating Freud distinguished those who were more disturbed than neurotics, with "minds trembling in the balance between reason and madness" from the insane because they were without "appreciable intellectual derangement" (Rosse 1880, p. 32). This ability to think was seen as a potential resource for treatment (Hughes 1834).

Adolf Stern (1938) was the first to use the term *borderline* to describe these patients and outline the symptoms, most of which we still associate with that diagnosis. Like Janet, he saw that "actual cruelty, neglect and brutality by the parents of many years duration" are factors found in these patients. Although he emphasized their "inordinate hypersensitivity and emotionality," he did comment that education and using "whatever there is of healthy ego functioning" are important approaches (pp. 56–73).

Ego functioning was a major interest of Hartmann, who suggested that people have a third drive, for learning and curiosity, or ego energy in addition to the drives of libido and aggression (Bieber 1980). However, as conceptual thinking about the borderline diagnosis continued, more focus was put on the complex internal dynamics of these patients (i.e., Kernberg 1975, Mahler 1979, Masterson 1981). Cognitive approaches in psychodynamic thinking evolved primarily into methods for shoring up ego functioning so that exploration of internal conflicts could proceed usefully.

Recent studies have found that as many as 81 percent of women with borderline diagnoses have suffered trauma in their developmental years (Bernard and Hirsch 1985, Herman et al. 1989), forcing us to reread the literature on borderline patients with a new perspective. We now have concrete evidence that these patients do indeed suffer from the developmental effects of real, traumatic experiences (Davies and Frawley 1994, Herman et al. 1989, Linehan and Kehrer 1993). It is the impact of trauma on a child's development that brings us back to the importance of cognitive approaches.

The constructivist theories of cognitive therapy suggest that the child's sense of self is built up of repetitive bits of information about herself that she gleans from interaction with the environment. Particularly important are people in the environment who she can see are consciously aware of her. She uses their perception of her as a mirror in which she can see information about herself (Guidano and Liotti 1985). Secure attachment to one or two others acts as a vehicle for information on the self and as an organizing and integrating power. Even before this stage of emerging self-knowledge, the child develops tacit (or unconscious) knowledge: a model, or schema, of reality based on her earliest experience. This schema determines the patterns in which the child organizes or makes sense of her experience (Mahoney 1991). If all goes well enough, the child develops a "full sense of self-identity and an inherent feeling of uniqueness and historical continuity" (Guidano and Liotti 1985, p. 103).

When a child is born into a dysfunctional family, where her experience is fragmented and painful, there is no secure attachment figure and a variety of sadistic, ambivalent, or detached awarenesses of herself are mirrored back to her. The child's "cognitive structures are coalescing and evolving in a terroristic environment in which she feels held hostage and isolated from her peers" (Fine 1988, p. 6). It is likely that her tacit schema of reality is distorted by expectations of harm, distrust, and self-blame. If the child is being regularly abused, she may develop the saving ability to dissociate away from her painful experience. However, dissociation acts to further fragment her sense of identity and her personal history.

Because of her tortuous childhood, the adult survivor finds herself caught in styles of information processing that lead to pathological views of current reality. Incorrect conclusions that often lead to troublesome behavior can be drawn by abstracting elements of an event out of context (selective abstraction); ignoring important evidence in order to make emotionally needed conclusions, for example, concluding that "my current boyfriend is good to me" while ignoring the number of times he gets drunk and hits her (arbitrary inference); over- or undergeneralizing evidence or assuming a cause–effect relationship where there is none ("I didn't say hello to my landlady yesterday so she raised my rent today"); or, finally, missing a cause–effect relationship that does exist.

The survivor can terrify herself with catastrophizing ideas ("My father is not at home; he must be coming to get me"), or get into trouble by not seeing real danger (e.g., driving a car with faulty brakes, ignoring an injury). She can also upset herself with "all or nothing" thinking ("I didn't like what my therapist said today. She's a really bad therapist and I should find a new one"). One of the most difficult types of distortion is "egocentric" thinking, or assuming everything that happens in life is because of her. Its most painful form is assuming that she was responsible for her abuse and is now going to continue to be abused because she is such a terrible person (Davies and Frawley 1994, Fine 1988, van der Kolk·et al. 1996). This can be seen as both a cognitive distortion and a defense against full knowledge of her helplessness as an abused child. It is crucial for children to see their parents as competent and loving so the child must always blame trouble on herself.

The most disturbing of these perceptual distortions are focused around self, self-other, and other-other interactions (Fine 1988). This makes sense because trauma is a series of relational events from which the child gleans her most important information about herself and others, yet from which all possibility of negotiation, experimentation, or play has been removed. Correction of the survivor's basic schema must also happen in the context of a relationship, but this one must be safe enough to allow for testing information, moving in and out of connection, and playing out of sadistic and masochistic themes. In general, the therapist must provide the space within which old assumptions are given up and new schemas can be spontaneously created. Cognitive interventions will be helpful only to the extent that they occur in this kind of compassionate relational context.

PHASES OF TREATMENT

Most trauma therapists conceptualize treatment of their patients in three phases. These may differ slightly in timing and purpose among different theoreticians, but they generally follow Richard Kluft's (1993) outline: establishment of safety, remembering and mourning, and, finally, reconnection to the present social world. Establishing safety is a complex and sometimes lengthy process of preparing the patient for doing the intense work of remembering the trauma. First, a safe and consistent therapeutic alliance must be formed with a survivor who has learned that others can be expected to hurt her. In these situations it is very difficult for the survivor to believe that her wishes and needs are primary. Survivors are so exquisitely attuned to the wishes and motivations of authority figures that a therapist could take them through an entire year of therapy, never realizing that the survivor was submitting herself to what she thought her therapist wanted.

When the woman presents for treatment, she may be flooded with physiological agitation, pain, or flashbacks. She may be experiencing depression, manic depression, or intense anxiety that needs to be medicated. She may be addicted to drugs, alcohol, food, or other substances, which needs to stop before any therapy can begin. Education about her diagnosis of PTSD or dissociation or dissociative identity disorder is crucial at this point so she can gain some understanding and mastery over what is happening to her.

The survivor also needs extensive information in this first phase on how her trauma has affected her ability to think in a present, reality-based way. Her difficulties as a child with processing information in a chaotic and traumatizing field has led to the development of cognitive distortions that can create more difficulties for her. For example, if the woman reacts to her flashbacks with panicky fears that she is crazy, one would provide her with education on the role of flashbacks and work with her on her catastrophizing style of thought. (One would not, at this point, explore the flashback.)

Catherine Fine (1991) suggests that survivors be taught to test reality with the experimental model: "What is the evidence for this belief of mine? What other explanations are possible? What were the reasons for my original, distorted belief?" (p. 664). As the woman learns to notice and correct her own errors in information processing, she begins to gain a sense of mastery and control over what has seemed an overwhelming and chaotic inner experience. This first phase is like weaving a net over a canyon: there needs to be something for her to hold on to as she descends into the depths.

A preliminary understanding of how trauma affects the brain will help to anticipate the work of the second phase of treatment. When someone is caught in an actively abusive situation, the central nervous system is overstimulated to the point that there may be permanent neuronal changes that negatively affect "learning, habituation and stimulus discrimination" (Kolb, cited in van der Kolk et al. 1996). Abuse may be even more destructive for children who are developing the brain functions they will need as an adult. One way this kind of damage is evident is that many survivors have an abnormal startle response to a stimulus that would be neutral for nonsurvivors. Their reception of sensory stimuli is no longer connected to appropriate evaluation and action.

In addition, survivors of child abuse have experienced such continuous physiological arousal that they can no longer use internal signals, such as their own emotions, as information that will alert them to danger, guide their response to others, or signal their own needs. Much of their energy goes to fight/flight responses or to numb their hyperarousal (van der Kolk et al. 1996). Much of the cognitive work in treatment is directed toward helping survivors learn that their emotions have meaning, are connected to previous events, and can be used to guide their responses. This kind of clarification helps the survivor feel less victimized by internal chaos and more able to take control and direction in their lives.

The work of recovering traumatic memories can be better understood with knowledge of how these memories are stored in the brain. A traumatic experience is so overwhelming that there is no space to organize a string of impressions into a narrative in explicit memory, which occurs in memories of ordinary events. During trauma, the victim's level of upset is extreme, and his or her attention is narrowly focused so that only the perceptual details of the experience are retained. The ego is so overwhelmed that these details, or trauma fragments, cannot go through normal memory processing, but are split off from ordinary consciousness in such a way that they cannot be represented by speech. Fragments of smells, strong emotions, sounds, and visual or kinesthetic images float in and out of consciousness without a context.

These concepts of memory disturbance seem to be validated by neuroimaging studies of the brains of people with PTSD who were remembering trauma. While trauma memories were recalled, the activity in Broca's area (where sensory experience is transformed into speech) was reduced. At the same time, areas in the brain thought to process intense emotions and visual images (the limbic system) were significantly activated (van der Kolk et al. 1996, p. 287). The work of therapy, put simplistically, is to reduce limbic stimulation and reactivate Broca's area so that the sensory trauma fragments can be processed into a narrative.

The process of recovering memories is a long and painful task of experiencing and reexperiencing the same painful images, sensations, and emotions, sometimes as vague shadows and sometimes as a flood of intense emotion, body pain, and sound. Eventually these fragments, like pieces of a jigsaw puzzle, can be joined to other fragments so that a pattern begins to emerge. However, continuing to review memories without challenging the survivor's fixed traumatic ideas can be retraumatizing. Helpful techniques include contradicting traumatic ideas while a memory is going on; encouraging the survivor to describe the fragments; and asking, "What do you think about that?" or "How do you imagine that could have happened?" These questions stimulate the observing ego to begin to master these events.

During this time it is also critical to interrupt and correct such cognitive distortions as "I must have been such a bad child." "My mom said it happened because I was a girl. I wish I were a boy!" Survivors must be reassured constantly: "It was never your fault," "Your parents were very sick people who did not know how to love people," "We are born into families by accident; it had nothing to do with something you did wrong," "You were just a little girl with normal needs and wishes to be loved; there is nothing wrong with that." As these litanies begin to make sense and more pieces of the puzzle are retrieved it becomes possible to verbalize what happened, until finally the fragments of trauma become a recognizable story.

One of the questions for treatment is how much to use traditional desensitizing techniques for abuse memories. For those who have experienced onetime trauma in their adulthood or who have severe anxiety disorders, exposure to the feared memories, coupled with incompatible new information, has been useful in some cases (Rothbaum and Foa 1996). For example, Resnick and Schnicke (1992) developed cognitive processing therapy for survivors. They say that PTSD is more than an anxiety reaction, but includes anger, disgust, humiliation, and guilt. When clients are encouraged to have memories of their trauma with all the associated feelings, they then confront the person's conflicts and maladaptive beliefs with new formulations, information, and cognitive restructuring.

Programs like these may be helpful to victims of onetime trauma, but may not be appropriate to survivors of childhood abuse. Meichenbaum (1985), who developed stress inoculation training (SIT), comments that emotions related to the trauma should be experienced in a safe situation, the pace should be tolerable, and new cognition about the experience should be available. He cautions the therapist to be aware of the use of self-blame by the survivor, and to be sure to work with this and related cognition. He comments that the trauma experienced by survivors of childhood abuse is so extensive and complex that attempts to stimulate recall could actually result in flooding and retraumatization.

Catherine Fine (1991) suggests that memories be recovered in a process of "fragmented abreactions." The therapist and patient talk about a major memory that they decide together to work on, and divide it up into manageable segments. This planfulness allows the survivor to feel some control over her painful experience. As each segment is reviewed and the emotions are experienced, the segment is connected to the history known to this point and the cognitive distortions are corrected. Dr. Fine relates this process to systematic desensitization, but it is done in the context of a therapeutic relationship and at a pace that is comfortable to the woman.

As the second phase of treatment gradually comes to an end, the survivor finds that she is no longer held prisoner by the floating, intrusive images, sounds, and experiences. She can now tell her personal history, and evaluate where the blame belongs and what she will forgive and not forgive. In the third phase of treatment she is in the business of making meaning of her life, of restoring the soul trampled by cruelty, violence, and neglect. Janoff-Bulman (1992) points out that a major impact of trauma is to shatter one's previous assumptions, especially those about a belief in personal invulnerability, the perception of the world as meaningful and comprehensible, and the view of the self as positive. Her concepts apply particularly to survivors of onetime adult trauma, but survivors of childhood trauma may now be able to create a version of these assumptions for themselves.

It will continue to be important to work with cognitive distortions in this phase of treatment. One important arena will be distortions associated with developing relationships with others. The tendency to split, to see oneself as the central cause of all events, and to engage in self-blame can continue to cause problems. It is also very difficult for people to give up the habit of dissociation, even though it is no longer necessary. Survivors must be taught how to face and bear reality, how to engage in planful action, and how to accept the responsibilities of being an adult in the world. They may have to adjust around the damage of the trauma that they still carry such as hyperarousal, memory problems, physical injuries, or stress-related illness. In addition to working with all the feelings associated with these issues, learning to think about them is essential.

Another, not so arduous, task, is what van der Kolk and colleagues (1996) refer to as "the accumulation of restitutive emotional experiences" (pp. 433–434). These women have lived their lives focused on surviving terror and disorganization. Now is the time for something as frivolous as finger painting or as consuming as climbing a mountain. New areas of exploration and play can be free of the traumatic past and make it possible to experience pleasure, mastery, and re-creation. However resistance to these new vistas is likely, and even they may need cognitive exploration.

CLINICAL EXAMPLES

The following case examples illustrate the way cognitive techniques are used during the course of a therapy session. The first vignette illustrates the beginning of therapy when the client is oriented to the structure and style that will be needed to do the work. The second illustrates working with a flashback as it comes up in a session.

Vignette 1

Mary C. came into the office for her first appointment appearing quite anxious but determined. She explained to the therapist: "I've been to therapists many times in my life and have never gotten the help I need. I must be a hard person to help! I heard you were an expert so maybe you'll know what to do. I've been tempted to give up on therapy but it's been hard to live with my depression and this terrible anxiety. I have a very orderly life and try to do what I should but sometimes things happen and I just don't know what to do."

After some reflecting and reassurance from the therapist she went on: "These strange things have been happening to me the last month or so. One day I was just making the bed when all of a sudden I saw a picture in my head of my uncle standing in the door with his . . . his, you know, in his hand and staring at me with this weird look on his face, like a photograph, just a picture, then it was gone. And then a couple of weeks later when I was driving to church, I saw his face really big in front of me. I think I must be going crazy, doctor, because I could hear his voice too, and he's been dead these seven years. I'm afraid God is punishing me"—she becomes tearful—"because I didn't like that uncle and I pretended not to see his wife last month and I know I've made her lonely now. Please help me! I'll do anything you say. I know my other therapists were no good and you are an expert so you will know what to do."

A number of issues are presented in this brief vignette. The woman's long history of therapy with no improvement, her efforts to remain rigidly in control of her life, and the possibility of the disturbing incidents being flashbacks suggest that she may indeed be an abuse survivor. There are also a number of cognitive distortions that are typical of survivors. Almost immediately she indicates her low self-esteem and her tendency to blame herself for her problems by saying she is "a hard person to help." She expresses fears that she is "crazy," which is common in survivors. She has an interesting but egocentric and self-blaming fantasy that God is punishing her for ignoring her uncle's wife and has made an invalid assumption, because there is no evidence, that she has made her aunt more lonely.

Another troublesome distortion is the way she is splitting her former therapists and this new "expert." She draws the emotionally needed conclusion that this new therapist will be her savior, then places herself in a submissive position with respect to the therapist. Making this naive assumption that a new person will give her what she needs, without waiting for appropriate evidence, is what draws many abuse survivors into retraumatizing experiences. In this case her assumption leaves her open to exploitation and possible exacerbation of her symptoms, or worse, if the therapist is untrained or unprofessional.

This material is open to any number of psychodynamic formulations. However, it would be unwise to make even the gentlest of interpretations. Survivors often experience interpretations of unconscious material as confusing, intrusive, and controlling, even later in the therapy. At this point some education about the possibility of abuse (always leaving the question open for more exploration at this stage), beginning work on her cognitive distortions, and working toward a therapeutic alliance need to come first. The therapist might reply:

> TH: Well, I can hear that you've given this whole matter a lot of thought! It's really a helpful skill, you know, to be able to think about what is happening to you and try to understand it. I think you're saying that you need some more information on what might be happening to you. (*A positive reframe pointing toward the use of cognition and downplaying the expertise of the therapist*) Your experience of seeing your uncle and hearing his voice is consistent with having some very upsetting interactions with him, and it does not mean that you are crazy! It may have to do with the way your mind copes with disturbing memories, but we need to gather a lot more information before we can say anything for sure. I wonder if you could say more about your thought that God is punishing you?

From both a psychodynamic and cognitive perspective, this kind of pathological guilt, or self-punishing assumption, is not helpful. Understanding it cognitively, we can see it as part of a self-blaming schema around which she organizes her perceptions of her abuse experiences (which we will assume occurred for the purposes of this chapter). Addressing it is a way to evaluate Mary's ability to work with her cognitive distortions, defocus the intrusive memories for now, and begin to build a therapeutic alliance.

M: What I always learned was that God teaches us to love our elders, to be very good and do anything we can to please them. If we get selfish, or want our own way, that is sinful and God punishes us by making bad things happen to us. I shouldn't have ignored my aunt, I should love her but I just didn't want to talk to her, and now look at what is happening to me!

Th: So your view is that you are seeing pictures of your uncle and hearing his voice because God is punishing you for ignoring your aunt?

M: That's right. Yeah. My mom always told me that when they did things I didn't like it was because I had been bad and they were punishing me before God did. Sometimes I didn't know what I had done that was bad but I knew it must have been something!

Th: So you must have gotten pretty good at figuring out how to be good so your parents didn't do the things you didn't like. That helped you figure out that you are "seeing things" because you made your aunt lonely.

This is, again, a positive frame around her skill at creating survival strategies. We could hypothesize that, in addition to her uncle, her parents also abused her under the guise of "correcting her sins." This is a particularly cruel, but common, abuser strategy that reinforces the tendency of children to blame themselves for what goes wrong. At this time we are not going to ask her for details of what her parents did because that could lead to a retraumatizing memory when she first needs a lot of cognitive, or ego, structuring. The veracity of the memories is also not an issue at this time.

M: Yeah, I guess I had to be good at that, although I never thought about it that way.

Th: Well, you know, I'm a little confused. I don't quite understand how you know your aunt is lonely.

M: I knew she had to be because I didn't talk to her. Huh! (*pauses a minute*) I guess she could have other people to

talk to her, maybe she's not lonely! But then I don't understand why I'm having these bad things happen to me.
I must have done something else wrong.

TH: There may be another way to look at it. When bad things
happened to you with your parents, they always told you
that you had done something wrong. So you got good at
figuring out what you had done, and making sure you
didn't do it again. You got so good at seeing the connection between doing something wrong and getting punished
that you began to assume that any time something bad
happened to you, you must have done something wrong
to cause it! I wonder if there could ever be a time when
something bad happens and it has nothing to do with you?

M: It feels kind of scary to think about bad things happening to me and not knowing how I caused it. Or you're
saying maybe I didn't cause it?

TH: Well, what do you think? Are you one of those people
who make it rain every time there's going to be a picnic?
(*A little humor usually helps!*)

M: (*Smiles*) There are times I find myself apologizing when
it rains! But this whole thing makes me feel afraid.
Shouldn't we be talking about the memories, Doctor? I
don't understand.

What is frightening to Mary is the idea that she might not
be responsible for bad things happening, which means she
had no control over her abuse. She then would have to know
that her parents were cruel and she was helpless. She is not
ready for that realization, which is usually resisted successfully until near the end of memory work. It is encouraging
that Mary is able to pick up on the cognitive work so easily,
indicating that she has intelligence on her side.

TH: I think you're feeling scared because you're so used to always being able to figure things out, even if it had to mean
you were bad. I guess I'm suggesting that there might be
a number of ways to think about what causes what.

M: It's hard to give up what I know. Is that what you're saying, Doctor? It is. I've always prided myself on being able
to figure things out.

Th: You certainly don't have to give up that skill! A lot of
what we will do together is try to figure things out. I'm
just saying perhaps we can think more openly, with some
new possibilities in mind. It might also be nice if we could
help you feel less bad about yourself some of the time!

M: I sure would like that! I feel better, now, because I can
see that you're really just trying to help me think in some
new ways (*pause*). Nobody ever talked about the way I
think before. They just wanted to hear my memories. Then
one doctor said he didn't believe I had any hidden memories and all he wanted me to talk about was my childhood.

Th: It may be important to talk about your memories at some
point, but I find it helps a lot to work on some new ways
of thinking before we do that. Also, it is important for us
to get to know each other! Talking about memories can
be quite upsetting and it is very important for you to feel
familiar and safe with me first.

M: I guess you're right, Doctor. I never thought about trying
to feel safe except by hiding. (*Gets up to leave*) Thank you.
(*Session ends with setting up next appointment.*)

The session ends with Mary successfully backing away from
the frightening idea that her abuse might have been the fault
of her parents. She is able to retain her idea that she is "good
at figuring things out," which is very important for therapy
work. The emphasis on thinking has helped her feel
grounded. It has also defused her dissociative panic around
the flashbacks of her uncle and the magical thought that God
is punishing her. There is the beginning of a therapeutic
alliance, helped along with light humor that can be shared
and with the therapist's use of the word "we" to indicate
"we're in this together." The ground is set for the beginning
stages of therapy to proceed.

Vignette 2

Claire had been in treatment for eight months. She had begun therapy with complaints of depression, acute anxiety including agoraphobia, feeling "different from other people," and alcohol abuse in remission with a twelve-step program. She said that as soon as she stopped drinking six months previously she began to feel more depressed and anxious, sometimes feeling "so creepy I just want to jump out of my skin." When her depression deepened into suicidality she saw a psychiatrist who put her on a calming antidepressant that had "helped some but I still can't sleep and I feel like I want to yell or cry most of the time."

Claire described a chaotic family situation when she was a child. Her father was a raging alcoholic whom her mother divorced when Claire was 6. Her mother remarried a man who seemed safer, but she had felt uncomfortable with the ways he approached her. She said they moved frequently after that and her memory for the next several years was very spotty. She said she was not sure why, but "I never want to go near that man [her stepfather]; he gives me the creeps!"

During the first six months she and the therapist had worked on stabilizing some relationship issues in her life, using some cognitive techniques. Claire had exhibited many of the cognitive distortions consistent with a disturbed childhood, increasing the therapist's concern that she had some history of abuse. About two months before the session to be described, Claire had been talking about her discomfort with a man she had just met, because he reminded her of her stepfather. As she talked she suddenly had a frightening image of the stepfather: "It's like he's right here! Get him away!" She sounded like a frightened child as she cried that he was coming toward her "with a terrible look on his face." This flashback ended as abruptly as it started, leaving Claire very upset and frightened to go home.

Since that time the therapist had helped Claire understand what flashbacks are and had agreed with her on some

ways to feel safe when they happened outside of therapy
sessions. Claire agreed to keep a journal of her experiences
that would help her begin to process the memories in verbal
form. She and the therapist agreed on a signal they could
both use when the flashback was becoming too overwhelming. These signals consist of one word like "Stop!" "Safety!"
or "Close!" and are a mild hypnotic technique that functions
as a way to help the client feel in control of memories of previously uncontrollable events. They also agreed on a vision
of a safe place where Claire could take herself in her mind
when she felt afraid.

Claire had only a few brief flashbacks since that time,
which she and her therapist used to practice the above skills.
They had addressed the self-blame issues intensively but
Claire still believed in the course of the flashbacks that she
had done something wrong, a natural problem since the flashbacks contained her beliefs at the time the event was happening. It had become clear to both of them that the stepfather had approached her sexually but to this point there had
been no explicit memories of the abuse.

These flashbacks were becoming more intensive recently
because she was going to see her stepfather in the next month
at a family wedding. In the days previous to this session,
Claire had become increasingly agitated, unable to sleep, and
was calling the therapist frequently with panicked but un-
clear demands. She came into the office, her usually neat
appearance somewhat disheveled, looking pale and tearful.

C: I couldn't sleep last night! I kept getting flashes of pain, or
   I'd hear these weird sounds. I finally got up and made some
   tea but that didn't help much. What's wrong with me?
Th: Perhaps you're experiencing little fragments of memory.
   Sometimes memories return as bits of sensation, sounds,
   or even smells, without any visual picture. It can be pretty
   upsetting, especially when you can't sleep. Do you think
   anything happened yesterday after we talked that upset
   you?

The therapist is trying to help her connect emotion to events, while suspecting a major memory is on its way. They are often preceded by a period of turbulence and disturbing memory fragments.

C: I felt better for a little while after we talked, but then it all started again. I feel weird, I feel like everything is getting dark (*speaks in childlike voice*) . . . oh no . . . not you! Get away! He's coming in the room, oh help!

TH: (*Soft, reassuring voice*) I'm right here with you. Here, I'm moving my chair a little closer. I'm with you. You're having a memory.

C: (*Does not visibly respond*) Nooo! (*Continues to talk, indicating that a sexually abusive act is occurring*) Why are you doing this? Bad! I'm so dirty!

TH: (*Speaking as Claire moans and indicates the abuse is continuing*) You are not bad. He is the bad one! You never did anything bad enough to deserve this. You are just a little child wanting love and protection. I'm still here with you.

C: (*Weeps*) I want my mommy! Where is she? (*Silence for a few moments; Claire continues to cry.*)

TH: What's happening now?

C: It hurts! My body hurts! Why did he do that to me? He said it was my fault! I put on a bad dress, tear up that dress!

TH: You did absolutely nothing to make that happen! He's telling you a lie! There is nothing wrong with any of your dresses. They are pretty and just right for a little girl like you. Your stepfather is a very sick man, that's the only reason he did that!

C: (*After a period of silence*) My mommy never came.

TH: No, she never did. That makes you feel really lonely. Your mommy should have been there. (*pauses*) I think it might be time for you to come back to the room now. It seems that the memory has passed. Why don't you sit up and look around the room?

C: (*Sits up from her half-reclining position on the couch, blinks, and looks around*) Uh . . . I had a memory? Oh, I'm cold (*begins to shiver, picks up an afghan and wraps it around her*). What happened?

TH: What do you remember?

C: My stepfather . . . he came in the room . . . (*shivers*) Ugh! Oh my God! He really did those things to me, didn't he?

TH: You seemed to have a powerful experience. What do you remember of it?

It is very important not to say or do anything to elaborate on or change the memory experience. This is a point where therapists can cause confusion or disturbance in the memories even by repeating back what they think they heard. This is the critical time for the client to be translating the implicit memory to narrative memory where it can be worked through.

C: He was coming in my room. It was in the blue house. . . . I must have been seven. . . . I think it was night. . . . He threw my teddy bear across the room! He was mad . . . . he said I was bad, it was the pink dress with the lace. I hated it! I cut it up with scissors! (*begins to cry*) He did this terrible thing to me . . . . I feel like throwing up, I feel so sick.

TH: What do you remember? I know this is painful but it's very important.

C: I'm embarrassed to say . . . . it's so gross! He . . . (*describes some explicit details*). I can't say any more to you . . . I feel so dirty!

TH: I know, it's so hard to talk about! It sounds like you're feeling embarrassed, maybe even ashamed of being that little girl. I wonder whether you're concerned about what I'm thinking about you, do you think so?

C: Well, I guess so, I mean here I am saying all these gross things. You must think I'm a terrible person.

TH: No, in fact I'm thinking what a brave person you are to

go through this really hard work! I know it wasn't your fault that this happened. I know you were just a little girl and you had to do what your stepfather told you. You couldn't help it.

C: I always thought I was a bad girl . . . my mother told me I was dirty . . . she always made me take baths . . . she scrubbed me . . . you know (*begins to cry again, reverting to little girl voice*).

TH: It's so sad that your mommy wasn't there to help and protect you the way mommies are supposed to!

C: I bet you wouldn't let that happen if you were my mommy, would you?

TH: No, I wouldn't! I'd come to see what he was doing and when I saw him I would pick you up and take you right out of there, and I would call the police!

C: Would they come and get him and put him in jail? (*Smiles with pleasure*)

TH: They sure would! And we would take a nice soft bubble bath, and then we would go out for ice cream! What kind do you like?

C: Ummmm. Peach! With whipped cream and a cherry! (*Pauses, begins to look more adult, sighs*) That's so nice to think about . . .

TH: Well, what's important is that you know that is what you deserved, even though it couldn't really happen for you. It looks like we've got about eight minutes left. Let's talk about what you are going to do when you leave today. And I want it to include a bowl of peach ice cream!

There are many important aspects of this vignette. It illustrates one of the major guidelines for treatment of abuse, which is that the experience of remembering must change the trauma; the memory must be reworked. This ensures that the experience no longer stays trapped as wordless fragments in the implicit memory but becomes part of a verbal narrative.

The therapist changes the situation right away by declaring

herself a witness to Claire's memory: "I'm right here with you." Claire will then not have the retraumatizing experience of being alone, without recourse. There is also a very powerful meaning in being witnessed. The therapist has seen the truth of Claire's experience of this moment of inhumanity and can testify to it. Ideas of justice, restitution, and support are associated with the concept of witnessing. These ideas are not explicit in the session, but form a context in which the work is done.

Therapeutic reworking of the memory depends on the therapist's recognition that the memory feels to Claire as though the trauma is happening in the present time. Talking "above" the memory as it is occurring feeds new information into the experience that contradicts the message given by the abuse. The psychodynamic understanding of this is that the adult ego observes uncovered memories and emotions and is able to evaluate them differently than the childhood ego did.

In this vignette the therapist first provides information to a potential observing self that this is a memory, not an actual event. She then contradicts the beliefs Claire is verbalizing in very strong terms—"He is the bad one!"—and provides comfort—"I'm still here with you." This reminds Claire that her mother was not there and did not protect her and she becomes very sad. While, in a regular therapy session, one might want the client to stay with her emotion, in this case the therapist does not allow silence to go on very long because other cognitive distortions or unspoken traumatic images may be running through Claire's mind. In fact, Claire was experiencing body pain and believing that the trauma happened because of her dresses (we take a chance here that the dresses were, in fact, appropriate for her; a detail to check out later).

The therapist is very watchful for the time when the memory is over and the dissociation is no longer relevant. Survivors with chronic PTSD often have the habit of remaining in dissociated states for long periods of time. A crucial area for treatment is to help them learn how to be in the present. The client can focus on the present with such grounding techniques as looking around the room, noticing colors or shapes in pictures, looking at what she or the therapist is wearing, picking up a "koosh" ball or other hand-held object, standing up and walking around, or getting some tea or juice. In this case Claire did not have much difficulty returning to a present orientation.

Repeating elements of the memory in "present time" is an essential part of knitting the information into the narrative of her life. As she repeats the memory she remembers the time and place that it happened, and adds details, such as the teddy bear and more information about her dress. In fact, the information about her dresses is a potential clue to why Claire always wears pants.

Although it is distasteful for Claire and difficult for the therapist to hear, it is also essential for Claire to repeat whatever details she can of the actual sexual abuse, partly for desensitization and partly to move these images out of the split-off, nonverbal portion of her mind. She then has painful access to the profound shame engendered by the abuse. The therapist begins to address this shame in the present by gently inquiring how she feels about the therapist knowing, and then providing reassurance and empowering information. If the therapist had not inquired about the shame, Claire could have left with it untouched and had a very difficult time returning. In this situation the reassurance probably allowed Claire to bring up another painful fragment.

It is not unusual for the client to return to a dissociated state during discussion of the memory, as Claire did when the painful subject of her mother came up again. The therapist chose not to follow the physical details this time, but to stay with Claire's feelings of abandonment. Claire's impulse to reimagine the situation with the therapist as her mother is a sign of her own self-healing abilities. Images have a powerful impact on the mind, with the unconscious often accepting them as reality. The therapist plays with the story as though Claire is a child, adding details of what should have happened (calling the police, putting the stepfather in jail, then comforting the child).

It is very helpful to leave a few minutes at the end of the session to allow the client to gain some distance from the material and to reinforce her orientation to the present. The playful addition of a bowl of ice cream reminds Claire of the potential for positive self-care and of the presence of the therapist.

CONCLUSION

As these vignettes demonstrate, the use of cognitive techniques does not necessitate a distant or strictly rational approach. Many of the techniques used here (desensitization, psycho-education, self-soothing, etc.) can be folded seamlessly into a supportive, psychodynamic treatment process. Typically, the psychological and social development of abuse survivors is transformed indelibly by real events in childhood. These events have significant, predictable cognitive sequelae in addition to the affective and behavioral sequelae that are prominent in the symptoms of their presenting problems. The cognitive sequelae include cognitive distortions such as catastrophizing, "all or nothing" thinking, egocentric thinking, arbitrary influence, erroneous or missed assumptions about cause–effect relationships, selective abstraction, and perceptual distortions and flooding. The successful use of cognitive techniques to modify these distortions can best occur within the context of a psychodynamic treatment frame that also recognizes the significant developmental and affective sequelae of abuse. This necessitates the use of contemporary and developing knowledge in the areas of posttraumatic syndrome disorder, the complex formation and maintenance of perceptual schema and cognitive distortions, the effect on the brain of psychophysiological hyperarousal, and the importance of narrative versus implicit memory. This focus on skill building in the areas of affect modulation and self-soothing allows the possibility for the survivor to tolerate the affects aroused during both the uncovering and the working-through phases of treatment. Likewise, the cognitive approaches outlined here help survivors learn how to modify their views of themselves and the world in ways that are both reorganizing and empowering.

REFERENCES

Bernard C., and Hirsch, C. (1985). Borderline personality and victims of incest. *Psychological Reports* 57:715–718.

Bieber, I. (1980). *Cognitive Psychoanalysis*. New York: Jason Aronson.

Davies, J., and Frawley, M. (1994). *Treating the Adult Survivor of Childhood Sexual Abuse: A Psychoanalytic Perspective*. New York: Basic Books.

Fine, C. (1988). Thoughts on the cognitive perceptual substrates of multiple personality disorder. *Dissociation* 1:4:5–10.

——— (1991). Treating stabilization and crisis prevention. *Psychiatric Clinics of North America* 14:3:661–675.

Guidano, V., and Liotti, G. (1985). A constructivist foundation for cognitive therapy. In *Cognition and Psychotherapy*, ed. M. J. Mahoney and A. Freeman, pp. 102–125. New York: Plenum.

Herman, J. (1992). *Trauma and Recovery*. New York: Basic Books.

Herman, J., Perry, D. J., and van der Kolk, B. A. (1989). Childhood trauma in borderline personality disorder. *American Journal of Psychiatry* 146:4:490–495.

Hughes, C. H. (1834). Moral insanity. In *Essential Papers on Borderline Personality Disorders*, ed. M. Stone, pp. 17–31. New York: New York University Press, 1986.

Janet, P. (1889). *L'Automatisme Psychologique*. Paris: Felix Alcan. Reprint: Société Pierre Janet/Payot, Paris, 1973.

Janoff-Bulman, R. (1992). *Shattered Assumptions: Toward a New Psychology of Trauma*. New York: Free Press.

Kernberg, O. (1975). *Borderline Conditions and Pathological Narcissism*. New York: Jason Aronson.

Kluft, R. (1993). The treatment of dissociative disorder patients: an overview of discoveries, successes and failures. *Dissociation* 6:2/3:87–101.

Linehan, M., and Kehrer, C. (1993). Borderline personality disorder. In *Clinical Handbook of Psychological Disorders*, ed. D. H. Barlow, 2nd ed., pp. 397–426. New York: Guilford.

Mahler, M. (1979). *The Selected Papers of Margaret Mahler. Vol. II*. New York: Jason Aronson.

Mahoney, M. J. (1991). *Human Change Processes: The Scientific Foundations of Psychotherapy*. New York: Basic Books.

Masterson, J. (1981). *The Narcissistic and Borderline Disorders*. New York: Brunner/Mazel.

Meichenbaum, D. (1985). *Stress Inoculation Training*. New York: Pergamon.

Resnick, P., and Schnicke, M. (1992). Cognitive processing therapy for sexual assault victims. *Journal of Consulting and Clinical Psychology* 60:5:748–756.

Rosse, I. (1880). Clinical evidences of borderline insanity. In *Essential Papers on Borderline Personality Disorders*, ed. M. Stone, pp. 32–41. New York: New York University Press, 1986.

Rothbaum, B., and Foa, E. (1996). Cognitive-behavioral therapy for P.T.S.D. In *Traumatic Stress*, ed. B. van der Kolk, A. McFarlane, and L. Weisaeth, pp. 491–509. New York: Guilford.

Stern, A. (1938). Psychoanalytic investigation of and therapy in the borderline group of neuroses. In *Essential Papers on Borderline Disorders*, ed. M. Stone, pp. 54–73. New York: New York University Press, 1986.

van der Kolk, B., Brown P., and van der Hart, O. (1989). Pierre Janet on post-traumatic stress. *Journal of Traumatic Stress* 2(4):365–378.

van der Kolk, B., McFarlane, A., and Weisaeth, L. (1996). *Traumatic Stress*. New York: Guilford.

9

Treating Older Adults

Thomas W. Johnson

Old age ain't no place for sissies.
                                            —BETTE DAVIS

INTRODUCTION

As detailed in previous chapters, there are many compelling arguments for integration in psychotherapy theory and practice, particularly within the psychoanalytic perspective. Contemporary fiscal attitudes call for the expenditure of increasingly scarce mental health dollars, including Medicare and Medicaid dollars, on treatments that are brief, practical, and easily explainable. Therapists of all theoretical orientations need to give closer scrutiny, in the form of outcome research, to some of the cherished assumptions of theory and practice, and develop a data-driven picture of the strengths and weaknesses of the approach. Integration of the components of other theory and practice perspectives is a likely result of this examination.

The current sociocultural context also calls for a more comprehensive and complex approach to the theory and practice of psychotherapy. Postmodern critiques of mainstream assumptions about people and their psyches have loosened some long-standing theoretical anchors about the world, leaving people with the notion that "truth" may be "up for grabs" (Gergen 1985,

1991). Within psychoanalysis, the contributions of the relational theorists (Aron 1996, Ghent 1989, 1992, Mitchell 1988) and the feminist revisionists (Benjamin 1988, Goldner 1991, Harris 1991) have reexamined psychoanalytic premises about gender, neutrality, transference, countertransference, and interpretation.

These changes in the practice, reimbursement, and sociocultural contexts have important implications for the psychotherapy of older adults. The values of the managed care movement have made their way into Medicare reimbursement policies. Long-standing psychoanalytic ideas about the treatment relationship, about personality, and about development are as open to revision in the treatment of older adults as they are in the treatment of their younger counterparts. Premises about the psychoanalytic treatment of seniors also need closer examination, and the integration of other empirically validated treatment perspectives is a likely outcome here too.

TREATMENT OF OLDER ADULTS

Older adults are no small group. As of the early 1990s, a quarter of the United States population was over the age of 50, and one eighth was over the age of 65 (Myers 1991). It is expected that those over 65 years of age will represent 21 percent of the U.S. population by the year 2020, and the 85+ cohort is the fastest growing portion of the aged population (Atchley 1985). The overwhelming majority of older adults (95 percent) live in the community (cited in Blazer 1990), and most function with only minimal degrees of impairment despite the presence of a number of chronic illnesses like diabetes, hypertension, heart disease, or arthritis (Huntley et al. 1986). Even though the size of this population is considerable, mental health practitioners are woefully underprepared for this work, and many endorse negative standpoints about treating them (Lasoski 1986, Storandt 1977, Zarit 1980, Zivian et al. 1992). However, research indicates that older adults benefit from many varieties of psychotherapy (Gatz et al. 1985, Smyer et al. 1990), including both psychodynamic (Kernberg 1984, Myers 1984, Newton et al. 1984) and cognitive treatments (Thompson et al. 1986, Thompson et al. 1991).

A number of issues might account for the gerontophobic reaction of many practitioners. One important theme is the clinical complexity that often leaves therapists overwhelmed and puzzled. For example, older adults face a daunting array of normative life-stage challenges, particularly a parade of biological changes that can affect quality of life, personality, and identity. Clinicians working with older adults must always consider the impact of disease, medications, sensory changes, and cognitive changes in their presenting problems. In addition, there are enormous psychosocial changes immediately in front of the older adult. Older clients may be dealing with retirement, relocation, role changes, dramatic losses, social/family network changes, and fixed or diminished financial resources all in one fell swoop.

A second theme that might help to explain professional distance from this population is the frequent difficulty in engaging elders in treatment. There may be generational or cohort issues in the underutilization of mental health services by older adults (Gatz et al. 1985, Lasoski 1986), revealed in statements like: "In our family no one went to see a therapist. We coped. We talked to our relatives or to our minister when we felt poorly. Therapy was for crazy people." However, reluctance to use psychotherapy might also reflect a developmentally normative resistance to face the narcissistic injury inevitably involved in introspective work, especially when aging already represents such a steady stream of narcissistic injuries to be weathered without the increased self-consciousness that therapy entails.

A third theme in our professional distancing emerges in the fact that psychotherapy with older adults must be inordinately flexible, given interruptions in treatment expected by illness in self or family members, a high likelihood of the need for crisis intervention because of the unstable biopsychosocial context of aging individuals, a need to liaison frequently with other professionals because of the typical complexity of service needs, and a need for therapists to play an educator role because of the acute need for information by older adults and their families in meeting the crises of later life. These kinds of demand characteristics might create anxiety, for example, in a mainstream psychoanalytic therapist with rigid ideas about preserving neutrality and the purity of the transference.

RELEVANCE OF PSYCHOANALYTIC TREATMENT TO OLDER ADULTS

Given the psychosocial complexity of the lives of older adults, does psychoanalytic treatment have anything to offer them? Freud (1905) had doubts about the utility and effectiveness of psychoanalysis for aging individuals, and doubted their suitability as analytic patients: "On the one hand, near or above the fifties, the elasticity of the mental processes, on which the treatment depends, is as a rule lacking—old people are no longer educable—and, on the other hand, the mass of material to be dealt with would prolong the duration of the treatment indefinitely" (pp. 258–259).

Freud's view is quite ironic given that his later life was marked by considerable creativity and productivity. However, there is a clinical literature that echoes his view and suggests that the treatment of the aged has very limited possibilities for success (for review see Silberschatz and Curtis 1991). The limitations revolve around the putative characterological and intellectual rigidity of the aged, and their alleged massive resistance. Gutmann (1980) maintains that this bias reflects a catastrophic view of aging. This bias also underpins the notion that the most effective intervention in the elderly is psychopharmacological, or that, at best, treatment should be palliative or supportive.

However, many psychoanalytic writers maintain that older

patients are in fact excellent and possibly superior candidates for analytic treatment compared to their younger counterparts, given their wealth of life experiences and strong motivation to change in the last chapter of life (for review see Myers 1984, 1991, Silberschatz and Curtis 1991). Many well-known psycho-analytic theorists like Abraham, Jung, Grotjahn, Kernberg, and Kohut contend that psychoanalytic treatment has much to offer patients in later life. According to Myers (1984, 1991) and to Silberschatz and Curtis's review (1991), older adults are no more resistant than any other group, and are not more characterologically and cognitively rigid than younger patients. Myers maintains, however, that older adults may initially present as rigid and defensive, but that this dissipates as the therapeutic alliance is established. Older patients actually may bring more motivation to treatment because of the sense of finitude concerning the amount of time left, and Silberschatz and Curtis (1991) contend that older patients may even be more daring and ambitious in their approach to treatment because of the greater awareness of time limitations. The above authors also suggest that older patients may show more flexibility in interpreting life experiences and greater empathy for others because of an increased experience with problem solving and an increased diversity of role enactments over their life history. The authors also suggest that the increased span of time since early-life trauma may also afford older patients enough defensive distance to address these painful experiences in a more in-depth manner. In support of this premise, I have worked with many older female and male patients who have disclosed early experiences with sexual abuse trauma for the first time in older adulthood.

Myers (1984, 1991) maintains that the criteria for assessing an older patient's ability to work productively in a psychoanalytic approach are the same as the criteria used to assess younger patients: the degree of object relatedness, the attunement to unconscious processes, and the level of motivation to change. However, I believe that an older patient's ability to satisfy the criteria for analyzability is not enough to ensure the success of a psychoanalytic treatment. The psychoanalytic psychotherapy model needs to be tailored in a certain number of important ways. First, treatment must prioritize the reinforcement of mastery, competence, and self-efficacy given the normative challenges that aging entails. Muslin (1992), a self psychologist, maintains this view, and argues that treatment with this group must revolve around facilitation of "the cohesive elderly self." Muslin also contends that this perspective becomes essential in light of the decreased visibility and possible loss of power older adults face in the larger sociocultural context.

Related to this first point is my second belief that the treatment relationship with an older patient must be marked by a spirit of collaboration. This becomes important given the above issues around mastery and competence and the ambivalent attitudes toward treatment that this group often endorses. In addition, transference is often complicated in the treatment of older patients. Because of the need for periodic crisis intervention, liaison work, and education, the therapeutic relationship must accommodate multiple role configurations and multiple transferences and countertransferences. A purist approach to transference is often not realistic. Instead, as described in the relational approach, a collaborative analytical relationship, in which there is the ability to shift relationship gears and move from transference–countertransference exploration at one moment to problem solving and supportive coaching at the next moment, makes more sense.

A third modification is that the analytic treatment must incorporate the building of skills in self-soothing and self-regulation in consideration of the high likelihood for crisis and interruption in treatment occasioned most frequently by physical illness. A fourth modification involves the importance of incorporating education into the relationship, given the frequency with which older patients need information about medical concerns, caregiving resources, and community services. At times the education may need to be imparted in a multisensory approach because of the higher possibility of the presence of sensory problems in this population.

Psychoanalytic purists may exclaim that if a psychoanalytic psychotherapy requires these substantial modifications, then it is no longer psychoanalytic. However, psychoanalytic theory and practice are undergoing considerable modification, as exemplified by the work of the intersubjectivists (Stolorow et al. 1994), who have emerged out of a self psychology perspective, and the relational school (Aron 1996, Mitchell 1988), whose roots lie in the object relations and interpersonalist traditions. Some of the premises of the relational approach will serve as an illustration.

The relational perspective shares with both the object relations and interpersonal traditions the core premise that the basic motivation of life is to attach and connect. However, theorists like Mitchell have extended the interactionist position even further and maintain that the mind is an interpersonally shared entity and that people are best described by a two-, three-, or four-person model of psychology. In this view the analytic relationship is a collaborative and mutual experience in which the separate selves of the patient and the therapist are simply subsystems of a relational field. The therapeutic relationship is both a real relationship and a transitional space where patient and therapist "play" with projections and associations in order to understand more about self. The therapist is not constrained to protect neutrality and to limit his or her role behavior to the role of container for the patient's experiences and associations. It seems that all patient–therapist experience is valid grist for the therapeutic mill. The modifications I suggest for psychoanalytic psychotherapy with older adults are more easily accommodated within this kind of perspective.

Even with the revisions offered by contemporary psychoanalytic "reform," some important ingredients to the skill base needed to treat older adults effectively are still missing. Cognitive therapy offers some helpful techniques that could be added to a psychoanalytic psychotherapy.

INTEGRATION OF COGNITIVE THERAPY TECHNIQUES

The most crucial missing ingredient in psychoanalytic models of the treatment of older adults is the absence of techniques for self-regulation and self-soothing during crises, particularly medical crises. These crises also often entail an interruption in treatment because of hospitalizations or periods of at-home recuperation, and the actual therapy relationship may not be accessible in vivo. Thus older adults frequently find themselves on their own, coping with anxiety, obsessional rumination, insomnia, and reduction in pleasurable and personally meaningful activities as a result of illness in self or in a significant other. Standard psychoanalytic thinking maintains that the ability to self-regulate and manage destabilizing affects occurs as a function of the internalization of the soothing aspects of the therapeutic relationship. However, older patients are likely to need these abilities right away, before much time elapses in the therapeutic relationship. Older patients also often need acute measures to reduce the limiting aspects of medical illness such as chronic pain, gastrointestinal distress, or hypertension. Behavioral medicine techniques, particularly cognitive-behavioral methods of relaxation training, pain management, or diaphragmatic breathing, offer immediate methods to reduce symptoms that interfere in the patient's quality of life and the ability to make productive use of the therapeutic relationship. Often older adults and their therapists do not have the luxury of waiting the time required for the treatment alliance to intensify and for the ego-supportive attributes of the therapist to be internalized by the patient.

In addition, therapists of older patients are often called upon to convey important information about medical and medication issues, services, and resources. This is particularly the case with older adults who present with caregiver burden related to their care of older relatives with progressive debilitating illnesses like dementia. There is no model within the psychoanalytic perspective about how best to convey educational material. This is particularly crucial as older patients may need multisensory approaches given the normative sensory and cognitive processing deficits that occur for many persons in later life. Not only does psychoanalytic theory not provide models about the educator role, but psychoanalytic theorists caution against the educative role for therapists because of its interference with analytic neutrality and its potential contamination of the transference. A traditional analyst might suggest that the analyst refer a patient to a geriatric case manager or a health professional for relevant information, and avoid the role conflict involved in transmitting information to patients. However, many older adults may not have other sources of information or people to help them translate confusing medical data. In addition, these patients might be loath to add yet another professional to the parade of service providers in their already bureaucratized lives.

Some geriatric mental health clinicians maintain that older adults prefer treatment models that emphasize pragmatic self-sufficiency, and collaborative work that describes the spirit of cognitive therapy (Yost et al. 1986). These authors contend that this preference derives from this population's ambivalent attitudes about seeking help and from their need to feel some measure of control when life can feel so unstable and stressful due to the predictable changes and demands of later life.

Cognitive therapy offers some techniques to address the weaknesses of psychoanalytic approaches to treating older adults. The model prioritizes skill acquisition and education, offers some practical ideas about imparting psychoeducational material, and gives detailed guides to acute interventions that reduce a variety of symptoms (Barlow 1993, Beck et al. 1979, Freeman et al. 1990, Gallagher-Thompson et al. 1991, Thompson et al. 1991, Yost et al. 1986). Cognitive therapists have also been diligent about performing outcome studies, and many of their approaches demonstrate significant effectiveness and utility with older populations (Gallagher-Thompson et al. 1991, Thompson et al. 1986, 1987).

Teaching older patients the cognitive model, in the straight-forward manner articulated by Burns (1980), offers them an approach to self-regulation of overwhelming affects and to self-soothing. Specific techniques used to apply this perspective to the patients' day-to-day experience include daily mood monitoring, weekly activity scheduling (for depressed patients), the DTR (Dysfunctional Thought Record), and specific relaxation techniques such as progressive muscle relaxation or diaphragmatic breathing. The relaxation methods fall under the rubric of behavioral treatment, but are often used in cognitive approaches to a variety of problems.

These sorts of cognitive-behavioral techniques can be integrated into a contemporary psychoanalytic psychotherapy approach that includes the following aspects: exploration of the vicissitudes of the therapeutic relationship, both in terms of "real relationship" issues as well as issues emerging from the transference–countertransference matrix; exploration of genetic and developmental material; exploration of the meaning of various relational experiences both inside and outside the therapeutic relationship; exploration of unconscious motivation and meaning; and exploration of resistance and defense.

Discussion of a case from the author's practice will illustrate the integration. Many identifying details of the patient and her life have been disguised to protect her privacy and anonymity.

CASE ILLUSTRATION

Presenting Problem and Demographic Information

Rose was a 77-year-old Italian-American woman married for fifty nine years who presented for treatment with overwhelming anxiety and an unrecognized depression. She was seen for about a year and a half of individual psychotherapy. Rose had three sons, two daughters, seven grandchildren, and one great-grandchild, and her social network was limited totally to her nuclear family. Rose had worked outside the home only for a few years, as a saleswoman in a milliner's shop before her marriage. Her 79-year-old husband had been retired from his lifelong employment as a carpenter and construction worker for about ten years, and they lived comfortably on social security and a pension. Rose was quite embarrassed about her own and her husband's working class background. But she was quite proud that all of her children were successful high achievers. One daughter was a geriatrician, a son was a pediatrician, and another daughter was a successful attorney. Despite her pride, Rose felt that she embarrassed her children because she saw herself as intellectually their inferior.

Rose presented as a petite woman, stylishly and impeccably dressed. Her hair was attractively colored and she appeared to be much younger than her age. It was clear she devoted considerable time to her appearance. She related in an anxious, self-deprecatory, and deferential style, frequently apologizing for not understanding questions or "not explaining myself better." She frequently stated that I probably was feeling impatient and frustrated with her.

She suffered from insomnia, constant fear that she would suffer a heart attack or stroke, chronic feelings of fatigue, and difficulty performing her usual busy day-to-day routine. Rose prided herself on being an "immaculate housekeeper," and was disturbed that she no longer took the same level of care of her house. She reported that her husband and children teased her, saying that no one would know that her functioning had fallen off because of how spotless her house still remained. Rose cried softly throughout the first interview when talking about how tired she was of worrying about having a medical catastrophe: "I'm really not afraid of dying—I just don't want to suffer or to lose my dignity. Hospitals scare me so much—you feel so out of control."

Rose came to treatment at the urgent behest of her primary physician. Although she had been an anxious worrier most of her life and had always maintained a sensitive and compulsive personality style, her anxiety magnified about three years before she came in for treatment. The precipitators for the exacerbation of her anxiety seemed to be her husband's back surgery and long recuperation, which required considerable caregiving on her part. In addition, she had begun to suffer from angina, but she was anxious about taking medication for her mild coronary artery disease. She presented a few times in local emergency rooms with chest pain that was determined to be related to panic attacks. She reported obsessional ruminations about having a heart attack.

Rose tried individual therapy twice during this time. She found both treatments unhelpful "because the therapists never really told me anything, and didn't seem to be particularly interested in me. The last therapist put me in a group after a month or so, and I hated that. I felt lost, and the other people's troubles just made me feel more nervous." Her primary physician had convinced her to try psychotherapy again by referring her "this time to someone with experience with old people."

Her physician and her family had become more concerned because her anxiety went unabated, and she was becoming more tired, demoralized, sleepless, and hopeless. Just prior to this treatment her situation had worsened when her husband began to develop prostate difficulties and her physician indicated that he wanted to try angioplasty with Rose to reduce her episodes of angina.

Past History

Rose was the youngest of seven daughters. She reported that she was very close to and very dependent on her mother, whom she described as a continuously disgruntled, disappointed, anxious, and suspicious woman. Her mother was deeply ashamed of Rose's Italian immigrant father, and frequently criticized and dismissed him. He spent a great deal of time out of the home because of his work hours and his intense involvement with a neighborhood group of friends.

Rose indicated that she always suffered from severe self-doubt and feelings of incompetence: "And instead of helping me, my mother just did for me." Rose's mother often expressed worry about Rose's health and saw her as a fragile child who needed protection.

Rose met her husband in adolescence and married him at age eighteen. She described herself as a devoted wife and mother. Her home was always spotless, and she described herself as a good cook. Her husband often dealt with her anxiety about her performance with humor and dismissal. She felt secure that her husband loved her, but she often felt embarrassed by his rough language and simplicity. She felt that she was his intellectual superior and that she had married beneath her. Rose managed the finances in the family, and was usually the one who made the important decisions despite her self-doubt.

Her social relationships outside the family were minimal. She found her female acquaintances to be envious and "gossipy," and at times she worried that they flirted with her husband. She also reported considerable social anxiety throughout her life. She dreaded relating to people outside the family for fear that she would embarrass herself and appear stupid: "I was always so sensitive to being criticized and rejected that I thought it was easier not to bother too much with people, except for my family." Rose had little extended family left at the time she began treatment. One sister lived in California, and contact was infrequent.

Rose also had had many somatic worries over her life, and periodically suffered from headaches, gastrointestinal distress, and severe menstrual pain. She found her husband and her children to be unsympathetic.

Diagnosis

Rose's view of her problems was that she felt helpless to deal with her own changing health, and felt overwhelmed at providing care to her husband. She indicated that she had no idea how to stop herself from worrying so much, how to begin to trust her ability to cope and survive crises, and how to stop the self-attack from which she so frequently suffered. She saw herself as anxious, but did not think she was depressed despite her neurovegetative symptoms.

The diagnosis was a mixed anxiety disorder with features of generalized anxiety disorder and panic disorder. She also suffered from an underlying dysthymia that went unrecognized and untreated. In terms of characterological functioning, she evidenced strong narcissistic traits and histrionic features.

Treatment

Rose was not easy to engage. She had a history of poor treatment experiences, and initially complained about how overwhelming it was to drive the ten miles required to come to my office. She was also quite overwhelmed with her anxiety, her sleeplessness, and her exhaustion. Her ability to self-soothe was poor, so the immediate focus of treatment was a holding/empathic approach in which she was given ample time to explain her experiences and her needs. I mirrored every possible evidence of coping, and attempted to normalize some of her symptoms as stress responses to all the caregiving demands and medical instability she was enduring. In response to her high level of anxiety and insomnia, I taught her diaphragmatic breathing techniques, which she practiced, totally on her own decision, on a daily basis. I talked about the biogenic substrate of anxiety and sleep problems, but she still refused medication. We began to look at how her long-standing sense of inadequacy mitigated against her ability to learn ways of managing her considerable stress. In essence, we talked about how her sense of herself set her up to short-circuit when she was challenged. I offered to teach her some techniques for managing her obsessional worry, but we talked about what that would mean in terms of her long-held inadequate vision of herself, which had been laid down in her family early in her life. At Rose's request I talked about the cognitive model (including content such as the Burns [1980] list of dysfunctional thoughts, the cognitive triad, and automatic thinking) and began to help her apply it to the process surrounding her insomnia and her obsessional ruminations about having a heart attack. We used the DTR (Dysfunctional Thought Record), which helps patients identify and record the dysfunctional thoughts that underpin symptomatic behavior, clarify the acute cognitive process that precipitates worry and sleeplessness, and generates alternative and more functional cognitions. Rose began to report some improvement in her insomnia, and her immediate response was a deepening of trust in the therapeutic relationship and a mild idealization of me.

With the slight reduction in symptoms she appeared more ready to attach to me and to begin the process of internalizing the soothing functions established in the relationship. She became willing to try a psychopharmacological consultation, and agreed to try Paxil. Her symptoms reduced even more dramatically, and her trust and connection in treatment deepened. She more often began to articulate some increasing ability to handle her worries and demands.

In the next phase of treatment Rose began to examine the operation of shame in her sense of self and in her relationships. The increased mastery facilitated by the cognitive techniques and the medication allowed her to shift gears from an acute focus on symptom relief to a more introspective focus. She addressed how her shame and inadequacy related to her inability to separate from her mother, and how she had internalized her mother's own shame and her mother's contemptuous dismissal of Rose's father. She talked about having no venue to learn how to trust herself in her early life. She also talked about how her shame operated in the therapeutic relationship: how her shame led her to fantasies that I was tired or bored or frustrated with her "slow pace in learning all of this stuff." She feared my criticism and disappointment, believing that I would dismiss her as her mother had done with her father. She began to test my attachment to her by revealing shameful memory after shameful memory, including stories about soiling her pants because of an embarrassed inability to ask someone for directions to a bathroom, and stories about premarital sex with her husband. We humorously referred to this phase of the treatment as "Rose's dance of the seven veils." Rose missed a session during this period of the treatment and quizzed me about whether I saw her as irresponsible and unmotivated. We "played" with the fantasies of what would happen if I were angry at her or she were angry at me. In most ways this phase of treatment was fairly typical psychoanalytic psychotherapy from a relational/Winicottian perspective. However, I believe that the shift to this kind of focus was made possible by the earlier cognitive-behavioral focus on symptom reduction and mastery. Psychoanalytic traditionalists might maintain that the transference was contaminated by my lapse in neutrality and by my functioning in an "omnipotent" and "grandiose manner," but the patient did not reveal this content either directly or indirectly in the year-long treatment, and her introspective work was marked by a fairly normal level of resistance.

About nine months into her treatment Rose's physician felt that angioplasty was indicated to treat her persisting coronary artery disease, and Rose became very anxious again. I reintroduced the DTR, and she began to use the technique on her own to calm herself about her worries regarding the procedure. She stated: "I'll really need this way of thinking when I'm sitting in the hospital before the procedure and when I have to go through all the preoperative tests. After all, you won't be there to talk me down." She made it through the procedure with flying colors and reported feeling much better. Soon after, however, Rose's husband was diagnosed with prostate cancer, and she became overwhelmed at the prospect of his physical and emotional dependence on her. We talked about services available for him that might offer her some relief, and developed a plan of action for various contingencies in his recovery. Again, we used cognitive techniques to address Rose's attitudes about caregiving and she began to identify dysfunctional beliefs she held about the level of responsibility she must assume in her family. When she returned from a month's absence due to her caregiving responsibilities, she used treatment to understand more about her anger, irritability, and contempt for her husband. She was able to understand processes like projective identification, and her replication of her mother's contempt toward her father as it was replicated in her own marriage. She also became aware of her own longing for her husband to care for her as completely as her mother had.

After about a year and a half's time, Rose reported that she was consistently feeling better, that she understood and believed in herself more, and that she felt "less scared by life." Rose continued and expanded her leisure interests and felt ready to end therapy. Her goals had been accomplished, "and I want to test my wings on my own." We ended therapy on a positive note, reflecting on the gains she had made and on the positive mutual attachment that had developed between us.

CONCLUSION

This case illustration offers a broad-stroke impression of how cognitive techniques can be woven into a contemporary psychoanalytic psychotherapy, specifically with an older adult. Use of the treatment relationship and other critical tenets of both traditional and revised psychoanalysis are modified for this population. Cognitive techniques, such as self-soothing, relaxation training, psychoeducation, DTR, and weekly activity scheduling, are utilized within the context of a psychodynamically informed treatment. These techniques alternated with more standard insight-focused analytic technique. My overall impression was that this shifting of theoretical and technical gears operated smoothly with no obvious transference contamination. Rather, the flexibility of the clinician's therapeutic stance allowed for exploration of relevant affects, modification of cognitions, and alleviation of the debilitating anxiety and depression that initially brought her to treatment. Meanwhile, we used her developmental and psychological history to identify unconscious repetitions and dynamics, allowing the successful use of cognitive techniques.

REFERENCES

Aron, L. (1996). *A Meeting of Minds: Mutuality in Psychoanalysis.* Hillsdale, NJ: Analytic Press.

Atchley, R. C. (1985). *Social Forces and Aging.* Belmont, CA: Wadsworth.

Barlow, D. H., ed. (1993). *Clinical Handbook of Psychological Disorders.* 2nd ed. New York: Guilford.

Beck, A. T., Rush, A. J., Shaw, B. F., and Emery, G. (1979). *Cognitive Therapy of Depression.* New York: Guilford.

Benjamin, J. (1988). *The Bonds of Love.* New York: Pantheon.

Blazer, D. (1990). *Emotional Problems in Later Life: Intervention Strategies for Professional Caregivers.* New York: Springer.

Burns, D. D. (1980). *Feeling Good: The New Mood Therapy.* New York: William Morrow.

Freeman, A., Pretzer, J., Fleming, B., and Simon, K. M. (1990). *Clinical Applications of Cognitive Therapy.* New York: Plenum.

Freud, S. (1905). On psychotherapy. *Standard Edition* 7:257–268.

Gallagher-Thompson, D., Lovett, S., and Rose, J. (1991). Psychotherapeutic interventions for stressed family caregivers. In *New Techniques in the Psychotherapy of Older Patients,* ed. W. A. Myers, pp. 61–78. Washington, DC: American Psychiatric Press.

Gatz, M., Popkin, S. J., Pino, C., and VandenBos, G. R. (1985). Psychological interventions with older adults. In *Handbook of the Psychology of Aging,* ed. J. E. Birren and K. Warner Schale, pp. 755–785. New York: Van Nostrand Reinhold.

Gergen, K. (1985). The social constructionist movement in modern psychology. *American Psychologist* 40:266–295.

―――― (1991). *The Saturated Self*. New York: Basic Books.

Ghent, E. (1989). Credo: the dialetics of one-person and two-person psychologies. *Contemporary Psychoanalysis* 25:169–211.

―――― (1992). Foreword. In *Relational Perspectives in Psychoanalysis*, ed. N. J. Skolnick and S. C. Warshaw, pp. xiii–xxii. Hillsdale, NJ: Analytic Press.

Goldner, V. (1991). Toward a critical relational theory of gender. *Psychoanalytic Dialogues* 1:249–272.

Gutmann, D. L. (1980). Psychoanalysis and aging. In *The Course of Life: Psychoanalytic Contributions Toward Understanding Personality Development. Volume III: Adulthood and the Aging Process*, ed. S. Greenspan and G. H. Pollock, pp. 489–517. DHHS Publication No. ADM81-1000.

Harris, A. (1991). Gender as contradiction. *Psychoanalytic Dialogues* 1:187–224.

Huntley, J. C., Brock, D. B., Ostfeld, A. M., et al. (1986). *Established Populations for Epidemiologic Studies of the Elderly: Resource Data Book*. Washington, DC: National Institute on Aging, NIH Publication 86-2443.

Kernberg, O. (1984). *Severe Personality Disorders*. New Haven, CT: Yale University Press.

Lasoski, M. C. (1986). Reasons for low utilization of mental health services by the elderly. *Clinical Gerontologist* 5:1–18.

Mitchell, S. (1988). *Relational Concepts in Psychoanalysis*. Cambridge, MA: Harvard University Press.

Muslin, H. L. (1992). *The Psychotherapy of the Elderly Self*. New York: Brunner/Mazel.

Myers, W. A. (1984). *Dynamic Therapy of the Older Patient*. New York: Jason Aronson.

―――― (1991). Pychoanalytic psychotherapy and psychoanalysis with older patients. In *New Techniques in the Psychotherapy of Older Patients*, ed. W. A. Myers, pp. 265–279. Washington, DC: American Psychiatric Press.

Newton, N. A., Lazarus, L. W., and Weinberg, J. (1984). Aging: biopsychosocial perspectives. In *New Techniques in the Psychotherapy of Older Patients*, ed. W. A. Myers, pp. 95–108. Washington, DC: American Psychiatric Press.

Silberschatz, G., and Curtis, J. T. (1991). Time-limited psychodynamic therapy with older adults. In *New Techniques in the Psychotherapy of Older Patients*, ed. W. A. Myers, pp. 95–108. Washington, DC: American Psychiatric Press.

Smyer, M. A., Zarit, S. H., and Qualls, S. H. (1990). Psychological intervention with the aging individual. In *Handbook of the Psychology of Aging*, ed. J. E. Birren and K. W. Schale, 3rd edition, pp. 375–404. San Diego, CA: Academic.

Stolorow, R., Atwood, G. E., and Brandchaft, B. (1994). *The Intersubjective Perspective*. Northvale, NJ: Jason Aronson.

Storandt, M. (1977). Graduate education in gerontological psychology: results of a survey. *Educational Gerontology* 2:141–146.

Thompson, L. W., Davies, R., Gallagher, D., and Krantz, S. E. (1986). Cognitive therapy with older adults. *Clinical Gerontologist* 5:245–279.

Thompson, L. W., Gallagher, D., and Steinmetz-Breckenridge, J. (1987). Comparative effectiveness of psychotherapies for depressed elders. *Journal of Clinical and Consulting Psychology* 55:385–390.

Thompson, L. W., Gantz, F., Florsheim, M., et al. (1991). Cognitive-behavioral therapy for affective disorder in the elderly. In *New Techniques in the Psychotherapy of Older Patients*, ed. W. A. Myers, pp. 3–19. Washington, DC: American Psychiatric Press.

Yost, E. B., Beutler, L. E., Corbishley, M. A., and Allender, J. R. (1986). *Group Cognitive Therapy: A Treatment Approach for Depressed Older Adults*. Elmsford, NY: Pergamon.

Zarit, S. H. (1980). *Aging and Mental Disorders: Psychological Approaches to Assessment and Treatment*. New York: Free Press.

Zivian, M. T., Larsen, W., Knox, V. J., et al. (1992). Psychotherapy for the elderly: psychotherapists' preferences. *Psychotherapy* 29:668–674.

10

Treating Depression

Dennis Miehls

INTRODUCTION

I really wanted to do it this time. I couldn't get the thought out of my mind . . . just floor the damn thing. Ram the car into the side of the building . . . then they'll take me seriously. Then they'll see some blood and guts. I can't believe not one of them takes me seriously. I can't believe not one of them listens to me. I suppose I know why they don't . . . I wouldn't listen to me either. Who would listen to such a loser? I haven't had a new case for months. I'm not bringing any money in . . . they're going to let me go anyway. I might as well go out with a bang . . . do it right there in front of our office . . . I guess they would notice then.

So begins a session with Peter, a 32-year-old lawyer who increasingly feels his career is on the line. As therapist, I respond in a number of ways to the material. I initially think, "Here we go again" . . . he seems to be talking more and more about hurting himself; then I feel some guilt for having this thought. I am aware that I am frightened for Peter; I worry about his increased suicidality. He seems more desperate today than usual. What has precipitated this? I recognize his despair and hopelessness and realize that the treatment of this increasingly depressed man is no easy task.

Brigette, a 26-year-old Burmese-Canadian woman, comments during her psychotherapy session:

He did it again, he called me at work. He knows I'm often with customers. I can't work retail and have him constantly calling me. I started to cry right there . . . right at the sales counter. I don't think he'll ever get it . . . why can't he leave me alone? I guess I should go and visit more often. He's an old man. My mother doesn't know what to do with him either. I know I cannot be free until he dies. . . . I know, I know, it's okay for me to have my own life, you've already told me that.

I had not remembered saying this to Brigette so directly, although I certainly could acknowledge to myself that I did think it was okay if she had her own life. I knew that it was not so easy. She had been struggling to make a place for herself in this city for a while. She had contemplated moving back to her hometown. She had been trying to convince herself that it wasn't so bad there after all and that she might feel less depressed if she was closer to her parents.

This chapter demonstrates how the integration of cognitive techniques into the psychodynamic treatment of these two depressed individuals proved beneficial for the clients' well-being. The marriage of cognitive techniques with psychodynamic therapy of depressed individuals provides the context for a natural partnership. Specific challenges in working with depressed individuals can be met effectively when one appreciates the impact that cognition plays in the development of the views of self and other that often hold our clients prisoners in their interaction with the world.

In this chapter I will put forward some working definitions of depression, highlighted by a brief literature review of depression from both psychodynamic and cognitive theories. Essential elements of treatment from these two broad perspectives will be summarized, and through the elaboration of the above clinical illustrations, specific interventions will be demonstrated to show the clients' accelerated progress when cognitive techniques were interwoven with their psychodynamic therapies and the benefits derived from this combination of approaches.

WORKING DEFINITIONS

Depression, as a feeling state, is something that most, if not all of us, have experienced at different points in our life. Fundamentally, depression is a mood. Our moods influence the ways in which we think, feel, and act in the world. Milrod (1988) elaborates that a mood is an ego state that colors all ego functions, substructures, and modes of emotional discharge. Sadness is considered the emotional response of the ego to suffering, either fantasized or real. Depression, as a clinical entity, is fundamentally a syndrome that has persistent and ongoing impact in our psychological worlds.

Symptomatically, depressed individuals experience a range of physical and emotional characteristics. Usual symptoms are persistent changes in sleeping, eating, and sexual habits. Depressed individuals may have difficulty concentrating, may seem preoccupied, may feel tired and apathetic, and are unable to enjoy previously pleasurable activities and relationships. They have a critical view of themselves and may be suicidal. Depressed individuals may demonstrate irritability, ruminative thoughts, and excessive worry over their physical health.

In the *DSM-IV* manual (1994), the American Psychiatric Association publication of mental disorders, depression is primarily considered a mood disorder. In this diagnostic system the range of depressions include Major Depressive Episodes, Bipolar Disorder, cyclothymic and dysthymic disorders, and depressive personality disorders. Of these, it is important to note that there is widespread agreement that bipolar disorders and major depressive (affective) disorders clearly have biological etiologies (Gabbard 1994, O'Neil 1984). Following from the idea that some individuals have a genetic (family) predisposition to depression, individuals often find relief through engaging in a course of pharmacological intervention. It is not unusual to treat individuals in psychotherapy while they are concurrently taking medication to manage acute symptomatology of depressive disorders (Willinger 1997).

For the purpose of this chapter, I will use the definition that Berzoff and Hayes (1996) put forward with regard to depression. They note that a diagnosis of depression is responsibly utilized when an individual experiences an alteration in at least two of the following three broad mood states: a loss of interest, a loss of energy, and a loss of pleasure.

LITERATURE REVIEW

Psychodynamic theory makes a distinction between "normative" mourning processes and depression. In *Mourning and Melancholia*, Freud (1917) noted that the grieving individual experiences many feelings and symptoms of depression. As discussed in Mendelson (1974), a grieving individual, in contrast to a depressed individual, does not experience a marked shift in self-esteem or self-regard. Individuals who experience melancholia (depression) as a result of a real or symbolic loss of an important object are thought to have ambivalent feelings toward the lost object. The hostility that aims for expression to the lost object is turned inward so that the depressed individual experiences increased self-reproach, loss of capacity to love, guilt, and expectations of punishment (Karasu 1990). The more intense the individual's unconscious hostility toward the lost object, the more marked the tendency for the individual to have guilt and self-reproach for the felt destructive impulses.

In discussing Abraham's contribution to the literature concerning depression, Brenner (1991) mentions that depressed individuals have likely experienced some form of neglect or abandonment by primary caregivers earlier in life. Similarly, Karasu (1990) cites Abraham as noting factors that contribute to the etiology of depression: "a constitutional overemphasis on oral eroticism, fixation of psychosexual development at the oral stage, early and repeated childhood disappointments in love, occurrence of first major developmental disappointment before oedipal wishes are resolved, and repetition of primary disappointment in later life" (p. 134).

Other psychodynamic theory development included and emphasized the importance of object relations in the development of depressive etiology. Discussing the narcissistic injury that depressed individuals experience, Rado (1928) felt that depressed individuals had been unsuccessful in repairing the relationship with the love object. Depression occurs when the individual's self-image is dependent upon the craving and need for external gratification from the significant others (Mendelson 1974, Zaiden 1982). Similarly, Arieti and Bemporad (1978) postulated that if an individual lives for a "dominant other," as opposed to oneself, he or she will experience repeated failure to please the other and become depressed. Ego psychologist Bibring (1953) suggested that depressed individuals have set unrealistically high standards and expectations for themselves. He comments that the repeated blows to one's ego ideal as precipitated by persistent failures to meet these unrealistic expectations leads to an ongoing battering of one's self-esteem. Depression is the consequent response to the repeated feelings of helplessness felt when goals and aspirations are not actualized.

In Bibring's formulations, the depression is located in a conflict within the ego; it is not an intrapsychic conflict between ego and superego. The importance of self-esteem regulation and feelings of wishing to be in control of oneself naturally lead to the conceptualizations of cognitive theoreticians in terms of depression. Here as well, the conflict is primarily an ego conflict. Cognitive theorists posit that depressed individuals develop belief systems (schemata) about themselves, the world, and the future that fundamentally alter their perceptions and experiences in their interactions with others (Altshuler and Rush 1984). Primarily based on the formulations of Beck and his colleagues (Beck 1991, Beck et al. 1979), depression is thought of as negative thinking patterns in the "cognitive triad" of self, world, and future; dysphoria is fundamentally conceptualized as a disturbance of cognition, not mood (Karasu 1990). Here, defective information processing leads to depression. One views oneself as being essentially worthless, boring, defective, and undeserving. Others are seen as demanding, rejecting, and perhaps hypercritical. Last, the future holds little promise of positive change; there is little value or meaning attached to future goals (Karasu 1990).

With these underlying assumptions, individuals distort their experience in varied ways. Beck and his colleagues (1979) elaborate: individuals may selectively abstract information (take things out of context), overgeneralize, magnify or minimize responses to contribute to denigrating self-fulfilling prophecies, or personalize events in a self-referential and devaluing manner. Individuals who are depressed are more likely to see situations in absolute terms and use dichotomous thinking. They may also infer conclusions based on little, contrary, or no evidence to support the extent of the critical thinking of self, other, or the future.

TREATMENT TECHNIQUES

Psychodynamic treatment techniques focus primarily on the use of insight to make the unconscious conflict(s) become conscious. In the context of an established treatment alliance with the therapist, symptom relief is expected when the unconscious aggression and hostility toward the lost objects is realized and expressed. The ambivalence toward the lost object is understood, elaborated, and worked through (Altshuler and Rush 1984, Gabbard 1994, Karasu 1990). The vehicle for the therapeutic work is at least partially realized through the development of the transference relationship and the working through of same. Also inherent in the psychodynamic model, the narcissistic wishes for love and excessive expectations are eventually understood by the client as being unrealistic and misguided. The demand for perfection for oneself and the unrealistic ego ideal aspirations are examined and modified. One becomes more comfortable with the expression of aggression and has less need to internalize feelings of disappointment and ambivalence. Rather, the assertive expression of expectations in interpersonal relationships becomes another vehicle for repair to the intrapsychic and interpersonal world of the client.

In cognitive treatment the therapist is considered to be an active partner in the process; a transference relationship is discouraged. The major modus operandi of the treatment is logical analysis of the faulty information processing that the client is using to understand his or her interactions with the world. The treatment approach is highly collaborative and structured. Clients are often asked to keep journals of their experiences so they can cite the context, frequency, and reasoning of their "distorted thoughts." Self-reports and discussion with the therapist offer the framework for investigation and challenging of themes, inaccurate perceptions, beliefs, and automatic thoughts that contribute to the individuals' depressive characteristics. Using a problem-solving approach, the client–therapist team will jointly agree to the selection of a target problem(s), and will find more rational explanations for behavior, thoughts, and feelings. There will be an effort to control and isolate illogical thinking, especially as related to the cognitive triad. Automatic thoughts related to negative self-attributions ("I am a failure," "I am disgusting") need to be challenged directly (Oei and Shuttlewood 1996). Instances in which a client is overgeneralizing, catastrophizing, and/or personalizing responses in interpersonal relationships are challenged; in so doing, the worker and client disrupt the vicious cycle of depression. As depression increases in the individual, the assumptions (schemata) that the individual specifically holds will have become more negative. The therapeutic work will assist the client in challenging the faulty information processing that he or she has automatically utilized in understanding interpersonal relationships (Beck et al. 1979). Thus the client begins to feel a sense of mastery and self-control and will generalize the learning to other aspects of faulty cognition and belief (Beck et al. 1979, Kwon and Oei 1994, Oei and Shuttlewood 1996). The negative cognitive attribution needs to be replaced by less absolute thinking, less personalization of interactions, and less overgeneralization.

VIGNETTE 1: PETER

Background

Peter, introduced earlier, was seen in twice-weekly treatment over a course of two years. His original presenting concern was his increased feelings of depression and anhedonia, secondary to the breakup of an intimate relationship. He described himself as an overachiever who could never meet the standards of his family, especially his father. He had been to see his family doctor, and while they had some discussion of pharmacological treatment, Peter had determined that he wished to pursue psychotherapy first. We agreed that we would keep an open mind concerning the potential benefits of pharmacological treatment as an adjunct to the psychotherapy. He also disclosed, during the assessment, that he was gay, that he had come out to his family only about five years before, and that he was still passing as heterosexual in his work environment. He described that he and his previous partner had often argued about his passing at work. He also described that he felt hopeless about ever finding a partner who would accept him or who his family would accept.

In his treatment, we reconstructed his history as being largely determined around the false self he adopted to feed his mother's wishes for Peter to be her narcissistic extension. His mother was often depressed, would criticize him for asserting any autonomy, and was also critical of his choice of profession. She had wanted him to be a physician; a lawyer in her mind was "second-best." His father was a demanding businessman who was largely absent from the home. He was verbally abusive to Peter and Peter's only sibling, a younger sister. His father often ridiculed Peter for having "nonmasculine" interests, and at times his father would openly demean him in the neighborhood and/or at family functions. Peter was a good student but had few friends during high school. In his mid-twenties he had been hospitalized once with a depression, after having attempted suicide. His suicide attempt had occurred after he had begun to have sex with men. He had two long-term relationships, the most recent dissolving when his partner precipitously left to resume a relationship with a former lover.

Peter's work history had been more positive. He had attended law school in Toronto and returned to his home city to take a position with a large firm. While he had hoped his parents would be pleased that he had moved back closer to them, and that he had secured a job with a good firm, his perception was that he was still unable to please them. He felt that his work colleagues, many of whom were older men like his father, also were not pleased with his performance. His work record, however, indicated that he had surpassed "usual" career expectations and was a responsibly functioning professional within his firm and the larger legal community. He clearly had distorted ideas about himself in the workplace.

Psychodynamic Treatment

Peter's initial treatment focused on his grief response to his partner's withdrawal from the relationship. While Peter had initially thought of the relationship as having broken up precipitously, we eventually reconstructed that he had had some warning signs of trouble. After his initial relief through ventilation, support, and insight about his intimate relationship, Peter seemed to feel less depressed. However, in attempting to move his treatment toward some family issues and the anger he had repressed toward his parents, Peter became more and more depressed, seeming more and more suspicious of me in the transference. Why was I so determined that he was angry, why was I not seeing how the senior partner in the firm was "on" to him in terms of his lack of success, why did I not understand what it was like to be a gay man in an "old-boys law firm"? These sorts of questions punctuated his ongoing treatment, which did appear to be at a stalemate. I concurred with Peter that he seemed to be increasingly suspicious of his work colleagues and that he was having more difficulty in maintaining a positive therapeutic alliance with me.

Integration of Cognitive Techniques

With the increase in his suicidality (as noted in the opening vignette), I began to think that I had perhaps moved too quickly in interpreting his unconscious hostility toward his parents. He seemed to be unable to allow for expression of his hostility. He also still seemed to be emotionally tied to his mother especially, leading me to think that my sense of his ability to be autonomous from her was perhaps ill-founded. Since he seemed unable to work actively with insight about his hostility toward his parents or me in the transference, I joined with his more intellectual approach and began to integrate cognitive techniques into his psychodynamic treatment. Peter agreed to look for specific demonstrations that his work colleagues were undermining him, and was an eager record keeper of events. He began to document, in detail, his interactions with his colleagues, and to listen for signs in his interactions with others that he was attributing denigrating comments to himself. He also began to perceive that in some instances his senior partner was favoring him in work-load assignment. He began to appreciate that he was negatively attributing meaning to interactions as a result of his distorted sense of self, and acknowledged thoughts of himself that were grounded in self-blaming, self-denigration, and, at times, self-loathing.

With these ongoing revelations he began to challenge some of his beliefs around himself; he started to explore some of his own internalized homophobia. With an emerging sense of self that was not so self-accusatory, Peter began quietly but assertively to challenge those in his professional environment who had become used to positioning him as the boring, sullen, and insignificant partner. We actively examined his tendency to exaggerate detail out of context (selective abstraction), to appreciate instances of disagreement with colleagues as "normative" in working with a team of professionals (magnification), and to realize that he had previously personalized comments when in fact his colleagues had attempted to show him that they appreciated his wit. He used part of a session to practice a speech he was going to give at a business luncheon. With obvious pleasure he reported the favorable response he received when he combined some tongue-in-cheek lawyer humor with the substantive material he was delivering. The challenging of his generalizations about himself and others had a definite positive impact on his depressive phenomenology.

Ongoing Treatment

With some beginning mastery in his work environment, Peter consciously began to look for patterns in his interaction with his parents. He spent many painful months examining, in detail, his own attributions and perceptions concerning his family interactions. What he began to integrate, affectively, were the painful reminders of how he had been denigrated in his family. He more fully realized that he was tremendously ashamed of himself, especially his sexual orientation. We began to explore his internalized homophobia. In this phase of his treatment, we talked at length, in a psychoeducational manner, about homosexuality, the social construction of his identity, and the repressed anger and hostility he had internalized toward himself and other gay men. He was able to see how he had sabotaged his intimate relationships since he fundamentally hated himself.

With a more integrated sense of himself as a gay man, Peter was eventually able to revisit his family-of-origin issues. Though the process was painful and at times slow-moving, he was finally able to grieve the lost objects of his childhood. He recognized the context of his position as the triangulated child between his unhappy parents. He had been used as a confidant by his mother, which further distanced him from his father and lent fuel to his father's sadistic feelings toward the more emotional side of his son (and himself). During the remainder of his treatment, Peter was able to masterfully utilize insight about his unconscious world while keeping a focus on his attributional style in his interpersonal relationships.

VIGNETTE 2: BRIGETTE

Background

As noted earlier, Brigette appeared to be getting more and more hopeless about ever having a life of her own. She perceived her father as intrusive and controlling, and herself as helpless in meeting his requests for further loyalty to him and her mother. Brigette's self-image was extremely poor. She conceptualized herself as a stupid, ugly young woman destined to live alone only to eventually be responsible for her parents as they aged. As the eldest and only daughter of three in her family, she felt that she was predestined to be the caregiver for her parents. She felt imprisoned by her circumstances and was increasingly depressed. She had come to treatment after experiencing panic attacks in her workplace. She felt an increasing sense of dread in going to work and was beginning to think that her only recourse was to go back to her hometown, live with her parents, and perhaps find work as a housecleaner. Psychotherapy for Brigette had become her last resort before going back home.

In the beginning treatment, Brigette had disclosed to me her earlier history, which had demonstrated her achievement in school. In fact, she had been considered bright. She also reported that she was often sought after by young men. She

had struck me as being quite attractive; her self-perception
as an ugly woman had been exacerbated by her father and
two younger brothers who had teased her mercilessly about
her appearance. As a biracial woman, Brigette identified as
a woman of color and was often surprised when Anglo men
would ask her out. The family history revealed that her father had been in a Japanese prisoner of war camp and had
emigrated to Canada after the war. Brigette described how
her father often recounted the hardships of his confinement,
inducing guilt if she requested any material things. Her description of her early years was that she had been raised as
if she had been in prison, with few of the clothes, make-up,
or other material possessions her other middle-class friends
enjoyed.

Cognitive Technique

In Brigette's treatment, cognitive techniques were the focus
of the beginning therapy. She began to document her panic
attacks and was a ready and eager participant in tracing the
events, context, and incidence of her panic. She was so desperate to have symptomatic relief that she readily began to
keep detailed notes about her experiences. She also began
to recognize the pattern of her panic, and to appreciate that
she often misunderstood customer requests (selective abstraction). She often felt as if the customers were treating her like
a servant, someone they could demean as a result of her perceived incompetence. This was a clear example of personalization that I began to get her to challenge, that is, to observe the interactions of customers with her co-workers.
Much to her surprise, she discovered she was not being
singled out in the store: customers often approached sales
clerks with questions. Some were rude, but she saw that perhaps she had been attributing attitudes toward customers
that were ill-founded. She began to see her dichotomous
thinking about customers, that they were either rude (bad)

or, in her eyes, indifferent (good). Documenting her interactions with her co-workers, she was surprised again, realizing that they sought her opinions on clothing, films, and music.

Psychodynamic Work

During the course of the cognitive work with Brigette, we were able to attach insight to her panic attacks. She was able to acknowledge the symbolic aspects of her panic: she seemed to panic when people wanted help from her, which was symbolic of her unconscious hostility toward her father for his demands that she be the sibling who would care for her parents in their old age. She also began to understand that she did not need to feel survivor guilt for wanting a life of her own (Weiss and Sampson 1986). She had a great deal of hostility toward both parents: she felt that her father used his own history to imprison her, that her mother had not protected her against the father's excessive demands for loyalty. As Brigette mastered her feelings in the panic attacks, she was able to use her insight to solidify her evolving sense of self. In consultation with her family doctor, she stopped taking her anti-anxiety medication. Her treatment is ongoing, with decreased feelings of panic, less depression, and a beginning sense that she can perhaps have a profession. More recently she has started to discuss her biracial heritage and the meaning it holds for her.

CONCLUSIONS

This chapter has demonstrated, through clinical vignettes, the benefits of integrating cognitive techniques in the psychodynamic therapy of two depressed individuals. As mentioned in the introduction, the partnership is a natural one. It is true that cognitive style and attributions play a major role in the self-definition of individuals. One's object relational world of self and other is influenced by affective and cognitive experiences (Altshuler and Rush 1984, Berzoff and Hayes 1996, Bowlby 1980, Karasu 1990, O'Neil 1984). The symptom picture of depressed individuals clearly demonstrates self-denigrating thoughts, suspicion of others, and a hopeless view of the future (Arieti and Bemporad 1978, Beck et al. 1979, Gabbard 1994).

As demonstrated in the vignettes, it is often true that clients become further resistant to insight-oriented work when therapists prematurely interpret unconscious hostility toward significant others. Until clients can integrate a sense of themselves as individuals with some ego strength, they will not be able to withstand interpretations concerning hostility. Psychodynamic therapists recognize that timing is essential in interpretations; what is clear in the integration of the cognitive and psychodynamic approach is that cognitive techniques can enhance the benefit of the potentially insight-oriented treatment. For Peter, his resistance was softened when cognitive techniques were used. For Brigette, cognitive techniques around her panic were fundamental to setting the basic foundation for dynamic work. For both, the integration of cognitive and psychodynamic theory proved beneficial. The benefits of a collaborative, and at times psychoeducational, approach for both clients was also beneficial. It is clear that the integration of theory proved useful in the individual treatment of these two individuals. It is also increasingly clear that no one theory can ever hope to adequately offer treatment suggestions that will inform all clinical situations and individual presentations (Saari 1997). This chapter has demonstrated the benefits of the integration of cognitive theory and psychodynamic theory in working with depressed individuals.

REFERENCES

Altshuler, K., and Rush, A. J. (1984). Psychoanalytic and cognitive therapies: a comparison of theory and tactics. *American Journal of Psychotherapy* 38(1):4–16.

Arieti, S., and Bemporad, J. (1978). *Severe and Mild Depression.* New York: Basic Books.

Beck, A. (1991). Cognitive therapy: a 30-year retrospective. *American Psychologist* 46:368–375.

Beck, A., Rush, A., Shaw, B., and Emery, G. (1979). *Cognitive Therapy of Depression*. New York: Guilford.

Berzoff, J., and Hayes, M. (1996). Biopsychosocial aspects of depression. In *Inside Out and Outside In*, ed. J. Berzoff, L. M. Flanagan, and P. Hertz, pp. 365–396. Northvale; NJ: Jason Aronson.

Bibring, E. (1953). The mechanism of depression. In *Affective Disorders*, ed. P. Greenacre, pp. 13–38. New York: International Universities Press.

Bowlby, J. (1980). *Attachment and Loss. Vol. III: Loss, Sadness and Depression*. New York: Basic Books.

Brenner, C. (1991). A psychoanalytic perspective on depression. *Journal of the American Psychoanalytic Association* 39(1):25–43.

Diagnostic and Statistical Manual of Mental Disorders (1994). 4th ed. Washington, DC: American Psychiatric Association.

Freud, S. (1917). Mourning and melancholia. *Standard Edition* 14:237–260.

Gabbard, G. (1994). *Psychodynamic Psychiatry in Clinical Practice: The DSM-IV Edition*. Washington, DC: American Psychiatric Press.

Karasu, T. B. (1990). Toward a clinical model of psychotherapy for depression. I: Systematic comparison of three psychotherapies. *American Journal of Psychiatry* 147(2):133–147.

Kwon, S., and Oei, T. (1994). The roles of two levels of cognitions in the development, maintenance, and treatment of depression. *Clinical Psychology Review* 14(5):331–358.

Mendelson, M. (1974). *Psychoanalytic Concepts of Depression*. 2nd ed. New York: Spectrum.

Milrod, D. (1988). A current view of the psychoanalytic theory of depression. *Psychoanalytic Study of the Child* 43:83–99. New Haven, CT: Yale University Press.

Oei, T., and Shuttlewood, G. (1996). Specific and nonspecific factors in psychotherapy: a case of cognitive therapy for depression. *Clinical Psychology Review* 16(2):83–103.

O'Neil, M. K. (1984). Affective disorders. In *Adult Psychopathology: A Social Work Perspective*, ed. F. Turner, pp. 148–180. New York: Free Press.

Rado, S. (1928). The problem of melancholia. *International Journal of Psycho-Analysis* 9:420–438.

Saari, C. (1997). Editorial. *Clinical Social Work Journal* 25(2):131–135.

Weiss, J., and Sampson, H. (1986). *The Psychoanalytic Process: Theory, Clinical Observation, and Empirical Research.* New York: Guilford.

Willinger, B. (1997). Psychopharmacology and clinical social work practice. In *Clinical Social Work: Theory And Practice,* ed. J. Brandell, pp. 423–441. New York: Free Press.

Zaiden, J. (1982). Psychodynamic therapy: clinical applications. In *Short-Term Psychotherapies for Depression,* ed. A. J. Rush, pp. 251–310. New York: Guilford.

11

Treating Chemical Dependence

Clayton T. Shorkey

Over the past twenty-five years therapists have applied a broad range of theories and treatment procedures in their work with alcoholics and other substance-abusing clients. Interesting therapeutic contributions have come from Gestalt therapy (Boylin 1975, Browne-Miller 1993, Buchbinder 1986), reality therapy (Bratter 1974, Glasser 1976, Wubbolding 1985), transactional analysis (Selavan 1976, Steiner 1971), family therapy (Dulfano 1982, Steinglass 1987), and many other approaches. Psychodynamic therapy has the longest history of research and practice dedicated to understanding the historical antecedents involved in the development of dependence on chemicals. The psychodynamic approach places major emphasis on the analysis and understanding of factors involved in both the initial use of chemicals and the repetition of the behavior. Awareness and understanding of contributing psychological factors for any emotional problems opens the door to a better selection of problem-solving strategies. Some problem-solving strategies flow from the theory that is applied, while others may arise from the dependent individual's introspection and intuition. The therapist may also borrow elements from other theoretical perspectives and incorporate them into a planned therapy process. Psychodynamic theorists recognize the incredible diversity of individuals, which is due both to innate characteristics and to environmental influences. Psychodynamic theory provides a methodology for exploration and hypothesis testing in a search for the best fit between the individual's unique experience of disordered behavior and the assessment of major historical antecedents that may be used to guide the treatment process. Although psychodynamic treatment is based on an extensive repertoire of theoretical concepts for identifying possible sources of dysfunction, it has a relatively limited range of techniques for achieving stable changes that transfer to functioning in the external world.

In contrast to the psychodynamic perspective, cognitive-behavioral theories have rarely been applied to study the development of chemical dependence. The theoretical base of the cognitive-behavioral approach generates empirically testable techniques for the modification of affective and cognitive and motor behavior patterns rather than providing tools for the analysis of factors involved in creating these behaviors.

Psychodynamic theory brings a rich range of theory that helps to identify factors contributing to the development and persistence of the problem of substance dependence; cognitive-behavioral theory contributes empirically tested strategies to modify and maintain positive changes in these disordered behavior patterns. In practice, these two approaches complement each other well (Kaufman 1994, Keller 1996). Graduate-level social workers with training and experience in clinical practice can select theoretical concepts and practice techniques from these two approaches to arrive at the best treatment package for chemically dependent clients. An understanding of and an ability to integrate psychodynamic and cognitive-behavioral methods, along with current knowledge of biochemical contributors to chemical dependence, is a prerequisite for increasing the probability of success with this challenging population.

This chapter is organized into five sections. The first reviews psychodynamic theories organized into categories of dysfunction according to the underlying dynamics associated with chemical dependence. In the second section psychodynamic treatment issues and general treatment guidelines are presented. Section three provides an overview of cognitive-behavioral theories related to chemical dependence, and the fourth section presents an overview of cognitive and behavioral techniques. The final section gives examples of the use of cognitive-behavioral techniques to bolster effectiveness of change related to selected areas of dysfunction. It is recognized that no current approach to chemical dependence treatment comes near the desired level of successful outcomes that we would like to see in this field. Therefore, integration of the most promising components of existing strategies is a necessity.

PSYCHODYNAMIC THEORIES

In most textbooks devoted to the study of chemical dependence there is little substantive treatment of the etiology of alcohol and other drug dependence from the perspective of psychodynamic theory. The information presented is often simplistic and many times distorted by an emphasis on long-outmoded formulations that related dependencies to repressed homosexuality or oral fixation. One early theory described by Karl Abraham suggested that chemical dependency persists because it removes repression or resistance to underlying "perverse component instincts of the sexual drive such as homosexuality, exhibitionism, sadism, masochism, and incest" (Bryan and Strachey 1927, pp. 82–83). Although this hypothesis received extensive discussion in early literature, it is not addressed in more recent works. Early analytical theories focused attention on alcohol and morphine dependence. These works employ theoretical concepts that were easily extended and modified for dependency on all types of chemicals. As a result, the current psychoanalytic literature, which includes both early and contemporary theoretical concepts, is of interest to professionals concerned with analysis of possible factors related to development and maintenance of dependence on a broad range of legal and illicit chemicals. Although the following sections of this chapter review several categories of psychodynamic concepts related to chemical dependence, most practitioners use a broad range of theory and practice.

Autoeroticism: Somatic-Psyche Connections

"Autoeroticism" is the primary concept Freud used to explain alcohol dependence. According to Freud, alcohol is ingested via the highly cathected (invested with psychic energy) lip-zone, which initially unites both the drive for self-preservation and the drive for sexual gratification. In early developmental stages stimulation of this zone provides generalized libidinal gratification unconnected to stimulus objects. Later, the erogenous significance becomes independent of the self-preservation function. Stimuli associated with ingestion of alcohol may become highly cathected for this zone. Other activities and substances may become connected to this zone, such as smoking and "perverse" kissing (Brill 1938, pp. 585–587). Along with the lip-zone, other areas of the body such as the nose and the skin serve both self-preservation and erogenous functions. Chemicals smoked, sniffed, snorted, or injected act similarly on other areas, such as the nose and skin, and can become highly cathected objects for these sites. The biopsychosocial perspective is highlighted in early psychoanalytic theory related to chemical dependence. In psychoanalytic thinking, genetic characteristics and social factors are viewed as interacting with psychological factors to produce chemical dependence (Bryan and Strachey 1927). Common cultural connections between choice of chemicals and gender, as well as other cultural factors, are represented in the early psychoanalytic literature, such as "There are wide circles in which to be a hard drinker is looked upon as a sign of manliness, even as a matter of honor. Society never demands in this way that women should take alcohol" (Bryan and Strachey 1927, p. 80).

Individual physiological characteristics combined with the pharmacological properties of specific chemicals are viewed as playing a part in the variation of the addiction process. Fenichel (1945) notes that dependence on drugs is especially complicated because of the unique chemical effects of each drug. The importance of genetic and chemical factors is greatly increased with polydrug-addicted persons. Although mediated by genetic predisposition and culture, continued use of chemicals is fostered by autoerotic gratification under the control of the pleasure principle. The chemicals and the paraphernalia associated with their use become highly cathected for their zone of administration. Dependence is seen as an unending cycle of attempts to consummate the sexual drive. Failure leads to unending repetition (Blum 1966).

Displeasure and Emotional Disturbances

The pleasure principle or its reverse, avoidance of displeasure, also accounts for much chemical use. Fenichel hypothesized that individuals who are dependent on chemicals for this function are intolerant of tension. "They cannot endure pain, frustration, or situations of waiting. They seize any opportunity for escape more readily and may experience the effect of the drug as something much more gratifying than the original had been, interrupted by the precipitating pain or frustration. After the elation, pain or frustration becomes all the more unbearable, introducing a heightened use of drugs" (Fenichel 1945, p. 377). In discussing the effects of chemicals on the body, Freud (1930) pointed out the biological and pharmacological aspects of drugs related to pain and discomfort: "It is a fact that there are certain substances foreign to the body which, when present in the blood or tissues, directly cause us pleasurable sensations, but also change the conditions of our perceptivity so that we become insensible to disagreeable sensation. These two effects not only take place simultaneously, they seem to be closely bound up with each other" (p. 18). Freud also speculated on the presence of naturally occurring chemicals in the body that produce similar effects. Research findings on the presence of endorphins confirmed Freud's view that "there must be substances in the chemical composition of our bodies which can do the same" (p. 18).

A major source of psychic pain is produced by the presence of emotional disorders. Alexander and French (1946) documented a psychoanalytical case study of a 56-year-old woman dependent on alcohol. The major factors identified in development and maintenance of her dependency were feelings of failure and inadequacy and the subsequent depression that developed through her relationship with a hostile, rejecting, and punitive husband. She used alcohol to regress to an "infantile nirvana-like existence" (p. 272). Another early case study presented by Alexander (1948) emphasized regressive gratification of dependence cravings under conditions of extreme emotional stress. The client's inability to master demanding social situations triggered intense inferiority feelings, which in turn produced massive guilt. Chemicals may first be used to deal with inferiority feelings, which are considered to reflect early presocial conflicts between becoming an adult and the longing for an early dependent form of existence. Guilt on the other hand is viewed as a later consequence resulting from failures in actual attempts at social adjustment. Addiction may be seen as a maladaptive attempt to deal with basic feelings of inferiority and guilt due to ineffective problem solving. Other emotional disturbances may include stress, trauma, depression, anxiety reactions, or anger and resentment (Schiffer 1988). "Getting sober means facing the full impact of one's pain while renouncing the central means of coping one has learned to use" (Bean 1981, p. 91). Some contributors to psychodynamic thinking on chemical dependence emphasize emotional disturbances as consequences of the addiction rather than as antecedent factors. Numerous authors argue that a large part of personality dysfunction seen in chemically dependent individuals is directly caused by physical and psychological consequences of the disease. From this perspective, although some psychopathology may predate the dependence, physical and psychological disturbances due to chemical use override the original causes and must be given primary attention, as physical damage to brain cells, which causes confusion and memory loss and other problems, may also be involved.

Deficits in Ego Ideal and Superego Dysfunctions

A more recent conception of the interaction of eroticism and underlying conflicts is presented by Wurmser (1984a,b, 1995). This conception emphasizes neurotic conflicts generated by interacting deficits in the structure and functions of the superego, including the ego ideal and both the critical and approving/affirming aspects of the superego. According to this concept, early conflicts related to a sense of self-worth are magnified by harsh and punitive introjections of the critical component of the superego, while at the same time the superego mechanisms for approval and affirmation of self-worth are absent or inadequate. This results in a "narcissistic crisis" related to doubt of self-worth that leads to global feelings of anxiety, pain, and shame. These conflicts are triggered by a broad range of stressful conditions or interpersonal interactions in daily life. Khantzian and colleagues (1990) presented a similar theory about the role that an inadequate sense of self-worth plays in chemical dependence, emphasizing a poorly developed or fragile ego ideal and deficits in the approval/affirming component of the superego due to failure of internalization of the "admired and being admired experience of childhood" (p. 12).

Deficits in Affect Regulation and Object Relations

Disturbance of the ego function of affect regulation is also presented as a major feature of emotional disturbances contributing to chemical dependence. Central to this conception is the hypothesis that individuals vulnerable to chemical dependence are characterized by "alexithymia," or a condition in which recognition of basic feeling states is impaired. Deficits in the ability to detect and interpret emotional signals eliminates the use of feelings of inner states and needs as a guide for self-understanding and action. Deficits in self-observation of feelings combined with inadequate ego functions associated with the interpretation and management of emotions result in the use of chemicals to eliminate unwanted feeling states. According to

Krystal (1975), "A major cause of their (drug-dependent individuals) use of drugs as an affect-blocker is their basic impairment in affect tolerance" (p. 181). Similarly, Khantzian views chemical dependence as self-medication to control depressed affect, hyperactivity, and emotional liability (Khantzian et al. 1990).

Object relations deficits in healthy ego functioning are also viewed as related to the development of chemical dependence. According to this theory, chemicals are used in a symbolic process of incorporation and separation with the primary maternal object. The basic deficit underlying this conception is an inadequate ego ideal caused by failure of normal development in the separation-individuation process. Brehm and Khantzian (1992) write that chemically dependent individuals "are experts in disguising their need for nurturance. . . . They tend to go to either extreme of totally depending on and being subservient to the other, or they isolate themselves in a standoffish position" (p. 114). Krystal (1978) views chemical dependence as a variant of a borderline personality disturbance created by severe problems in early development. Chemical use functions as a primitive attempt at merger with early maternal object for security. This ineffective solution is repeated over and over. The disturbance causes deficits in ability to function autonomously and impairs ability to relate to others. Interpersonal relations are characterized by an ambivalence in which others may first be idealized and later devalued and attacked.

PSYCHODYNAMIC TREATMENT

There is a dearth of information related to specific treatment techniques and procedures in the current literature for psychodynamic psychotherapy with substance-abusing clients. A major emphasis is placed on identifying different foci for therapeutic work with little regard for details of procedure. It must be assumed that most clinicians rely on variations of traditional psychodynamic techniques. Basic skills for working through resistance such as free association, active listening, interpretation, clarification, and confrontation (Greenson 1974–1975), are used to develop insight into pattern dynamics in current behavior and connections between current functioning and historical antecedents. "Working through resistances to insight gained in analysis in the therapeutic relationship makes it possible for the insight to lead to lasting change in the client" (Greenson 1965, p. 282).

Over the past twenty-five years, general consensus has developed to view chemical dependence as a disease in itself rather than as symptomatic of an underlying disorder. Because of this change in view, detoxification and abstinence with a healthy appreciation for slips and lapses is viewed as prerequisite for psychotherapy (Gedney 1984, Vaillant 1981). Some resistance to change in the perspective on addiction is still evident in the literature. Johnson (1992), for example, reports on successful psychoanalysis with a patient with active alcoholism. Silber (1970) restates his early (1959) contention that chemical dependence should not be viewed as a disease in itself, but, according to the medical model, substance abuse should be viewed in the same dynamic way as symptoms of other disorders. He does forgo the emphasis on transference neurosis in early stages of therapy because of the focus on repair of damaged ego functions due to chemical abuse. One contemporary specialist in the substance abuse field, Wurmser (1985), concurs with Silber on maintenance of the traditional view of substance abuse and argues that psychic conflict explains the origin of substance abuse and is the basis of the cure. Wurmser, however, recommends that psychotherapy be expanded to include both exploratory work and emotional nurturing to repair narcissistic injuries related to suppressed traumas in combination with education, self-help participation, and family counseling (Wurmser 1985, 1987).

A therapeutic alliance or working alliance is generally viewed as prerequisite for treatment by psychodynamic therapists working with substance-abusing clients (American Psychiatric

Association 1995). This relationship forms the basis for strengthening the client by addressing issues concerning safety, basic
trust, and mutuality in relationships (Murphy and Khantzian
1995). Transition is needed from the secure base of the therapeutic alliance to allow for later exploratory work using the
transference neurosis (Ball and Legow 1996). A working alliance is viewed as the preferable mode of therapist–client relationship in initial stages of treatment due to features such as
neurological impairments from chemical use, rigid defense
mechanisms, damaged ego functions, and/or object relations
deficits (Gedney 1984, Krystal 1978). A "pretherapy" stage of
counseling is suggested by some clinicians to enhance the client's
self-confidence, increase self-care functions, teach about feelings
(especially anxiety, fear, and depression), master fear of closeness, and accept responsibility for feelings of aggression (Brehm
and Khantzian 1992, Musholt 1988, Rothschild 1995).

Initial focus on development and maintenance of sobriety is
also emphasized as an appropriate starting place in psychotherapy. Many disorders such as low self-esteem, poor frustration tolerance, anxiety, and depression are viewed as outcomes
of the disorder that will often dissipate with continued abstinence (Wallace 1987). Levy (1987) suggests that emphasis on
early antecedents for substance use, whatever their origin, may
no longer be important. Resolution of psychological conflict is
not viewed as a necessary condition for maintenance of sobriety (Millman 1986). The focus of sobriety-oriented therapy emphasizes work on resistance to abstinence from denial, use of
projection, and rationalizations (Rothschild 1995, Wallace 1987).
Treatment should focus on restoration of "psychic integrity"
before assessment of antecedent factors can be addressed (Bean
1981, Gedney 1984).

COGNITIVE-BEHAVIORAL THEORY

In contrast with the psychodynamic theory of the etiology and
treatment of chemical dependence, the cognitive-behavioral

perspective has a fairly recent history, and its theoretical concepts and treatment techniques are limited and specific. Although there is little disagreement among theorists and clinicians related to major causal variables or useful treatment techniques, there are differences in emphasis in treatment. The focus of cognitive-behavior treatment of chemical dependence is clearly on techniques and skills for modification and maintenance of changes of existing behavior patterns rather than on analyzing and explaining historical antecedents of current functioning. Practice guidelines for treatment of individuals with substance abuse disorders, presented by the American Psychiatric Association, concisely identify the focus of cognitive behavior therapy as "(A) altering the cognitive processes that lead to maladaptive behavior in substance users, (B) intervening in the behavior chain of events that leads to substance use, (C) helping patients successfully deal with acute or chronic drug craving and (D) promoting and reinforcing the development of social skills and behavior compatible with remaining drug free" (APA 1995, p. 18).

Classical and Operant Conditioning Base

Most cognitive-behavioral therapists combine theory and techniques from classical conditioning, operant conditioning, modeling, and cognitive learning as a basis for their treatment. Genetic predisposition and underlying neurochemical factors are also acknowledged. Classical conditioning is seen as the major factor in developing physical and psychological craving responses and learned behaviors of chemical use (Morgan 1996, Steffen et al. 1986). Secondary and tertiary conditioning accounts for the association of a broad range of stimuli with the initial conditioned chemical stimuli. Association related to pleasurable reinforcing properties of unconditioned chemical reinforcers or to the reduction or elimination of aversive conditions affecting the individual can occur. This formulation is parallel with Freud's conception of the operation of the pleasure principle and cathexis of stimulus objects.

Operant conditioning of overt or covert voluntary behavior depends on the characteristics of chemical reinforcing stimuli. Specific physiological/psychological effects, intensity of the stimuli, presence of discriminative cues for responding, and frequency of reinforcement all influence the strength of the learned responses as well as their resistance to extinction (Lundin 1974). Thoughts, values, expectations, and goals are seen as voluntary behaviors that may be influenced by operant conditioning. Learning alcohol/drug use behaviors through modeling of cultural behaviors is the third major vehicle for developing chemical abuse and addiction (Bandura 1969). Observation of positive reinforcement for chemical use enhances learning through a facilitator effect.

Cognitive-Behavioral Contributions

Beyond concepts derived directly from operant and respondent conditioning and modeling, several prominent cognitive therapists have built on these concepts and have provided useful formulations. Both Albert Ellis and Aaron Beck view disordered thinking as the primary causal factor in emotional and substance abuse as an effort to cope with negative emotional states that arise as a result of illogical or distorted thinking (Rotgers 1996). Ellis hypothesizes that low frustration tolerance (LFT) is especially present in addictions. According to him, 20 percent of addicts are characterized by pure LFT, and must have their chemicals even if they are pernicious. Ellis suggests that in addition to a strong desire for chemicals, LFT is also experienced as a secondary level of LFT as a discomfort disorder. Many addicted individuals who experience withdrawal symptoms, craving, anxiety, depression, and feelings of hopelessness, resentment, and boredom convince themselves that they must have the chemicals to function. Ellis (1993) speculates that about 80 percent of chemically dependent individuals are characterized by this type of LFT. These individuals cannot stand the discomfort associated with these unpleasant emotions. When the substance-dependent person is deprived of the chemical, the individual engages in irrational thinking that produces the emotional and behavioral consequences of LFT. Irrational beliefs that foster LFT include: "I can't stand the withdrawal symptoms without...; I can't function due to anxiety without...; I am not strong enough to abstain from use of...; I can't control my craving for...; Because I feel so depressed, I am powerless to resist..." (Ellis et al. 1988, pp. 24–27).

Treatment must deal separately with the discomfort disorder and the original emotional problem. The term *intoxication coping* is used by Ellis to describe ineffective problem solving where chemicals are used to deal with discomfort. These painful emotions act as triggers for continued chemical use and may block out other aspects of one's existence (Steinfeld 1978).

Beck and colleagues (1993) use the term "core beliefs" to describe beliefs held by addicted individuals that interact with life's stressors to produce excessive anxiety, dysphoria, or anger. These core beliefs, such as "I'm trapped," "I'm helpless," or "I'm unlovable," act as facilitating beliefs for individuals who believe they cannot tolerate these unpleasant emotions and thus trigger urges and cravings for substances to reduce or eliminate them. Beck stresses the importance of expectations held by the individual that these unpleasant situations can be relieved only through use of the substances. Connors and Maisto (1988) extend Beck's concept of expectancy related to drug use by suggesting that two types of expectancy cognitions are present in addiction, those related to desired outcomes and those related to interpreting actual outcomes.

Support for Ellis's and Beck's hypothesis is presented in several research studies examining the underlying cognitive structure of chemically dependent individuals. Finnigan (1995) identified four major cognitive factors operating in a sample of heroin injectors. Beliefs reflected in these subjects were the use of heroin to reduce anxiety, to relieve boredom, to increase general self-confidence, and to improve communication and interactions with other people. In a sample of bulimic and drug-abusing women, Butterfield and LeClair (1988) found that the cognitive structure of these subjects was characterized by a negative view of the world, bleak outlook for the future, strong need for approval, perfectionist tendencies, and self-denigration. Finally, Denoff (1987) studied a sample of adolescent residents of a drug treatment program and found that catastrophizing about possible future misfortune and a dire need for approval were significant components of the cognitive structure of these substance-abusing teens.

Consistent with Ellis's conception of "intoxication as coping," several researchers identify deficits in problem-solving ability as an important factor in development and treatment of chemical dependence. Emotional problems may be viewed similarly as derived from environmental or resource factors or from problems in social interactions. When important life goals are blocked through frustration, individuals choose strategies to deal with the obstacles. Substance abusers have particular difficulty in dealing with interpersonal problems. "They have substituted extraordinary chemical solutions for more ordinary human ones, and as a consequence they need to discover in the context of human relationships . . . that their problems can be identified, understood and treated in more ordinary ways" (Khantzian 1985, p. 84). The selection of chemicals as solutions to frustrated life goals often reflects a lack of knowledge about the long-term effects of this problem-solving option. The initial use of chemicals as a solution to stressful life events or negative emotional states, and application of this increasingly maladaptive choice to a broad range of problem situations, highlights the importance of deficits in the cognitive-behavioral skill of problem solving in maintenance of addictions (Husband and Platt 1993, Intagliata 1978, Kunz et al. 1979).

COGNITIVE-BEHAVIORAL TREATMENT

The range of cognitive-behavioral treatment techniques used in the field of chemical dependence treatment is wide. Ellis and colleagues (1988) provide clear descriptions of many techniques.

Cognitive restructuring is the primary technique used by cognitive-behavior therapists. The procedure for identification and modification of drug-related beliefs frequently uses Ellis's A–B–C–D–E framework. With this procedure, clients are taught to examine the activating events (A) that currently result in irrational emotional responses and behaviors. An understanding of the concept of the term *irrational* is an important part of this process. In the context of this treatment approach, "irrational" is defined as "not in the best interests of the individual." Cognitions that lead to emotional and behavioral consequences that are not consistent with the values and goals chosen by the client would be irrational. Because of the importance of this definition in practice, chemically dependent clients may need preliminary work involving values clarification and goal analysis (Bernard and Wolfe 1993).

Generally, following specification of the activating event (A), the client is helped to examine the consequences (C), emotions, and behaviors that follow the A. Using the definition of "irrational" previously described, the client is taught to evaluate the effectiveness of emotions and behaviors at (C) in facilitating achievement of life goals. Step three (B, for "beliefs") involves teaching the client to identify and differentiate between rational and irrational beliefs concerning the activating event (A). A fourth step, disputing (D), introduces the client to a process of generating alternative rational attitudes, beliefs, and ideals to replace current irrational ones. The major techniques used in disputing (D) are (1) debating, or use of a logical-empirical method to examine the evidence supporting the belief; (2) defining or specifying beliefs characterized by overgeneralizations, absolutes, and loose semantics; and (3) discriminating or distinguishing wants versus needs, desires, and demands, hassles and horrors, and undesirable and unbearable events (Ellis 1977).

A final step, effect (E), involves practice by the client in evaluating the differential effects in the use of irrational and rational cognitions relating to the activating event selected. This step provides understanding and motivation for continued use of the process to reduce disturbances. With some chemical-dependent clients, additional work is needed to help the client identify or increase the capacity to identify, label, and evaluate the intensity of emotional responses. Steps 3 and 5 are dependent on the client's ability to identify and evaluate both rational and irrational feeling states. Clients with deficits in this area cannot discriminate the differential effects of rational and irrational beliefs and generally have little motivation to continue this process.

Numerous secondary techniques may be used to reinforce the cognitive restructuring method to achieve stable change in cognitions; for example (1) unconditional self- and other acceptance, (2) positive scanning, (3) imagery/rational emotive imagery, (4) forceful coping statements, (5) behavioral rehearsal/role playing, (6) cognitive distraction including relaxation, (7) psychoeducation using books and tapes, and (8) homework assignments including logs and journals (Ellis 1978a,b, Ellis et al. 1988). The *RET Resource Book for Practitioners* provides description, handouts, and exercises for many useful techniques, such as exercises to teach the client how to gauge the intensity of emotions, to clarify values, to differentiate between beliefs that help versus those that hurt, to increase tolerance of frustration, to decatastrophize, and to build positive self-regard (Bernard and Wolfe 1993). A series of self-help books related to rational emotive therapy techniques for dealing with perfectionism, anxiety, anger, shame, and depression is available for chemically dependent individuals from Hazelden Education Materials (Drilling 1992a,b, Hafner 1992, Perlman 1992, Sheehan 1992a,b).

Cognitive restructuring may also be combined with role-playing of social skills. After the client learns to identify irrational beliefs related to a specific situation, he or she is instructed to practice the situation using social skills rehearsal techniques illustrating the client's ideal self (Oei and Jackson 1984). Another combination includes the use of cognitive restructuring with imagery of performance in difficult situations related to chemical use (Collins and Carlin 1983). Other cognitive methods suggested are advantage–disadvantage analysis, daily thought record, activity monitoring and scheduling, and increasing cognitive dissonance between goals and current functioning (Beck et al. 1993, Whelan and Prince 1982, Whorley 1996).

Systematic problem solving is also used independently or in conjunction with cognitive restructuring to increase the client's ability to deal successfully with day-to-day frustration (blocks and obstacles) concerning achieving life goals (D'Zurilla and Goldfried 1971, Husband and Platt 1993, Intagliata 1978, Kunz et al. 1979). Several manuals provide practice guidelines for many of the techniques previously reviewed and include behavioral methods derived from operant conditioning, such as drink-refusal skills training, listening skills training, social skills training, and exercises for development of alternative behaviors (Monti et al. 1989, NIAAA 1992).

The last section of this chapter provides examples of the integration of cognitive-behavioral techniques in psychodynamic therapy with individuals recovering from substance dependence. Examples and suggestions are given for use with clients who exhibit clinical features related to disturbances underlying chemical dependence that were reviewed in the first section of this chapter. In each case a positive therapeutic alliance provides the basis for ongoing work.

INTEGRATION OF COGNITIVE-BEHAVIORAL TECHNIQUES INTO PSYCHODYNAMIC PSYCHOTHERAPY

Autoeroticism and Object Relations Deficit: Case 1

Hector is a 46-year-old Hispanic male who holds a mid-management position in a state social service agency. He is well respected in his community for developing innovative programs impacting the Hispanic population. His drugs of choice are LSD, marijuana, and alcohol. Hector has enjoyed the effects of these chemicals since adolescence and until recently never viewed his use as problematic. He was arrested three years ago for possession of a small amount of marijuana and completed a drug diversion program. No charges were filed. Recently he was arrested for DWI and again charged with possession of marijuana. He has completed an outpatient drug treatment program provided through the Employee Assistance Program serving his agency. He is required to continue treatment pending the court's decision related to his current offenses. He has elected therapy with a private practitioner who works with mental health and chemical dependence problems. Hector has lived alone in a small apartment for the last six years. He occasionally jogs alone and drinks at local clubs. He has avoided intimate relationships since the breakup of a relationship eight years ago. At the termination of the relationship, he sold his house, gave away his furniture, moved to a secluded property he inherited from his grandfather, and lived alone for approximately two years. He desires the "emotional" closeness of a relationship, but finds the sexual component an unpleasant requirement. He has a deep longing for a long-term emotional bond with another person, but has difficulty in the day-to-day aspects of relationships. He sees little value in casual relationships and friendships, and has a pessimistic attitude about investing his time in activities with others. He relies on chemicals for physical and mental relaxation and recreation and reports that they provide ideal conditions outside his workaday life. The client reports little difficulty stopping alcohol, but experiences anxiety and anger related to efforts at terminating LSD and marijuana use as he views them as his personal choice.

Significant factors in Hector's life history included being raised by his maternal grandparents. He never knew his biological father, and his mother turned over responsibility for his care to her parents when she married another man the year after Hector's birth. Her new husband would not accept responsibility for him. Hector's grandfather was a skilled carpenter and worked regularly. The family was a traditional Hispanic one with Spanish spoken in the home. Hector was the pride of his grandparents, who provided substantial emotional and financial support including assistance in obtaining a graduate-level degree. Hector experienced this continuity between his home and the predominant Anglo culture at school. He was academically oriented in school and well liked by teachers and counselors, but developed no close relationships with other students. He had casual friendships with a number of students who introduced him to chemical use. During high school he primarily used LSD and marijuana on a solitary basis. Alcohol use began in college.

Psychotherapy focused on feelings of rejection and abandonment by his biological father and by his mother. His inability to experience and express emotional closeness to his grandfather, difficulties in developing relationships with his peers, and his inability to express grief associated with his grandfather's death, which occurred shortly after he completed graduate school, were addressed also. Major features for work in psychotherapy include the reliance on chemicals for autoerotic gratification and deficits in development of object relationships needed to meet emotional and social needs through relationships with others.

A number of cognitive-behavioral techniques were incorporated into the treatment process. These techniques included values clarification using advantage–disadvantage analysis, positive scanning, self-monitoring, imagery, cognitive restructuring related to self- and other acceptance, and risk-taking exercises to develop emotional satisfaction in interpersonal relationships.

From a cognitive-behavioral perspective, definitions of behavior patterns as rational, adaptive, irrational, or maladaptive are determined by the extent to which they are consistent with achieving the basic values selected by the individual for his or her life. Ellis (1968) describes four levels of basic life values that most people choose: (1) survival, (2) pleasure,

(3) life in a social group, and (4) intimate relations with a few other persons. Hector admits that continued alcohol use, especially when driving, puts him at risk of physical injury or death and this motivates him to change this behavior. His reliance on acid and marijuana poses little threat to his physical survival and is experienced by him as his major source of pleasure. Based on the satisfaction of primary needs, it would be illogical and futile to argue the opposite. In Hector's case, chemical use becomes problematic at the level of higher values of satisfactory living in his social environment and in relation to this substitution for gratification in social, emotional, and sexual relationships with others.

Cognitive therapy with Hector involved a process of values clarification to increase his motivation for developing alternative nonchemical means for achieving psychosexual satisfaction (Bernard and Wolfe 1993). This process with Hector included analysis of the advantages and disadvantages of continued chemical use as it related to a satisfactory life. The disadvantages included the potential loss of his job, his comfortable financial status, and the respect he enjoys in the community. He also realized that continued use of chemicals reduced his motivation for interpersonal relationships. He viewed those risks and problems associated with continued use of chemicals as unacceptable to him, but continued to experience anxiety concerning life without them. From this advantage–disadvantage analysis, Hector's motivation increased enough for him to stop using marijuana and LSD and to try to increase satisfaction by building his capacity to enjoy social relationships as an alternative to chemicals and thereby reduce his risk of legal, job, and financial problems.

Unlike Hector, some clients will claim that they do not want any type of close social/emotional or especially intimate relationships with others, and define this as outside their value system based on personal preferences. Ellis (1968) suggests that when this occurs, it is usually motivated by the individual's fears of failure and rejection, and the situation requires exploration, questioning, and challenging. Using examples of current acquaintances, Hector was asked to write narratives about activities he might enjoy with people he knew, and to list all possible positive experiences he might have with them. After focusing on current acquaintances, he was asked to think of positive characteristics and potentially satisfying activities following interactions with new people and to write his recollections as an exercise in the evening. The second technique employed was imagery, in which he visualized himself enjoying various activities with some of his acquaintances. Finally, risk-taking exercises were used to get Hector started on spending time in activities with some of his acquaintances. The exercises include teaching and practice of both unconditional self-acceptance and acceptance of others. Hector was provided with reading material that illustrated these concepts. In Hector's case, acceptance of others as fallible human beings who sometimes do good things and other times do bad things was especially important. He worked at disputing demands that friends act like angels that never do things you don't like and are always thoughtful and attend to your needs. This client began to initiate as well as accept invitations to a variety of activities, including jogging, tennis, concerts, and movies. By increasing his awareness of the dynamics underlying presenting features of chemical use through uncovering techniques in dynamic psychotherapy, the client maintained motivation and experienced success in replacing chemical means of gratification with social and emotional satisfaction through increased interpersonal relationships after nine months of treatment. Issues related to long-term intimate relationships and increased sexual satisfaction remain to be addressed.

Displeasure and Emotional Disturbances: Case 2

Peggy is a 36-year-old female being treated for generalized anxiety and dependence on alcohol and sedative hypnotics. She began therapy at the urging of her husband because her nervousness, irritability, and sleep disturbances are increasingly impacting their relationship and her job as an administrative assistant. She completed a thirty-day drug treatment program at a private facility and continues psychotherapy. Over the last three years she has consulted a series of physicians who have prescribed medications for her.

Peggy's mother smothered her with attention and affection, but was perfectionistic in her expectations, which were magnified when Peggy's father was absent from the family due to military assignments. Psychotherapy focused on deficits in ego boundaries with her mother with emphasis on her self-perpetuation of demands for perfection and concomitant self-denigration when her goals are not fully met. Peggy's insecurity and ambivalence about her father were addressed, including a deep longing for emotional closeness and unexpressed anger and resentment.

From a cognitive-behavioral perspective, Peggy has two layers to her major disturbance that require treatment. The primary factor threatening a return to chemical use was anxiety; the second factor was the discomfort disorder related to symptoms of her anxiety disorder. Both needed to be dealt with separately. Following instruction concerning the impact of cognitions on feeling and behavior, the client was shown the two components of her disorder using examples she provided. Related to the discomfort disorder, cognitive restructuring using the A-B-C system was used to teach the client to identify beliefs (B) that produced and maintained the secondary anxiety. Peggy's beliefs were that she "could not stand or bear" her anxiety and that these symptoms were "horrible, terrible, and awful." Peggy practiced positive coping statements that she constructed; for example, "It is difficult to experience anxiety but I can stand it"; "Because it feels like I can't deal with my symptoms doesn't make it so"; "It's not easy but I can work at developing methods to enjoy my life despite the hassles of my symptoms." Peggy practiced disputing her irrational beliefs, used positive coping statements, and maintained a journal of her efforts. In addition, she learned to use rational emotive imagery to reduce her anxiety by seeing herself successfully manage anxiety symptoms.

Peggy was provided with audiotapes that dealt with etiology and change strategies for managing her primary anxiety disorder. Cognitive restructuring focused on unconditional self-acceptance and decreasing irrational thinking, including demand for perfection, self-denigration and exaggeration and catastrophizing of undesirable situations, and the dire need for approval from others. She was taught a variety of diversion techniques, including relaxation imagery, to help manage her experience of anxiety as she developed her ability to change the thinking patterns that generated much of her anxiety. Other distraction techniques included relaxing in her sauna and reading novels. Peggy made rapid progress in reducing her anxiety level and continued to work at achieving awareness and working through early contributing emotional conflicts. She maintained a record in her journal that emphasized her positive qualities and success in daily functioning, but also included areas for self-improvement.

Ego Ideal/Superego and Affect Deficits: Case 3

Lester is a 23-year-old African-American male who has been arrested twice for driving while intoxicated and several times for public intoxication. He is participating in a drug diversion court-ordered chemical dependency treatment program for polydrug abuse. In addition, he has been accepted as a client for psychotherapy of dysthymic disorder and drug abuse at a nonprofit clinic that offers long-term treatment. Lester is a follower in several groups of friends who have spent most leisure time together drinking, using whatever drugs are available, socializing, and cruising the city and surrounding areas in their cars. He is currently working evenings as a maintenance worker. His early environment was characterized by poverty and emotional deprivation, including the death of his mother when he was 5 years old. This client has developed a minimal conception of self, viewing himself as a person of no importance and with no personal goals. He is also unable to identify any positive attributes. He feels he has little control of his life and expresses the opinion that the bad things that happen in his life are not important. Unlike Peggy, who exaggerated and catastrophized unpleasant events in her life, Lester minimizes the significance of negative events, including the possibility of continued depression, addiction, or incarceration.

Lester shows flat or depressed affect; has difficulty connecting with positive feelings of joy, contentment, and self-satisfaction; and has great difficulty identifying or describing sadness or depressed feelings. He has little skill in problem solving and uses alcohol and drugs as a habitual panacea.

Psychotherapy with Lester focused on repressed grief related to the early death of his mother and subsequent emotional deprivation and lack of narcissistic supplies. Therapy also addressed childhood repression of conflicts underlying his "alexithymia" and began building positive components of his ego ideal and sense of self.

Use of the primary cognitive therapy technique, cognitive restructuring, was not indicated initially due to the client's inability to experience positive and negative feelings. Replacement of irrational thoughts with rational ones requires an ability to experience changes in affect associated with cognitive changes. Preliminary work was required to focus on identifying and getting in touch with feelings of hopelessness, sadness, depression, happiness, and satisfaction. Lester practiced describing and giving examples of emotional experiences using a list of basic feelings; he also kept a daily log of feelings and learned to rate their intensity on a scale of 1 to 5 with 1 signifying a minimal experience of the feeling and 5 signifying a maximum. He also worked on developing positive self-regard by listing and describing his positive characteristics and behaviors in his journal.

After Lester began to display greater ability in affect recognition and a more positive sense of self, he was instructed in the impact of beliefs on emotions and behaviors. Primary emphasis was placed on his beliefs that "I'm not important" and "Things that happen to me don't matter." Positive coping statements related to self-worth were prepared to counter these irrational thoughts. He developed a general daily activity schedule to provide structure and replace drug-related activities with other enjoyable activities. He also made a list of good things that he did each day.

The final component of cognitive-behavior intervention was having Lester identify short-term life goals and build his skill in dealing with obstacles to attaining them. He worked with the therapist on developing his problem-solving ability by identifying blocks to attainment of his daily goals. He practiced brainstorming and decision making for nonchemical solutions to frustrating situations and developed skills in task analysis to plan what he would do when he needed to do it, where, and how frequently. Following a year of treatment, this client displayed greatly improved affect and had maintained free of all chemicals except alcohol. He had two slips with drinking during the year but did not drive when drinking. He has expressed an interest in pursuing the training he needs to run a contract cleaning service and has developed a friendly relationship with several people who do not use alcohol or other chemicals.

The cases reviewed in this chapter illustrate the use of psychotherapy with clients demonstrating ego and superego deficits as well as concurrent emotional disorders including dysthymia and anxiety neuroses. Their presenting substance abuse problems necessitated the use of numerous cognitive-behavioral techniques to facilitate the process of "working through." These techniques included values clarification, goal analysis, problem solving, positive scanning, self-monitoring, journaling, daily activity scheduling, risk-taking exercises, skill development, diversion techniques, and cognitive restructuring.

Cognitive restructuring techniques yielded greater acceptance of self and other, decreased catastrophizing, and improved frustration tolerance. The clients' understanding and awareness of the early factors that contributed to their chemical use increased their motivation to work at achieving affective, cognitive, and behavioral changes using these cognitive-behavioral strategies.

REFERENCES

Alexander, F. (1948). *Fundamentals of Psychoanalysis*. New York: Norton.

Alexander, F., and French, T. M. (1946). *Psychoanalytic Therapy*. New York: Ronald Press.

American Psychiatric Association (1995). Practice guidelines for the treatment of patients with substance disorders: alcohol, cocaine, opioids. *American Journal of Psychiatry Monograph* 152(11):5–59.

Ball, S. A., and Legow, N. E. (1996). Attachment theory as a working model for the therapist transitioning from early to later recovery substance abuse treatment. *American Journal of Drug and Alcohol Abuse* 22(4):533–547.

Bandura, A. (1969). *Principles of Behavior Modification*. New York: Holt, Rinehart and Winston.

Bean, M. H. (1981). Denial and the psychological complications of alcoholism. In *Dynamic Approaches to the Understanding and Treatment of Alcoholism*, ed. M. H. Bean and N. E. Zinberg, pp. 55–96. New York: Free Press.

Beck, A. J., Wright, F. D., Newman, C. F., and Liese, B. S. (1993). *Cognitive Therapy of Substance Abuse*. New York: Guilford.

Bernard, M. E., and Wolfe, J. L. (1993). *The RET Resource Book for Practitioners*. New York: Institute for Rational-Emotive Therapy.

Blum, E. M. (1966). Psychoanalytic views of alcoholism: a review. *Quarterly Journal of Studies on Alcoholism* 27:259–299.

Boylin, E. R. (1975). Gestalt encounter in the treatment of hospitalized alcoholic patients. *American Journal of Psychotherapy* 29:524–535.

Bratter, T. E. (1974). Reality therapy: a group psychotherapeutic approach with adolescent alcoholics. *New York Academy of Sciences* 233:104–114.

Brehm, N. M., and Khantzian, E. J. (1992). A psychodynamic perspective. In *Substance Abuse: A Comprehensive Textbook*, ed. J. H. Lowinson, P. Ruiz, and R. B. Millman, 2nd. ed., pp. 106–117. Baltimore, MD: Williams & Wilkins.

Brill, A. A., ed., trans. (1938). *The Basic Writings of Sigmund Freud*. New York: Modern Library.

Browne-Miller, A. (1993). *Gestalting Addiction: The Addiction-Focused Group Psychotherapy of Dr. Richard Louis Miller*. Norwood, NJ: Ablex.

Bryan, D., and Strachey, A. trans. (1927). *Selected Papers of Karl Abraham, M.D.* New York: Basic Books.

Buchbinder, J. (1986). Gestalt therapy and its application to alcoholism treatment. *Alcoholism Treatment Quarterly* 3(3):49–68.

Butterfield, P. S., and LeClair, S. (1988). Cognitive characteristics of bulimic and drug-abusing women. *Addictive Behaviors* 13:131–138.

Collins, R. L., and Carlin, A. S. (1983). Case study: the cognitive-behavioral treatment of a multiple-drug abuser. *Psychotherapy* 20(1):101–106.

Connors, G. J., and Maisto, S. A. (1988). The alcohol expectancy construct: overview and clinical applications. *Cognitive Therapy and Research* 12(5):487–504.

Denoff, M. S. (1987). Irrational beliefs as predictors of adolescent drug abuse and running away. *Journal of Clinical Psychology* 43(3):412–473.

Drilling, E. (1992a). *Anxiety and Worry*, rev. ed. Center City, MN: Hazelden Educational Materials.

—— (1992b). *Perfection*, rev. ed. Center City, MN: Hazelden Educational Materials.

Dulfano, C. (1982). *Families, Alcoholism and Recovery*. San Francisco: Jossey-Bass.

D'Zurilla, T. J., and Goldfried, M. R. (1971). Problem solving and behavior modification. *Journal of Abnormal Psychology* 78(1):107–126.

Ellis, A. (1968). *Learning, Living and Loving*. Learning Resource Center, School of Social Work, University of Texas at Austin. Audiocassette.

——— (1977). The basic clinical theory of rational emotive therapy. In *Handbook of Rational Emotive Therapy*, ed. A. Ellis and R. Grieger, pp. 3–34. New York: Springer.

——— (1978a). *Rational Emotive Treatment of Addiction*. Learning Resource Center, School of Social Work, University of Texas at Austin. Videocassette.

——— (1978b). *Disputing and Other Cognitive Restructuring Methods*. Learning Resource Center, School of Social Work, University of Texas at Austin. Videocassette.

——— (1993). *Interview with Albert Ellis on Discomfort Anxiety*. Learning Resource Center, School of Social Work, University of Texas at Austin. Audiocassette.

Ellis, A., McInerney, J. F., DiGiuseppe, R., and Yeager, R. J. (1988). *Rational-Emotive Therapy with Alcoholics and Substance Abusers*. New York: Pergamon.

Fenichel, O. (1945). *The Psychoanalytic Theory of Neurosis*. New York: Norton.

Finnigan, F. (1995). The cognitive structure underlying heroin-injecting behavior. *Journal of Drug Education* 25(3):281–287.

Freud, S. (1930). *Civilization and Its Discontents*, trans. J. Riviere. Garden City, NY: Doubleday Anchor, 1958.

Gedney, M. (1984). The alcoholic patient in dynamic psychotherapy. *Issues in Ego Psychology* 7(1 & 2):11–17.

Glasser, W. (1976). *Positive Addiction*. New York: Harper & Row.

Greenson, R. R. (1965). The problem of working through. In *Drives, Affects, Behavior*, vol. 2, ed. M. Schur, pp. 277–314. New York: International Universities Press.

——— (1974–1975). Dynamics of the treatment situation. In *American Handbook of Psychiatry*, ed. S. Arieti, pp. 106-117. New York: Basic Books.

Hafner, A. J. (1992). *Anger*, rev. ed. Center City, MN: Hazelden Educational Materials.

Husband, S. D., and Platt, J. J. (1993). The cognitive skills component in substance abuse treatment in correctional settings: a brief review. *Journal of Drug Issues* 23(1):31–42.

Intagliata, J. C. (1978). Increasing the interpersonal problem-solving skills of an alcoholic population. *Journal of Consulting and Clinical Psychology* 46(3):489–498.

Johnson, B. (1992). Psychoanalysis of a man with active alcoholism. *Journal of Substance Abuse Treatment* 9:111–123.

Kaufman, E. (1994). *Psychotherapy of Addicted Persons.* New York: Guilford.

Keller, D. S. (1996). Exploration in the service of relapse prevention: a psychoanalytic contribution to substance abuse treatment. In *Treating Substance Abuse: Theory and Technique,* ed. F. Rotgers, G. S. Keller, and J. Morgenstern, pp. 84, 116. New York: Guilford.

Khantzian, E. J. (1985). Psychotherapeutic interventions with substance abusers—the clinical context. *Journal of Substance Abuse Treatment* 2:83–88.

Khantzian, E. J., Halliday, K. S., and McAuliffe, W. E. (1990). *Addiction and the Vulnerable Self.* New York: Guilford.

Krystal, H. (1975). Affect tolerance. *Annual of Psychoanalysis* 3:179–219.

——— (1978). Self representation and the capacity for self care. *Annual of Psychoanalysis* 6:209–246.

Krystal, H., and Raskin, H. A. (1970). *Drug Dependence: Aspects of Ego Function.* Detroit: Wayne State University Press.

Kunz, G. D., Coché, E. H. E., Hamme, P., and Korber, W. (1979). Problem solving training: a structured therapeutic modality for new drug and alcohol admissions. In *Addiction Research and Treatment,* ed. E. Gottheil, A. McLellan, K. Druley, and A. Alterman, pp. 34–39. New York: Pergamon.

Levy, M. (1987). A change in orientation: therapeutic strategies for the treatment of alcoholism. *Psychotherapy* 24(4):786–793.

Lundin, R. W. (1974). *Personality: A Behavioral Analysis.* New York: Macmillan.

Millman, R. B. (1986). Considerations on the psychotherapy of the substance abuser. *Journal of Substance Abuse Treatment* 3:103–109.

Monti, P. M., Abrams, D. B., Kadden, R. M., and Cooney, N. L. (1989). *Treating Alcohol Dependence.* New York: Guilford.

Morgan, T. J. (1996). Behavioral treatment techniques for psychoactive substance disorder. In *Treating Substance Abuse: Theory and Technique,* ed. F. Rotgers, D. S. Keller, and J. Morgenstern, pp. 202–240. New York: Guilford.

Murphy, S. L., and Khantzian, E. J. (1995). Addiction as a "self-medication" disorder: application of ego psychology to the treatment of substance abuse. In *Psychotherapy and Substance Abuse: A Practitioner's Handbook,* ed. A. M. Washton, pp. 161–175. New York: Guilford.

Musholt, D. M. (1988). Three crises in the psychotherapy of a recovering alcoholic. *Alcoholism Treatment Quarterly* 5(½):95–104.

National Institute on Alcohol Abuse and Alcoholism (1992). *Cognitive-Behavioral Coping Skills Therapy Manual* (DHHS Publication No. ADM 92-1895). Rockville, MD: National Clearinghouse on Alcohol and Drug Abuse.

Oei, T. P., and Jackson, P. R. (1984). Some effective therapeutic factors in group cognitive-behavioral therapy with problem drinkers. *Journal of Studies on Alcohol* 45(2):119–123.

Perlman, A. (1992). *Understanding*, rev. ed. Center City, MN: Hazelden Educational Materials.

Rotgers, F. (1996). Behavioral theory of substance abuse treatment: bringing science to bear on practice. In *Treating Substance Abuse: Theory and Technique*, ed. F. Rotgers, D. S. Keller, and J. Morgenstern, pp. 174–201. New York: Guilford.

Rothschild, D. (1995). Working with addicts in private practice: overcoming initial resistance. In *Psychotherapy and Substance Abuse: A Practitioner's Handbook*, ed. A. M. Washton, pp. 192–203. New York: Guilford.

Schiffer, F. (1988). Psychotherapy of nine successfully treated cocaine abusers: techniques and dynamics. *Journal of Substance Abuse Treatment* 5:131–137.

Selavan, A. (1976). Banal scripts in alcoholism. *Transactional Analysis Journal* 6(4):416–418.

Sheehan, T. (1992a). *Shame*, rev. ed. Center City, MN: Hazelden Educational Materials.

—— (1992b). *Depression*, rev. ed. Center City, MN: Hazelden Educational Materials.

Silber, A. (1959). Psychotherapy with alcoholics. *Journal of Nervous and Mental Disease* 129(5):477–485.

—— (1970). An addendum to the technique of psychotherapy with alcoholics. *Journal of Nervous and Mental Disease* 150(6):423–436.

Steffen, J. V., Steffen, V. B., and Nathan, P. E. (1986). Behavioral approaches to alcohol abuse. In *Alcoholism Development, Consequences and Interventions*, ed. N. J. Estes and M. E. Heinemann, pp. 426–435. St. Louis: Mosby.

Steiner, C. (1971). *Games Alcoholics Play: The Analysis of Life Scripts*. New York: Grove.

Steinfeld, G. J. (1978). Dope fiend irrationality: it takes one to know one. *Psychotherapy* 15(2):193–200.

Steinglass, P. (1987). *The Alcoholic Family.* New York: Basic Books.

Vaillant, G. E. (1981). Dangers of psychotherapy in the treatment of alcoholism. In *Dynamic Approaches to the Understanding and Treatment of Alcoholism*, ed. M. H. Bean and N. E. Zinberg, pp. 36–54. New York: Free Press.

Wallace, J. (1987). Working with the preferred defense structure of the recovering alcoholic. In *Practical Approaches to Alcoholism Psychotherapy*, ed. S. Zimberg, J. Wallace, and S. B. Blume, 2nd. ed., pp. 23–36. New York: Plenum.

Whelan, M., and Prince, M. (1982). Toward indirect cognitive confrontation with alcohol abusers. *International Journal of the Addictions* 17(5):879–886.

Whorley, L. W. (1996). Cognitive therapy techniques in continuing care planning with substance-dependent patients. *Addictive Behaviors* 21(2):223–231.

Wubbolding, R. E. (1985). Reality therapy applied to alcoholism. *The Counselor* 3(5):5–6.

Wurmser, L. (1984a). More respect for the neurotic process: comments on the problem of narcissism in severe psychopathology, especially the addictions. *Journal of Substance Abuse Treatment* 1:37–45.

——— (1984b). The role of superego conflicts in substance abuse and their treatment. *Journal of Psychoanalytic Psychotherapy* 10:227–258.

——— (1985). Denials and split identity: timely issues in the psychoanalytic psychotherapy of compulsive drug users. *Journal of Substance Abuse Treatment* 2:89–96.

——— (1987). Flight from conscience: experiences with the psychoanalytic treatment of compulsive drug abusers—Part one: Dynamic sequences underlying compulsive drug use. *Journal of Substance Abuse Treatment* 4:157–168.

——— (1995). *The Hidden Dimension: Psychodynamics of Compulsive Drug Use.* Northvale, NJ: Jason Aronson.

12

Integrative Brief Treatment

Adin DeLaCour

In recent years brief treatment has come to occupy the spotlight among psychotherapeutic innovations in the United States. This focus on brief intervention has evolved in response to factors largely external to the clinical situation itself, and related to sweeping changes in the fiscal arrangements of health care delivery. In the push to economize, preference is given to methods that can identify clearly delineated problems, realistic goals, and documentable strategies for reaching those goals within specified time limits. Often treatment is authorized a few sessions at a time, with provision of further sessions dependent on the demonstrated efficacy of treatment up to that point, as well as on clinical consultation and negotiation with a case manager employed by the payor.

These and many other procedural shifts in the frame of the treatment relationship favor clinical approaches that to some degree can be objectively planned, which presents a particular challenge for psychodynamic clinicians. Despite decades of research into the mechanisms and nature of change in dynamic therapy, the heart of the process remains largely unpredictable, relying as it does on the central impact of motives, desires, and fears that are not fully understood and do not operate logically. Caught between commitment to their work as they have practiced it and the demands of the new pragmatic environment, dynamic clinicians are struggling to make their work accessible and flexible while protecting the space necessary for an exploratory relationship. Defining the role of cognition in the process of change, as well as the technical means of maximizing the client's openness to new thoughts, perceptions, and beliefs, enhances the clarity and potency of dynamically oriented brief treatment.

Clearly, a full discussion of the relationship between psychodynamic and cognitive theory and technique is beyond the scope of this chapter. An effort will be made here to allude to a few central aspects of this relationship, drawing particularly on the recent work of Drew Westen. This overview will allow us then to consider the process of integrating cognitive-behavioral interventions into time-limited psychodynamic therapy. Several leaders in the field of dynamic brief treatment have begun to make these links explicit; the contributions of Hans Strupp and Jeffrey Binder (1984) and Leigh McCullough Vaillant (1997) will be noted in particular. I will then describe ways in which working within time limits naturally "pulls" psychodynamic technique in the direction of a more cognitively active relationship. Using clinical material to amplify the discussion, I will look at this in relation to two relevant aspects of brief treatment technique: the experience and use of the relationship, and the use of a central issue to shape the work.

Before I attempt to speak about psychotherapy in theoretical terms, it seems important to acknowledge the reality that when therapy is working well one's theory is invisible and, perhaps, as one grows more experienced, not even fully conscious in any given interaction. During training we absorb theories that make sense to us and are compatible with our experiential sense of what people want, need, and do. Our experiences with clients reinforce our theories, that is, when clients experience us as helpful, we rightly or wrongly attribute some of the credit to our guiding theory. When a clinician makes an explicit effort to examine how theory guides behavior, in order to sort out a problem, supervise someone, or write a paper, she works backward from responses that seem to have come naturally. Certainly these responses are not generally felt to be conscious efforts to reframe, model, examine faulty attributions, and so on. Thus, attempting to make clear and rational the process of integrating cognitive interventions with dynamic technique, for example, necessarily misrepresents the very process it attempts to describe. Nevertheless, we try, and in so doing practice that art of self-reflection that we encourage our clients to develop and engage in on their own behalf. As a clinician long identified with psychodynamic theory, I experience myself as either noticing the presence of, or integrating cognitive technique into, a preexisting home base. This process will be represented by highlighting the presence of cognitive concepts and technique throughout this discussion.

In his 1996 paper "Integrating Psychodynamic and Cognitive-Behavioral Theory and Therapy," Westen identifies three areas in which each treatment approach would be enhanced by integration with the other: the emphasis each places on small units of observable behavior versus broad, enduring patterns of functioning; the relative importance placed on the role of cognition versus motivation in behavior; and the relative emphasis placed on conscious versus unconscious processes in maintaining behaviors. For example, the tendency of dynamic clinicians to look at broad patterns—such as fear of success or survivor guilt—often overlooks the extent to which maladaptive strategies are reinforced and maintained by current responses of others to the client and the client's cognitive framework for interpreting (and misinterpreting) these responses. In addition, dynamic theory's focus on broad themes over detailed interactional sequences is usually considerably easier for clients, and often less useful. Clients working with broad constructs such as oedipal guilt are less likely to be brought forcefully face to face with the opportunity to comprehend the purposes and costs of such strategies. Without seeing why—and equally important, when and how—they operate, the automatic influence of these strategies over clients' behavior and perception remains intact.

On the other hand, the preferred focus on smaller units of observable behavior of cognitive treatment runs the risk of missing the deeper, less rational, and certainly less acknowledged sources of problematic behavior. Here the question of motivation arises, with dynamic theory offering a particularly rich view of the complex network of often contradictory and disavowed motivations underlying interpersonal relationship patterns that shape what we perceive and how we interpret it. Cognitive theorists refer to *person schemas*, while dynamic theorists speak of *object relations*. Cognitive theory's reliance on consciously accessible images of self and other misses the point that, as Westen (1991b) says, "there is little reason to believe, from either a motivational or a cognitive perspective, that people are generally aware of activated concepts of self that may be influencing their conscious thoughts, feelings, or actions" (p. 436). While both theories understand our relational strategies to be learned from the beginning of life, psychodynamic theory offers us a view of the conflicting beliefs and motivations that underlie our often inexplicably tenacious maladaptive responses.

This strength of dynamic theory, however, is gained at the price of an optimal focus on encouraging active learning in the current therapeutic relationship. While dynamic theory assumes that the reliving of early relationship patterns in the transference will result in learning about their archaic origins in ways that will facilitate relinquishing them, there is a bias in the approach against directively encouraging clients to *try new behaviors* and *observe their own and others' responses*. This is coupled with a bias against learning in the cognitive mode, which is seen as intellectualizing the process and severing it from its emotional roots. While the firsthand, affectively based learning that takes place in the analysis of transference may be effective for changing maladaptive patterns, it may also be relatively inefficient. Perhaps learning in the transference is enhanced when combined with an active curiosity about the current "networks of association" (Westen 1991b, p. 430), cuing inappropriate responses in the treatment as well as in all or most of the client's other significant relationships.

Westen's discussion of these associational networks emphasizes the central role affect plays in the evolution of our core relationship patterns. Interpersonal experiences generate feelings and our natural human tendency is to avoid experiences that are accompanied by bad feelings (e.g., anxiety, sadness, anger). We develop complex networks of association to our experiences that are affectively charged by the meanings we make of them. If asking for help as a child leads often enough to rejection, asking for help in an overt manner will decrease as a relational response. Since needing help is not something we can change, other more complex and disguised methods of help seeking will be devised, which is a way of describing defenses. As coming to a therapist constitutes an act of help seeking, it is bound to be loaded with the doubt, fear, suspicion, and anger such acts, and their inevitable discouraging outcomes, involve. This loading, particularly intense when what one wants help with is changing life itself, is what we call transference.

> Neurological evidence suggests that affective associative memory involves different neural pathways than conscious, explicit memory, and that affective associations may linger long after a conscious, declarative memory has dissipated. . . . These phenomena have substantial clinical implications, since they suggest the importance of techniques that allow the therapist and patient access to unconscious associational networks that may influence thought, feeling and behavior but be inaccessible to consciousness. [Westen 1996, pp. 24–26]

Other examples of this tendency to avoid pain by not "seeing" includes a family's collusion in the denial of an alcoholic member, or the way a couple's perceptions of their relationship tends to shift so rapidly and radically in the wake of a decision to separate. Perhaps encouraging clients to *notice, question, and test out their guiding assumptions* is no less neutral than waiting for misguided assumptions to be disproved without systematically calling conscious attention to them.

Within the brief treatment field, as mentioned above, steps toward the integration of psychodynamic and cognitive-behavioral theory have been taken. Strupp and Binder (1984) provide a clearly articulated integrated model, and the recent extension of their work by Hannah Levenson (1995) offers a wealth of clinical demonstration with accompanying theoretical discussion. Vaillant's book *Changing Character* (1997) offers the most extensively and systematically integrated model to date. She demonstrates with impressive clarity the process of helping clients to *notice the antecedents and consequences, both internal and external, of their interpersonal responses*. Direct exploration of affective responses, within a supportive and respectful relationship, is the quickest route to the warded-off tangle of motivations and their consequent defensive attributions.

In summary, it can be seen that the primary contribution of cognitive interventions to dynamic therapy lies in the area of encouraging more explicit learning. Cognitive clinicians encourage "collaborative empiricism" (Beck et al. 1990, p. 80); that is, they encourage clients to consciously notice and examine their emotional and behavioral responses. They train clients to utilize observing ego capacities. Thus they help them learn to interrupt faulty attributional patterns, to regulate affect and modify automatic responding, and to practice and try out new response sequences. They help clients to learn the process of implementing new behaviors, which is made possible through the insight achieved in the therapeutic relationship. Cognitive clinicians model these capacities in the relationship, using judicious self-disclosure, humor, rehearsal, and other strategies to help clients distance themselves from what has always seemed to go so wrong in their lives.

USE OF THE RELATIONSHIP

As in any psychotherapy, the brief therapist communicates both consciously and unconsciously about the nature of the relationship from its beginning. Thus, throughout the brief treatment literature, careful attention is given to the assessment process. Years ago I began using the metaphor of a camera's zoom lens to talk with students about assessment. First priority is given to establishing an atmosphere of trust and openness, as brief treatment does not allow the luxury of a leisurely testing of the relationship waters. As the therapist introduces herself and her role, by being in it as well as talking about it, she gathers information about the client. The therapist is interested in history, in getting a sketch of the big picture, which reveals the client's conscious narrative in its clearest form. Formative events and the client's conscious (and inevitably defensive) interpretations of their meaning and import (what they say about the self and the other) are laid out in some sequence, as well as beginning impressions of the key players in the client's life story. I ask permission to take notes in the first session, explaining that I want to concentrate on thinking about the details, not remembering them. In addition, I want to keep this early narrative available to refer to as we move into seeing things in other ways. This models an interest in the details of what actually happened at various significant points in the client's life. Details are key. As therapy begins to focus on the emotional residues of crucial events and relationships, it is the comparison of actual details with residual beliefs that helps to reveal patterns of faulty attribution. Referring back to the early story in the client's own words demonstrates change in patterns of perception and response, which shows that change is about shifting beliefs, that this can occur within a short period of time, and that it is the client doing the changing, which can and will continue after the therapy ends.

As sections of the life narrative emerge, the therapist "zooms" (tactfully) in for details. "When your big sister fought with your parents, what was going on inside you? How did you see yourself compared with her? What did you do? What did you want to do? The way you handled it, by getting quiet, is that something that still goes on in relationships? What's happening inside when you go quiet?" This attention to detail is absolutely essential in brief treatment, and is one of the ways in which time limits "pull" dynamic process toward cognitive activity. The focus shifts from the broad, enduring patterns emphasized in dynamic theory to the moment-by-moment variability of self-experience in response to current behavioral cues. From the start the therapist is asking the client to notice his or her feelings, the assumptions they arise from, and the responses they generate. In cognitive-behavioral terms, this is beginning to construct a picture of the client's operative person schemas; in dynamic terms it is about identifying object relations. This is often juxtaposed with alternative images of how the client would have wanted things to go. The client is invited (both explicitly and implicitly) to see him- or herself not only as the subject but as the student of the subject, that is, to develop self-reflective capacities, with the therapist as a carefully attentive and benignly curious participant. Change occurs within the client and through the client's willingness to seriously try out new ideas by engaging in new behavioral responses. This is all crucial in discouraging reliance on the therapist as the source of change. This dependency-inducing tendency to endow the therapist with the power to bring about the desired change is inherent in the role relationships of psychotherapy, and is particularly counterproductive in a brief relationship.

Strupp and Binder's *Psychotherapy in a New Key* (1984) is one of the definitive texts for the practice of brief treatment. The following excerpt from an assessment interview demonstrates the close attention the therapist pays, and invites the client to pay, to the client's inner process.

> *I:* How does that leave you feeling toward your husband? When he puts up with that?
>
> *P:* I get a little annoyed.
>
> *I:* A little annoyed? What do you do with it?
>
> *P:* Nothing.
>
> *I:* You don't say anything about it?
>
> *P:* No.
>
> *I:* How come?
>
> *P:* Well, because really it would not do very much good.
>
> *I:* How do you mean?
>
> *P:* We will continue to see the couple.
>
> *I:* You sound like you don't feel that your opinion would count

much with your husband in that situation. Is that a general feeling you have?

P: It depends on the situation. Sometimes he pays attention and then again he doesn't.

I: Do you see that as much of a problem? A big problem in your relationship?

P: I think I've learned to live with it.

I: That doesn't mean it's not a problem.

[Strupp and Binder 1984, p. 117]

This sort of focus differs from the less overtly shaping style of more traditional dynamic technique, which inclines toward following the client's associational process, which of course includes ample recourse to defensive delaying tactics. Again, the question of efficiency arises. The brief therapist is tacitly encouraging the client, within the limits of readiness and with respect for privacy (including individual differences in comfort level based on cultural, developmental, and other contextual forces in the room), to move toward the heart of the matter. This involves moving as quickly as possible into noticing and challenging defensive beliefs and patterns, one of the technical strategies that makes brief treatment an intensive and challenging experience for both client and therapist. Here the cognitive-behavioral focus on the details of relational thought patterns and interactional strategies appears in the foreground of dynamic brief treatment technique. Moving toward details is moving toward defenses, on the way to the beliefs that generate these defenses.

As with every aspect of the therapist's style and demeanor, this acute interest in detail will be experienced by the client in accord with his or her defensive stance and receptive readiness. It is quite a personal experience to be listened to and looked at so closely, and may initially be felt as threatening or rude, which will cue the therapist to adjust the pace. At the same time, it is quickly clear to the client that the therapist is genuinely interested in focusing on where and what the active problem really is, which is rarely if ever synonymous with the client's initially prepared description. (Otherwise there would be no need for treatment.) This wakes up the client and draws him or her into the situation. The experience of being unexpectedly seen generates hope as well as apprehension. As Westen (1991a) points out, use of cognitive-behavioral technique in the context of intensive psychotherapy neither interferes with transference-oriented work nor does it irrevocably "contaminate" the transference. "Therapeutically one can work with a patient's experience or distortions of the implications of various interventions on the part of the therapist, just as one works with patient interpretations and distortions of a relatively neutral stance" (p. 224).

Manifestations of the heart of the matter (i.e., the currently active maladaptive strategies interfering with the client's comfort or health) inevitably emerge in the unfolding relationship between client and therapist, and exploration of these manifestations is central to brief dynamic technique. However, the relationship is attended to differently than in open-ended treatment, and in ways that again encourage the client to specifically consider what he or she is thinking as well as feeling. Winokur and colleagues (1981) have described the way this works in relation to exploration of transference in brief treatment.

> Instead of waiting for the genetic links to emerge gradually . . . following a transference interpretation, in STDP [Short-Term Dynamic Psychotherapy] the therapist forcefully presses the patient to make these links and actively aids in the process by offering a generous number of reconstructions of his own. This rapid juxtaposition of the genetic material with the transference interpretation ensures that the feelings that emerge do not remain directed at the therapist. . . . In this way, the patient's feelings toward the therapist are allowed to develop into a crystallized attitude (transference neurosis). [p. 133]

The client is invited from the start to notice how she is constructing the relationship under the influence of what Westen

(1991b) refers to as "confirmatory bias," that is, the tendency to "seek information that confirms their hypotheses rather than look for disconfirming evidence" (p. 434). The invitation is to note that "reality," including all its self-defeating and frustrating dimensions, is being constructed under the guidance of outdated but automatically activated thoughts and beliefs. Even to notice this is a radical and usually ineradicable new experience of self, which is why, though it is a matter of ideas, it is an intensely affective process as well. The client is placed in a therapeutic paradox: she is free (for dynamic brief treatment, like its open-ended counterpart, avoids advice or exhortation) to go on being as before, but no longer believes the old arguments in the same way. To take a new step, and notice how it lightens things up, is to undermine a lifetime of commitment to the inevitability of things being the way they unfortunately are. As in Alice's Wonderland, motivations (known and unknown), thoughts, beliefs, and feelings all spin briefly before they reconfigure. Clearly this complexity cannot be fully articulated within cognitive theory's prime reliance on conscious learning processes, nor within dynamic theory's meager attention to the hold thought has on feeling.

USE OF A CENTRAL FOCUS

As mentioned earlier, all forms of brief therapy shape the treatment around a central goal or problem area. It is universally accepted that such a focus is a necessary part of limiting the domain of a treatment already circumscribed by time. This adherence to a central focus is one of the most powerful ways in which brief treatment naturally engenders a highly cognitive reflective process. The central issue is the pathway into, and becomes a sort of fluid blueprint of, the person schema (or the object relationship, depending on one's preferred language). In many forms of time-limited work the definitions of problem and of avenues toward solution are consciously delineated as part of the assessment process. In dynamic brief treatment the definition of both the problem and the experiences necessary to its amelioration involve careful thought and attention to the possible role of unconscious, warded-off, and conflicted desires and motivations. For dynamic brief therapists, the central issue is thought of as "a repetitive and maladaptive interpersonal pattern" (DeLaCour 1986), which can be seen as operative in the presenting complaints and distress of the client. Strupp and Binder (1984) give a definition of the central focus that virtually doubles as a definition of the cognitive theorists' "person schema":

> ... a focus must tell something about: 1) the kinds of distinctions the patient makes about himself or herself and others; 2) based on those distinctions, the kinds of actions (including making further distinctions) in which the patient characteristically engages; and 3) the ways in which these distinctions and actions are organized by the patient into a rigid and problematic interpersonal drama. [p. 70]

Implicit in this description is the idea that much of what fuels such interpersonal dramas is outside of awareness, in the form of a tangle of interpersonal wishes, fears, and confusion. The work of the brief therapy will be to begin the process of untangling, revealing, tolerating, and understanding these conflicting beliefs, hopes, and expectations. While Strupp and Binder provide a heavily cognitive description of the central issue, James Mann, in his earlier work (1973), emphasizes the affective dimension when he speaks of the central issue as the client's "present and chronically endured pain" (p. 18). Mann suggests two components to be stressed in articulating the treatment issue to the client: first, an acknowledgment of the client's longstanding efforts to end chronic distress, and second, recognition of the failure of these efforts, implied by the client having sought therapeutic help. Though the description is empathically put, it is also an immediate challenge to the client, who, as she is supported for diligent effort, is also asked to see that she does not yet understand the problem sufficiently. There is what is known (and of crucial importance to the therapist): the client's conscious, familiar if painful, life narrative, in which in some combination neither the self nor others behave or feel as the client would have them behave and feel. And there is what is not known, though alluded to in the articulation of the focus; the underlying *confirmatory bias* that, in its effort to avoid painful self-experience, authorizes a false, or at least woefully inadequate, story.

The development and use of a clinical focus is one of the clear differences between open-ended dynamic treatment and brief dynamic treatment, and often a chief source of long-term therapists' skepticism about brief work. Indeed, there is risk of the client seeing the therapist as the expert, the one who will make change come about, if the focus is presented authoritatively to the client. Ideally, in contrast, the therapist listens attentively, and attempts step by step to note discrepancies, puzzles, or mysteries as they emerge in the narrative. A young woman, for example, came to see me in a state of agitation brought on by her "obsession" with another woman. She felt impelled to become involved with this woman, and filled with guilt about hurting her current partner of six years. She was on the verge of moving across the country (indeed, we knew from the start we would be able to meet only six times), leaving behind her ailing grandmother and her parents, all of whom had escaped the Holocaust in tragic circumstances. She made it clear right away that she wanted to talk only about the immediate problem, which had nothing to do with her family history, which she felt she had already worked through sufficiently anyway. She explained in detail that she was "falling apart," agitated, not eating or sleeping, crying all the time. In the initial meeting I commented on the striking discrepancy between her description of crisis and her relaxed and articulate manner of relating it to me. A puzzle.

This kind of immediate attention to behavioral detail (in this instance, to defensive operations) is essential in establishing the lively, present-oriented climate of the brief treatment relationship. In addition, it is the most efficient way of searching out the shape of the central theme. Culture, class, gender, history, and so forth all influence a client's receptivity to being approached directly in this way. For this and other reasons, flexibility is the single most necessary ingredient in the brief therapist's attitudinal repertoire, as demonstrated by Alexander and French (1946) many years ago.

When I commented to the client on this behavioral paradox, she answered without pause, "Oh, I'm always like that. No one can ever tell when I'm upset." As I inquired further, this led into her sense of herself as the only source of light in her family, who, although they had escaped extermination, had lost most of their family and friends. She saw herself as the location and bearer of what was left of their hopes for the future. A straight cognitive approach would have taken her admonition about talking about her family at face value, and perhaps not have located the complex source of the crisis, that is, her impulse to leave her partner (who stands in for family) on the threshold of leaving her family, and her compulsion to do it in a way that causes her to feel guilty and unworthy. On the other hand, a straight psychodynamic approach would not have moved so quickly and directly toward active exploration (challenge, even) of current relationship strategies.

Other aspects of evolving and working with a therapeutic focus encourage integration of cognitively oriented treatment strategies into the relationship. I describe to clients at the start how developing interest in a focus allows the treatment to deepen, even though it unfolds in a brief time span. By attending to a particular tangle, it becomes possible to understand something useful about tangles in general, so that after treatment the client will be more adept at noticing the cues of conflict (anxiety, dread, guilt, indecision, procrastination, anger, for example), and of reflecting on what may not be obvious. In addition, the therapist's commitment to a focus indicates the relative modesty assigned to her role in the change process. That is, the fact that he/she offers to concentrate, albeit in a complex way, on a particular problem area and not on life in general implies that the client will be discovering not "The Answer" but methods of self-understanding.

As mentioned in relation to the assessment process, the therapist is faithfully interested in the details of the central maladaptive pattern as it unfurls itself in everyday behavior. Questions help the client see how to focus: "What did you feel when she said that? What did you imagine she was feeling? As you think about it here, at a safe distance, what would you have most liked to have done at that moment? What do you imagine might have happened if you had done that?" It is easy to see how these sorts of questions help to make visible a person schema that is operating in contradiction to the client's conscious intentions.

This sort of exploration also offers the opportunity for "homework," a classic component of cognitive-behavioral work. I often say something like, "It would be interesting to see what would happen if, this week, when your son leaves the dishes in the sink, you don't wash them. Sometimes you only really find out what you're afraid of in a situation by not doing what you usually do." This is an invitation to interrupt a maladaptive pattern in order to bring it and its consequences into focus. Often when clients are going to visit their families, I suggest they use the visit as a chance to notice new things, or to look at the relationship patterns between themselves and family members in the light of new ideas about what they may be seeking and avoiding. This suggestion usually comes late enough in the therapy for the client to be familiar with the sorts of cognitively oriented self-observing questions the brief therapist is full of. These questions and suggestions are examples of the cognitive restructuring techniques described by Heller and Northcut (1996) in their paper on integrative treatment of borderline clients. They refer to techniques that encourage the client's capacity to identify the process of cognitive splitting as it occurs, and then to identify its immediate triggers and a range of response options. Suggestions such as intentional self-observation during a visit to family need to be made with care, as either the therapist's stance (i.e., if the therapist appears to be invested in the client's behaving in a certain way) or the client's dynamics may result in the client's interpreting the idea as an expectation and resorting to either rebelling or complying, both of which slow things down. If the aim of the process is to foster the client's independent ability to self-reflect and choose among alternative behavioral responses, either rebellion or compliance institutes an attitude of dependence on the therapist (as the powerful one who must be resisted or obeyed), which becomes an iatrogenic detour. I often suggest that clients might find it helpful to write about what they notice during the week, again emphasizing the client as the agent of change and the client's life, not the therapist's office, as the location of change. The young woman who was moving in six weeks had said she didn't need to talk about her family, and I felt that not respecting that in our first meeting would rightfully lower my credibility in her eyes. I suggested that, since I needed at least some impressions of the people and events most crucial to her development, perhaps she could write a few things down during the two weeks before our next meeting and send them to me. Her unconscious orientation to the temporal structure around us as a stimulus to action, and her less than fully conscious motivation, were perhaps evident in the fact that her brief biography arrived thirteen days later, the day before our second session.

The relationship patterns that become the central subject of the treatment are often noted first in aspects of the client's history and current crisis, as the initial story unfolds. Attention to experiences outside the room is generally less anxiety provoking in the early stages of client and therapist getting to know each other. However, the central issue inevitably emerges in some form in the therapy relationship. These transactions will be shaped in part by the therapist's sensitivity to the circumstances of the case (including the client characteristics like ethnic, class, and gender expectations) and the circumstances of the moment in the particular treatment hour. At times, direct attention will be called to current interaction, as in my noting my client's striking presentation of herself as falling apart, all the while appearing composed and comfortable in her telling of the story. Here, learning occurs as unconscious defensive patterns are directly explored. At other times, however, calling direct attention to such patterns generates further defense. In such moments the therapist, rather than inquiring verbally, may choose to behave in a way that goes against the client's defensive expectations, thereby interrupting the automatic associational network and providing momentarily what Alexander and French call a "corrective emotional experience." Indeed, Alexander and French, writing in 1946, describe this process of deconditioning the client's maladaptive associational pathways of expectation with startling clarity.

> In the formulation of the dynamics of treatment, the usual tendency is to stress the repetition of the old conflict in the transference relationship and to emphasize the similarity of the old conflict situation to the transference situation. The therapeutic significance of the *differences* between the original conflict situation and the present therapeutic situation is often overlooked. And in just this difference lies the secret of the therapeutic value of the analytic procedure. Because the therapist's attitude is different from that of the authoritative person of the past, he gives the patient an opportunity to face again and again, under more favorable circumstances, those emotional situations which were formerly unbearable and to deal with them in a manner different from the old. [p. 67]

CLINICAL ILLUSTRATION

Sarah was 21 years old when she came to see me in September of her senior year of college. She described her previous summer at home with her parents as "a nightmare," during which she had painfully felt the absence of her parents' support with a difficult situation at her job. Over the summer she had settled into a state of depressed resignation. She mentioned two other precipitants: the return to college of a close friend who was suffering from cancer, and the imminent departure of her older sister (the sibling to whom she felt the closest), who was moving to a distant state. She described herself as "a needy, emotional person," wanting help with being less burdensome to her friends and boyfriend, and less hysterical in her phone calls home. She seemed eager to engage with me from the start, though I noticed immediately her tendency to laugh caustically while telling me painful stories. She seemed to be simultaneously asking for help and blocking any direct acknowledgment of the pain she wanted help with.

Sarah was the fifth of six children, one of whom had died before her birth and one during the year after her birth, precipitating a severe depression in her mother. She described her father as passive and relatively absent, and her mother as rigid and domineering, full of covert rules and expectations. When she was in fifth grade her mother had returned to work, and this was a memorably difficult transition for Sarah, who acted up until admonished by her sister. From this point on Sarah became a bit of a rebellious presence at school.

I begin this discussion with the question of the focus, as it is the central question in the brief therapist's mind at the start of treatment. My formulation was that Sarah, under the pressure of impending graduation and the loss of the home college had been for her, was beset by unresolved aspects of her relationship with her parents, particularly in the realm of dependence/independence. As a child she appeared to have coped with her mother's unavailability by trying to be good. Following her one period of protest she had been admonished, and thenceforth her protest was played out in the outside world. She confronted injustice on an institutional level, and these efforts were recognized and supported in the therapy at the same time that their defensive aspects were tentatively explored. At a more personal level her conflict was painful and confusing to her, and she continually oscillated between seeking help or support and pushing the other person away, after which she would feel frustrated and alone.

The therapy centered mainly on Sarah's defenses, which were complex and ever present in treatment in her interactions both with me and with others. She began the second meeting with a demonstration of the problem, as she came with her tearful readiness to seek my help and then dodged me each time I moved empathically toward her. I attempted to find out how close she would let me be, but also to begin drawing attention to her defenses. When I asked how her lifelong issue played out in her present life, she was able to share the problem with me in another way, by telling me about her boyfriend. She really seemed to want to feel better, and despite considerable wariness she was able to tolerate a fairly intense engagement. I offered a focus constructed along the lines of Mann's work (1973). This included her lifelong effort to form good relationships, her dependency needs, and her anger about their continual frustration. Gentle language was used in response to the strength of her defensive wish to see herself as good, even blameless, in her dealings with others. Despite the simplicity of the language, however, it did contain the confrontation: the plan was to help Sarah realize something about (1) how dependent and powerless she felt she was in her close relationships, (2) how angry she was about that, and (3) how her own defensive behavior helped to generate the responses she was troubled by. This was a tall order for twelve weeks. This central issue was somewhat easy to arrive at, given its pervasive presence in all major areas of her life. Yet I was aware that, no matter how empathically put, the very presence of a central focus would also at some point be experienced by Sarah as a limit, and thus as a stimulus for her defensive associational network. My hope was for her to begin to recognize how she fended people off, and how this was related to her expectation that people would reject her for wanting closeness. The inevitable subsequent conclusion she had drawn in childhood was that it was bad of her to want such things. This focus seems to me to draw together cognitive therapy's attention to the details of current interactional sequences, and dynamic therapy's attention to the embedded nonconscious roles in the person schema, which is activated again and again in the course of current emotional and relational experiences. Perhaps seeing this would enable her to be more tolerant of her needs and feelings, thus less frightened of rejection and more accessible for intimacy. I had no idea how much of her own contribution to the pattern she would be able to acknowledge, though I had a hunch how the struggle would evolve in our relationship.

Right from the start, as mentioned, I tried to bring Sarah's attention to her defenses and how they were preventing her from having satisfying experiences with people. Though this clearly was not what she wanted me to be doing, she managed to see some important things. At the end of our third meeting I commented directly on her primary defense, but it was my empathic recognition of her hardship during the infamous fifth grade year that visibly affected her. She felt close to me, a threatening experience, and we paid a price for this in the form of her strident externalizing of blame in the next couple of meetings. I continued to point out her evasiveness, and her active role in her drama with her mother. Once she was able to acknowledge her own participation in the fight with her mother, she began to feel the heat with me, worrying that I would criticize or reject her for being "less perfect." My attention to the focus thus facilitated the elaboration of her dynamic between us. By remaining neutral about her behavior, by emphasizing the importance of understanding it rather than hurrying to change it, I avoided her confirmatory bias toward expecting me to criticize her. In this unfamiliar moment, when the person schema was made visible by its unexpected absence, she was able to notice something new about how she pushed people away. She followed this with another test (Weiss and Sampson 1986) of my ability to avoid confirming her fears by demanding extra time from me, which I readily offered. Her cancellation of the next meeting I understood as yet another push toward the old pattern by interrupting a positive experience and frustrating the other person (in this case me). Again I was careful to challenge her only in the gentlest way.

As I understand it, in my relationship with Sarah my intention was to enter her object relational world with her, in order to help make it visible to us. This would, and to some extent did, allow her to feel and then understand its complex structure, which allowed her to begin to tolerate a wider range of her own feelings, and to begin getting out of her own way.

This formulation obviously arises from a psychodynamic understanding of internal life. However, the presence of the focus both allows and requires attention to the smallest transactional details, wherein lie the cues for the confirmatory bias. The more overt behavioral measures that characterize cognitive therapy have less play in a case like this, given Sarah's readiness to take them as invitations to either comply or resist. Made sensitive to the complexity of challenging her maladaptive patterns by my understanding of psychodynamic theory, I was better equipped to gently invite her to see, over and over again, how automatically she was impelled to distance me when fearful of needing and then being hurt by me, and then to interpret me as the unavailable one. Yet it is cognitive theory that most faithfully pursues this immersion in the subtle details of present relational experience.

CONCLUSION

Given the automatic unconscious operation of confirmatory bias, it is inevitable that therapists approach the clinical encounter set to see and respond to the client in ways congruent with a structure of expectations that is both longstanding and, it is hoped, continually evolving. This structure emerges initially from the clinician's temperament and lifetime of experiences, and is thus likely to be as sturdily resistant to change as any transference structure offered by a client. We are no more immune to confirmatory bias than our clients. Training only influences what is already there, inevitably sharpening some aspects of perception and obscuring others, which has been a theme throughout this discussion. Just as we believe in (and have seen the value in) respecting the power and usefulness of clients' defenses as an aid in helping to loosen the hold of those defenses, we may need such tolerance toward ourselves. We are living in an era of paradigms that come and go with dizzying speed, and the fiscal and organizational changes in the health care field require us to adapt. The task of integrating the creative depth of psychodynamic vision with the practical thoroughness and flexibility of cognitive theory is as challenging as it is likely to be rewarding.

REFERENCES

Alexander, F., and French, T. (1946). *Psychoanalytic Therapy: Principles and Application*. New York: Ronald.

Beck, A. T., Freeman, A., and Associates (1990). *Cognitive Therapy of Personality Disorders*. New York: Guilford.

DeLaCour, A. (1986). Use of the focus in brief dynamic psychotherapy. *Psychotherapy* 23:133–139.

Heller, N., and Northcut, T. (1996). Utilizing cognitive-behavioral techniques in psychodynamic practice with clients diagnosed as borderline. *Clinical Social Work Journal* 24:203–215.

Levenson, H. (1995). *Time-Limited Dynamic Psychotherapy*. New York: Basic Books.

Mann, J. (1973). *Time-Limited Psychotherapy*. Cambridge, MA: Harvard University Press.

McCullough Vaillant, L. (1997). *Changing Character*. New York: Basic Books.

Strupp, H., and Binder, J. (1984). *Psychotherapy in a New Key: A Guide to Time-Limited Psychotherapy*. New York: Basic Books.

Weiss, J., and Sampson, H. (1986). *The Psychoanalytic Process: Theory, Clinical Observation, and Empirical Research*. New York: Guilford.

Westen, D. (1991a). Cognitive-behavioral interventions in the psychoanalytic psychotherapy of borderline personality disorders. *Clinical Psychology Review* 11:211–230.

—— (1991b). Social cognition and object relations. *Psychological Bulletin* 109:429–455.

—— (1996). *Integrating psychodynamic and cognitive-behavioral theory and therapy*. Unpublished manuscript.

Winokur, M., Messer, S., and Schacht, T. (1981). Contributions to the theory and practice of short-term dynamic psychotherapy. *Bulletin of the Menninger Clinic* 45:124–142.

Afterword: Constructing a New Vision

Nina Rovinelli Heller and
Terry Brumley Northcut

We began this work from the context of a strong psychodynamic perspective. The combination of our clinical and academic experiences convinced us that we needed to reexamine that perspective. We did, however, have significant biases against what we had seen as the inflexibility and rote application of both cognitive-behavioral theory and technique. As we began to explore its theoretical origins, its continuing evolution, its varied techniques, and its potential flexibility, we began to see that the concept of cognition had something to offer clinicians who saw the exploration of affect as primary in therapeutic work. We realized that clients' cognitions were often eclipsed by a focus on their affects. In fact, an examination of cognition can help us to identify and elaborate on underlying affects. Furthermore, with the increased external pressure to "fix" people quickly, the field has increasingly focused on client behaviors without an understanding of critical determinants such as motivation, resistance, and internal conflict.

We began to notice that the nature, quality, form, and pattern of a client's cognitions are important, idiosyncratic, descriptive, and potentially predictive. We also found that two cognitive concepts, schemas and attributions, offered a detailed way of organizing and understanding multiple dimensions of the client's meaning systems. Together, these two concepts encompass elements of object relations and self-concept, two aspects of psychodynamic understanding we are loath to relinquish. Taken together, aspects of cognition, affect, and behavior as illustrated in schemas and attributions, are in reality intertwined. When these concepts are considered within an integrative theory, they can be conceptually intertwined as well. This is never more important than in the assessment process, described in Part I. Theory dictates a particular emphasis on certain aspects of assessment. Assessment in turn points the way to the choice of interventions. Therefore, the integration of technique requires an understanding of both the theory and the assessment that supports and rationalizes the use of particular techniques.

Also included in Part I are those areas worth preserving of both the psychodynamic and cognitive-behavioral traditions. An examination of strengths and limitations allowed for identification of areas of complementarity. However, we also found, in spite of the vast cognitive-behavioral literature, little discussion of when or how to incorporate specific techniques into integrative practice. We were delighted to receive our contributors' chapters, which demonstrated what we had begun to notice in our own practices. We had not in fact been practicing from as "pure" a theoretical perspective as we'd espoused. The cognitive-behavioral techniques described in Part II are all familiar to us and represent solid clinical practice. What is new to us, however, is the thoughtful and methodical, conscious and deliberate, use of specific techniques at particular points in treatment. Each clinician's articulation of how he or she uses cognitive-behavioral techniques forces us to examine the inherent compatibility of these approaches. It also gives us practice guidelines for the kinds of techniques apt to be useful in the treatment of certain clients with a particular set of problems.

A focus on the treatment relationship is one of the strongest contributions from our psychodynamic legacy. The practice applications in Part II also demonstrate a variety of ways that the cognitive-behavioral techniques can enhance or capitalize on the therapeutic alliance. For example, Kathryn Basham's chapter showed how cognitive-behavioral techniques help facilitate the formation of a therapeutic alliance. Jim Drisko used his understanding of the cognitive-behavioral training of collaterals to help improve relationships with child clients. Dennis Miehls used the cognitive-behavioral approach to further the treatment relationship and give a breather to a client reacting to the intensity of therapy.

A major strength of the cognitive-behavioral school also evident in the application chapters is the wide applicability of these techniques for multiple problems, varied populations, and short- and long-term treatment. Whether clients are older adults, survivors of trauma, chemically dependent, or rebellious adolescents, cognitive-behavioral interventions combined with a psychodynamic understanding of presenting problems, can lead to effective resolution.

While we hoped for and expected to conclude this process with practical chapters on integrative clinical work, we are surprised to find our theoretical position shifting in the manner that it has. One of the conclusions drawn from the chapters in Part I is the potential for integration within a constructivist framework. Both psychodynamic clinicians and cognitive behaviorists have made significant overtures into this arena. Because a constructivist perspective allows for multiple perspectives, we are challenged to think more on how clinicians and students could use this perspective in a way that captures the strengths of both the psychodynamic and the cognitive-behavioral schools.

The challenge remains to struggle further with the concept of defining an effective integration. From a purist perspective we are confident that what we have achieved is a folding in of cognitive-behavioral approaches into treatment that for a variety of reasons needs further structure and/or intervention. We suspect most clinicians don't care whether they are integrating, incorporating, or folding in different schools, being most concerned with pragmatics: Is the client responding positively? However, we all gain from this struggle if it yields new understandings about cognition, affect, and behavior and how social environments initiate, reinforce, or modify each.

It is quite appropriate that we are at a place in theory development where we can step back and consider the context from which we have developed our ideas. Perhaps it is a sign of the progress we have made in understanding our clients and ourselves that we can allow ourselves to reevaluate psychological and social theory, its social construction, its validity, and its applications to multiple gender, culture, and cohort populations. This scrutiny of theory is of course not new; Freud struggled with his own observations, misgivings, and reformulations, all in the context of turn-of-the-century Vienna. The ensuing theoretical battles are familiar to us all. Some wish to dismantle all of Freud's theories; others hold tenaciously to both the theory and the techniques of psychoanalysis. Regardless of one's position in this arena, what is clear is that no theory is infallible and that existing theory always falls short when trying to explain and predict all occurrences in human and social functioning. This awareness too brings us to a constructivist position that is informed by psychodynamic, cognitive-behavioral, and social theories. Central to this position for the psychotherapist is the belief that human beings are meaning-seeking, that similar phenomena have multiple etiologies and expression, that the client can be an expert, and that the treatment relationship forms an arena for exploration of the client's meaning. As social critics decry the loss of community and we see social phenomena such as the intertwining of Western and Eastern spiritual practices, the search for a theory of meaning is culture-syntonic. We have moved to a place that dictates our relinquishing the illusion of being therapeutically neutral or separate from the social context in which we practice. We can still offer our clients the best of what we have found to be effective with the challenge to discover what meaning, if any, that information has for them. Our most effective intervention may very well be our using whatever tools we have, including the treatment relationship, that allow our clients to construct a narrative that lets them more effectively "love and work."

Index